CHEF:
JERRY DRUM
516 627Q245

An American Taste of Japan

Also by Elizabeth Andoh:

At Home with Japanese Cooking

An American

William Morrow and Company, Inc., New York

Taste of Japan --=

Elizabeth Andoh

Color Photography by Aaron Rezny
Illustrations by Susan Blubaugh

Some recipes were originally printed, in slightly different form, in the following publications: *Gourmet, Food and Wine, Cook's Magazine, Bon Appétit, Cuisine, The Pleasures of Cooking,* and *The New York Times.* In addition, some of the recipes were excerpted in the June 1985 issue of *House Beautiful.*

Recipes for "Batter Fried Vegetable Bundles," "Eggplant with Pungent Bean Sauce," and "Eggplant and Green Pepper Sauté" originally appeared in *The Pleasures of Cooking.* Reprinted by permission of Cuisinart Cooking Club, Inc. Copyright © 1983 by Cuisinart Cooking Club, Inc.

Recipes for "Herbed Rice," "Kelp Squares with Fragrant Pepper," and "Honeydew Gelatin" originally appeared in *Gourmet.* Reprinted courtesy of *Gourmet.* Copyright © 1975, 1983 by Gourmet, Inc.

Library of Congress Cataloging in Publication Data

Andoh, Elizabeth.
  An American taste of Japan.

  Includes index.
  1. Cookery, Japanese. I. Title.
TX724.5.J3A518   1985   641.59′2′956   85-10558

ISBN 0-688-04369-0

Printed in the United States of America

First Edition

1 2 3 4 5 6 7 8 9 10

BOOK DESIGN BY GINGER LEGATO

A Note on the Romanization and Pronunciation of Japanese

There's a great deal of controversy and confusion over the best means of transcribing the Japanese language into the Roman alphabet. For the American cook and restaurant-goer who wants to buy Japanese ingredients and understand a menu, the lack of uniformity is very frustrating indeed.

In this book I have chosen to follow the well-known and respected Hepburn system for spelling, since it makes the most sense to speakers of standard American English. The Hepburn system is used here with the macron, or "long mark," over certain vowels that are meant to be extended in sound. This macron is useful in distinguishing words that would otherwise be spelled the same; *ōba* is a broad-leafed herb, but *oba* is an aunt.

In romanized Japanese, every letter in every word must be pronounced. Americans tend to forget this, particulary when they see a word ending in *e*, which is often silent in English but always pronounced "eh" in Japanese words. I've used an accent mark to remind the reader that *e* must be sounded—for example, *agé* should come out as "ah-geh," not the English word "age."

All hard "g" sounds (as in "good" or "great") are written with a *g*; soft "g" sounds (as in "gem") are written with a *j*.

Written Japanese is a steady flow of symbols rarely broken by spaces between words, or even by punctuation. No official system of romanization includes guidelines on how to break Japanese words on a page.

But since a lengthy string of unfamiliar combinations of letters is very discouraging to most readers, I've decided to break Japanese titles into units of meaning. Rather than write *torinomarumisoyaki* as one, impossibly long word, I've broken it into a series of five: *tori* (chicken) *no* (a possessive particle) *maru* (whole or round) *miso* (fermented bean paste) *yaki* (grill or roast). Whenever a close association of words causes a phonetic change, I've used a hyphen to create a compound word showing that special relationship. Alone, vinegared rice dishes are called *sushi*, but rolled *sushi* is called *maki-zushi* (*maki* refers to something that's rolled).

My system of romanization is meant to ease any difficulty you might have in pronouncing the original Japanese. I hope you find it helpful.

Acknowledgments

In writing this book I've been most fortunate to have so many sources of inspiration and information, and so many talented and supportive individuals to work with.

My good friend Eiko Ohta, my mother-in-law, Kiyoko Andoh, and my sister-in-law, Yohko Yokoi, have been extremely generous in sharing their knowledge of Japanese home cooking with me. I began my formal study of Japan's culinary arts in 1969 with Master Toshio Yanagihara and I am truly indebted to him, his family, and his staff for instructing me in the traditional ways of the Japanese kitchen and about Japan's culinary heritage. I consider it a great privilege and honor to have him as my mentor.

I am particularly grateful to Maria Guarnaschelli, my editor at William Morrow and Company, whose infectious enthusiasm and astute editorial comments had a catalytic effect on my work—they made me think, explore, and invent. I have many friends and colleagues at William Morrow whom I admire and appreciate: Brad Conard (Maria's able and affable assistant), Bruce Giffords (my meticulous copy editor), and John Ball, Cheryl Asherman, and Liney Li for their coordinated talents in the design and production of this book. My agent, Molly Friedrich, supportive of this project from its inception, conducted business for me in a smooth and professional manner, which freed me to concentrate my efforts on writing.

I am beholden to Lori Longbotham for her cheerful, diligent, and professional assistance in testing recipes and researching data. Matthew and Pamela Starobin first introduced me to the world of computers and they continue to help me when I'm confused and frustrated with word processing; their assistant, Michele Gray, has also gotten me out of many a tight technical spot. I'd like to thank my cultural experts, too: Miyuki Sekimoto for her patience in teaching me traditional Japanese tying techniques, and my three nieces, Yumiko, Kumiko, and Sumiko Yokoi, for their enthusiastic instruction in paper folding.

It was a pleasure to work with Susan Blubaugh, whose masterly drawings illustrate this book. I thank Shunyo Wakazono for her bold and stylish calligraphy; it contributes exactly the authentic yet contemporary Japanese design element that I sought. I've given a special page of credit (p. 317) to the artisans whose work appears in the photographs. Aaron Rezny is a gifted photographer, and his business representative, Jerry Anton, and studio assistants Michael Grand and Janet DiFabio saw that everything ran smoothly before, during, and after our photographic sessions. In addition, I'd like to thank Gloria Adleson for her inspired jacket design.

On a personal note, it gives me tremendous pleasure to acknowledge the help of my mother, Caroline Saxe, for her willingness to taste just about anything and her fine critical comments. After living abroad for so many years, it has been a joy to come home and discover such a capable resource so close by.

My husband, Atsunori, deserves a special word of appreciation, too. I am grateful for his recognition and acceptance of my unique perspective on Japanese cuisine; it couldn't have been easy watching me interpret so freely from his culture. Our daughter, Rena, with her boundless energy, unflagging appetite, and plentiful suggestions continues to be a constant source of inspiration to me.

Contents

The Recipes

An Introduction to Cross-Cultural Cooking

An American Taste of Japan is a collection of delicious recipes that make the most of what's best from two worlds—America and Japan. The dishes integrate Japanese ingredients, kitchen techniques, and culinary philosophy with American foodstuffs, kitchen appliances, and eating habits. The recipes here reflect the gastronomic excitement generated by continuing culinary exchange between Japan and the West. Recently, creative Japanese chefs working in the United States have been using indigenous American foodstuffs to prepare dishes in typically Japanese ways—the popular avocado *sushi* known as the California Roll is a classic in the making. At the same time, a growing number of restaurants in both Japan and America are serving Continental cuisine made with Japanese ingredients—the *enokidaké* and *shiitaké* mushrooms are happily finding their way into soups and sauces on both sides of the Pacific. These dishes are often, though not always, prepared by Japanese chefs trained in Europe. Japanese aesthetics, particularly the concern for beautiful table presentations, is an integral part of this emerging cross-cultural cuisine.

As an American trained in a Japanese kitchen and recently returned to the United States, I had many points of reference in researching and developing the cross-cultural recipes that appear in this book. Japanese culinary philosophy, which I find enormously appealing and remarkably compatible with contemporary American cooking and eating attitudes, was a major source. The irresistible abundance of America's fine foodstuffs was another of equal importance. Inspiration for original and interpretive cuisine came from contact with and generous sharing by creative food professionals in both cultures.

I first became seriously interested in cooking while living in Japan as a student, about twenty years ago. My early objectives were entirely self-centered. The dormitory fare was dreadful, my budget limited, and I longed for a chance to eat something—anything—that tasted good. I moved into a rented room with a tiny kitchen and my landlady, Eiko Ohta, patiently taught me the basic skills needed in a Japanese home kitchen. The women of the Andoh clan further educated me in the culinary ways of the Japanese home. Shortly after my marriage to Atsunori in 1969, I began formal training at the Yanagihara School of Classical Japanese Cooking. There I became enthralled with Japan's culinary culture and philosophy, and studied the history of Japanese food, too.

Master Yanagihara impressed upon me the importance of using the very best ingredients. Although this is a basic tenet of all fine cooking, the Japanese interpret the "best" to mean using whatever might be in season and special to the region in which they are. A deep and true appreciation of nature inspires the Japanese to make a varied feast from a limited number of seasonal and regional ingredients. The Japanese feel perfectly comfortable serving the same item—let's say eggplant—several times at the same meal. After all, chunks of eggplant nestled at the bottom of a soup bowl are so utterly different from herb-pickled eggplant slices, or *miso*-sauced and sesame-garnished sautéed slivers of the same vegetable, that there's no reason why all three dishes shouldn't appear on the same menu. By means of thorough familiarity with one's materials, skill, and ingenuity, those trained in a Japanese kitchen learn to transform simple ingredients into sublime and often complex creations.

In Tokyo, I began to write for other Westerners and to teach them about traditional Japanese cooking. My professional activities centered around translating and explaining classic Japanese culinary theory and practice to fellow Americans. My job was to transform the seemingly inscrutable into the feasible and fun. My first cookbook, *At Home with Japanese Cooking,* published in the fall of 1980, was written with that intent.

At that time, an unexpected turn in my husband's career brought me back to New York. I began teaching in the city at the Culinary Center and traveled to many other parts of the United States and Canada, demonstrating Japanese cooking and lecturing to various interested groups. It was as I traveled that I discovered the glories of regional American foodstuffs. In Seattle the fabulous chanterelles, salmon, and Dungeness crabs whetted my appetite, while in Hawaii the native macadamia nuts, pineapples, and *ahi* tuna lured me from the beach to the kitchen. Along the east coast soft-shell crabs, mussels, and lobsters inspired and impelled me to all sorts of culinary experiments.

At the same time, the huge influx of Japanese businessmen with their families meant that specialty grocery stores in America were stocking more and better-quality Japanese products. I was delighted that many items previously imported from Japan were being grown and harvested in the United States. Now, without a passport or a fortune in the bank, Americans have access to such gastronomic glories as short-grained Japanese-style rice, pale delicate *enokidaké* and dark woodsy *shiitaké* mushrooms, *gobō* (burdock root), *shiso* (a flat-leafed green herb), *daikon* (fat white radishes), *tsumamina* (radish sprouts), and many other Japanese herbs and vegetables.

In the past few years, I've had the remarkably good fortune to meet many fellow food professionals here and in Japan. They've been intrigued by what I had to offer them, and I've been inspired by what they have taught me. My own cross-cultural education is evident in the food and thoughts of *An American Taste of Japan*.

To begin, there's a guide to possibly unfamiliar ingredients and equipment called for in the book. You'll find descriptions of these foodstuffs and paraphernalia, and tips on what to look for when buying or storing your newly acquired culinary treasures.

Next are the recipes, which are organized by how you might serve them at an American table. In addition to detailed instructions on preparing the food, the recipes include information on the origins or inspirational sources for the dish, and specific suggestions on what to serve with it. There are chapters devoted to soups, appetizers, main courses, complementary side dishes, and desserts. The major exception to this plan is a chapter just on *sushi*, that splendid Japanese contribution to gastronomy that can be served alone or at the beginning, middle, or end of almost any meal.

After the recipes comes a chapter on table setting, where I share with you some of my thoughts on Japanese and American culinary aesthetics. I've catalogued some of the most frequently encountered Japanese decorative motifs to encourage you to expand your approach to setting the table. I've revamped some traditional Japanese folding and tying techniques to create original tabletop decorations.

An American Taste of Japan is a collection of delicious recipes and provocative ideas about cooking and serving food. I hope the information about Japan and its culinary traditions and practices will serve as a source of inspiration, kindling a spark of originality on your kitchen stove.

At the Market, in the Kitchen...

A guide to buying and storing Japanese foodstuffs and equipment, plus an explanation of certain Japanese cooking terms and techniques

There's now a greater variety and better quality of Japanese foodstuffs available in the United States than ever before, particularly in the larger urban centers along the east and west coasts. Oriental groceries and local supermarkets alike are stocking the basic materials needed for cooking Japanese-style food, and many specialty stores offer mail-order options to those living a distance from the bigger cities.

The recipes in this cookbook take advantage of unique and native American food products, combining their use with certain basic Japanese seasonings and techniques. Unfamiliarity with Japanese ingredients and equipment, though, can cause confusion when shopping, particularly since labeling is not always consistent, complete, clear, or in English. Here, then, is an alphabetical listing of information on the Japanese foodstuffs, techniques, and pieces of equipment you'll encounter in the recipe portion of this book. I hope you'll find this guide a useful reference when preparing a shopping list or working in your kitchen.

I have several general words of advice and caution for when you shop (or order through a catalogue):

1. Whenever possible, ask for the item you want using the Japanese name for it. English translations for the same product vary tremendously. There are also variations in the spelling of certain Japanese words; don't be surprised at *r* and *l* being switched around (as in *mirin* and *milin*), or at the interchanging of *n* with *m* in many names (*konbu* and *kombu* are the same kelp). Sometimes, products are given unnecessarily cryptic names, such as "alimentary paste" instead of "noodles."
2. Tell the clerk (or mail-order house) what it is you want to make with the product. Some products are labeled generically, like "seaweed" or "bean paste," even though all varieties of that item aren't necessarily suitable for your purpose. Also, some brands may be better than others at meeting your needs.
3. Many recipes given in English on Japanese food products don't take into consideration the difference in size between American and Japanese measuring cups. The difference is considerable; a Japanese cup is about four fifths the size of its American counterpart. Teaspoon and tablespoon measurements, though, are the same. All recipes in this book use standard American measures.

4. The freshness of a product is crucial, even when buying a dried food. It's always best to check the label for the date of manufacture. Most dates on Japanese products don't follow the Gregorian calendar. Rather, they use a system that counts the year in the reign of the Emperor. Emperor Hirohito is an elderly man, and 1985 is the sixtieth year of his reign, which is known as Shōwa (the era of "Bright Peace"). Dates often appear on packages as a series of numbers; a product manufactured on September 1, 1985, would be labeled 9160 or 9.1.60.

ABURA AGÉ (**Fried Bean Curd**). An inexpensive, highly nutritious and versatile food, *abura agé* finds its way into many Japanese dishes.

Abura agé is sold in clear cellophane packages stored in the refrigerator sections of most Oriental groceries. Two different sizes are available: One kind of package contains two or three slices, each measuring about 5½ by 2½ inches, while the other contains six or eight small, 2½-inch squares. Sometimes, fried bean-curd squares are labeled *inari agé* because one common use for them is in the making of a vegetarian *sushi* called *inari-zushi*. Some brands of *abura agé* are easier to pry open than others; when buying the fried bean curd for Bean Curd and Vegetable Bundles (p. 185), ask the clerk for the brand that will be easiest to open.

Fried bean curd should be kept refrigerated at all times and consumed within 3 days of purchase. Freezing changes the texture of the product and I don't recommend it, although you'll find fried bean curd imported from Japan in the freezer section of your Oriental market. Frozen fried bean curd tends to be unpleasantly spongy. Buy locally made bean-curd products whenever possible. Fried bean curd needs to be blanched just before using, to remove the thin film of oil that covers the packaged slices.

AKU NUKI. This term is used to describe a procedure for removing unpleasant bitterness from vegetables; it's most commonly performed on cucumbers by rubbing the stem end against the larger "fruit."

AMAZU SHŌGA (**Pink Pickled Ginger**). This mild but spritely ginger condiment is usually served as a palate cleanser at the *sushi* bar. It's an ingredient in several *sushi* recipes in this book, but could be served alongside any *sushi* dish. It also goes well with fish and chicken dishes.

Amazu shōga is sold in glass jars or hermetically sealed plastic tubs and bags. It doesn't have to be refrigerated until after the package has been opened. Most often, the pink pickled ginger is broadly and thinly sliced, but sometimes it's cut in julienne strips. Some brands are more intensely pink than others; the natural color is a very pale peach or yellow. Almost all brands use some food coloring to heighten the natural blushing shade that results from the chemical interaction between fresh, very young ginger shoots and rice vinegar. Pickled ginger will keep, covered and refrigerated, for many months.

AO NORI (**Sea Herb Flakes**). This is one of many sea vegetables and herbs the Japanese enjoy. This particular type of algae is harvested from shallow ocean beds, then it's dried and packaged in glass jars, alone or combined with terrestrial herbs and spices. I've called for sea herb flakes as a garnish in a few rice recipes where their fresh seashore aroma encourages hearty appetites. The Japanese use *ao nori* as a seasoning for potato chips!

Store your bottle of sea herb flakes on a dry shelf, away from direct sunlight or heat. It won't spoil, but its delicate sea-air aroma fades after several months. The full aromatic power of the herb can best be brought out by rubbing it between your fingertips or the palms of your hands just before using.

BENI SHŌGA (**Red Pickled Ginger**). This is a sharp, lively ginger pickle that's served as a garnish or condiment with many Japanese dishes. In this book, I've called for it in several *sushi* recipes. You might want to serve it as a condiment with cold meat or fish, too.

Red pickled ginger is usually sold whole, sliced, or julienne, in glass jars or sealed plastic tubs. *Beni* is a natural dye known from ancient days, when it was used for cosmetic as well as culinary purposes. *Kuchi beni* is the term for lipstick in Japanese; *kuchi* literally means "mouth" and *beni* is "red."

Once you've opened your package, store it in the refrigerator where it will keep, covered and in its original liquid, for many months. Drain just before serving.

DAIKON (Japanese White Radish). This white root is perhaps the single most versatile vegetable in the Japanese repertoire; it can be grated or shredded and eaten raw; it can be steamed or braised and sauced or included in stews; it can be pickled or dried, too. I've called for *daikon* in a number of recipes and I've included a wonderful recipe (p. 253) for using the peels left after other dishes are made.

There are several varieties of *daikon* available fresh in the United States. Most common is a kind of *ao kubi daikon* or "green-necked radish," which has a distinctive green coloring to the skin of the vegetable near where its shoots and leaves peek out of the earth. This variety tends to have a sharper taste than the more slender, all-white radishes, and is best for grating and pickling, though any variety can be used for the recipes in this book. All varieties of *daikon* should have a luminous quality to unbroken skin, and a firm, dense, and hefty feel in the hand. If you can find roots with their leaves stiffly attached, all the better.

Store your radish uncovered in the vegetable bin of your refrigerator. It will be crisp for 2–3 days (best for grating and shredding for salads), then get a bit limp (still fine for steaming and braising). The radish remains good for pickling for 1–2 weeks after purchase. Peels can be accumulated and saved for the spicy sauté on p. 253 for 10 days in a closed plastic bag.

DASHI (Basic Sea Stock). This subtle sea broth has always been essential to the traditional cooking of Japan and continues to play an important role in even the most modern and Westernized kitchens in Japan. Made from *kombu* (kelp) and *katsuo bushi* (dried bonito flakes), it imparts a delicate smoky-sea nuance to all foods cooked in it.

DASHI KOMBU. See *kombu.*

DOMBURI ("Big Bowl"). This is the name given both to hearty bowls of rice topped with various savory ingredients and to the big bowls in which the food is served. The bowl alone is also called a *domburi-buchi.*

ENOKIDAKÉ (Slender Creamy-White Mushrooms). These delicate fungi have almost a floral aroma to them and are used by the Japanese in soups and braised dishes. The Japanese never eat them raw, though they cook them only briefly (usually a matter of seconds; at most 2 or 3 minutes).

Enoki, as they're being called in the United States (the *také* or *daké,* by the way, means "mushroom" in Japanese), are grown in California nearly year-round. They come packaged in 100-gram (3½-ounce) clumps in sealed cellophane bags. The bottom of the bag is opaque, hiding the unattractive, but entirely normal, moldy growth of the stems. Peek through the cellophane and examine the small knoblike caps at the ends of the slender stalks; they should appear dry. If they look damp or slimy, the mushrooms are well past their prime.

After buying *enoki,* refrigerate them. They should stay fresh for 5–6 days, though that depends upon the age of the mushrooms when you purchased them. Just before using the mushrooms, rinse them under cold water, shake off excess moisture, and trim and discard the bottom halves.

GINGER. Fresh ginger is very different from the dried, pickled, and powdered forms. Pale-gold, shiny-skinned knobs of fresh ginger grown in Hawaii are now increasingly available in supermarkets throughout the continental United States. Choose firm knobs; break off a piece to check the aroma. You'll often notice a bluish rim on the inner edge of fresh ginger; that's fine and typical of certain botanical types. Since ginger often tends to be stringy, you'll find I recommend that you squeeze the gratings to extract the juice. A Japanese grater, called an *oroshi-gané,* with its well to catch the gratings and juice, is a convenient tool to have.

For the Felicity Swirls on p. 292, I call for candied ginger, and I prefer the moist crystallized ginger slices to the ones floating in syrup. Store crystallized ginger in an airtight jar in your cupboard.

GOBŌ (**Burdock Root**). This root vegetable is enjoyed throughout Japan, primarily in the fall, though young roots are edible in the spring months, too. Typically, *gobō* is sautéed or braised alone or with other vegetables and meat or fish. It imparts a subtle woodsy flavor to the dishes in which it's used.

Canned burdock root is tasteless and the texture is often stringy. Fresh burdock root is the only form worth buying. It's sold at many Oriental groceries. The best roots are no thicker than the average felt-tipped marker; roots with a diameter of more than 1 inch are usually spongy at the core. The roots can be as short as 8–9 inches but most are about 1 foot long. The vegetable should be sold (and stored in your home) with the dirt still clinging to it. Rinse and scrape just before using to retain as much aroma as possible. Store your burdock roots in a paper bag in your refrigerator and they should remain fresh for weeks.

GOMA. See sesame seeds.

GOMA ABURA (**Aromatic Sesame Oil**). This dark, nutty-flavored vegetable oil is best used to season foods, not for sautéing or frying. (There's a type of oil processed from white sesame seeds that can resist the high temperatures of a deep fryer, but it's very expensive and not appropriate for flavoring dishes.) Buy a small bottle of the deep-amber-colored oil unless you plan on using a great deal of it within 2–3 months. Store the oil on a cool, dry shelf in your cupboard.

HAKUSAI (**Chinese Cabbage**). This leafy, pale cabbage is popular throughout the Orient. Its English name shows that popularity in the West is due to its use in Chinese cooking. The *hakusai* grown and harvested in America is sweeter than its Japanese counterpart and quite delicious raw, in salads.

When buying, look for compact heads that feel fairly heavy. Ribs should be a pearly white (though speckling on the outer ribs of the vegetable is quite common) and leaves a pale to medium shade of green. Most produce markets will cut a large head in half or in quarters for you, if you need less than the average 2-pound head. Store your Chinese cabbage wrapped in a clean kitchen towel in the vegetable bin of your refrigerator. It will stay fresh for about 1 week.

HANDAI (**Wooden Rice Tub; also called** *Sushi Oké* **in Japanese**). These tubs are used for seasoning rice for *sushi* dishes. They're traditionally made from a kind of fragrant cedarwood that imparts a subtle aromatic nuance to the seasoned rice. The main advantage of these shallow but broad wooden tubs is their ability to absorb excess moisture from the steaming hot rice. Since the wooden tubs are hand-crafted in Japan, they're expensive (about fifty dollars for a 16-inch-diameter tub).

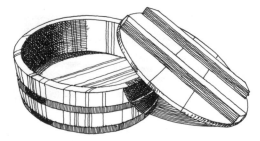

HARUSAMÉ (**Cellophane Noodles**). Literally translated, *harusamé* means "spring rain." This poetic name refers to the transparent, almost glassy appearance of the softened noodles. When these noodles are deep fried, they puff up to resemble mountain mists. I've used the noodles in both ways: as "spring rain" in a seafood casserole (p. 93) and in Misty Fried Shrimp (p. 93).

Harusamé are packaged in a variety of ways in Oriental groceries. Chinese packages often refer to them as bean thread noodles, made from the starch of mung beans. The Chinese product is typically packed in skeins of crinkly noodles held together by rubber bands and covered with cellophane wrap. The Japanese packages have straighter, thicker strands packed in an orderly fashion in a clear cellophane bag; the label often says "bean starch noodles," though occasionally "potato starch noodles." I prefer the Chinese noodles for deep frying, since they're more delicate, break into smaller pieces, and puff more fully. I choose the Japanese product for dishes that require the noodles to be softened in warm water before cooking.

These and other noodle products should be stored in an airtight container on a dark shelf. If the noodles should feel soggy, and you'll be wanting to fry them, take them from their container and spread them out in a 200-degree oven for 5 minutes to dry them out.

IKURA (Salmon Roe). This is the most prized of the red caviars in Japan. Red is a color of felicity and these large glossy globes are often served on happy occasions. Price is usually a good indication of quality. Each of the eggs should be nearly ¼ inch in diameter and full (no puckered look to them), the color a vivid, orangy one. Store fresh caviar in the refrigerator, covered, for up to a week.

JŌSHINKO (Rice Flour). Processed from glutinous rice, *jōshinko* is used extensively in the making of traditional Japanese pastries. Here, I've used it as a binder in making "ocean noodles" (p. 71) from scraps of fresh fish. Rice flour is useful as a thickener in making Continental-style white sauces, too.

There are various grades of rice flour available; price is a good indication of quality. Store rice flour as you would any flour, in an airtight container on a dark shelf.

KAMPYŌ (Dried Gourd Ribbons). Large, pale pumpkinlike gourds called *fukubé* are harvested and peeled into long ½-inch-wide ribbons and dried for several days. These are sold in cellophane bags containing very long strips (several yards), or short (6-inch) lengths. It's best to buy the uncut gourd ribbons since these are easier to use when tying up edible packages such as Bean Curd and Vegetable Bundles (p. 185).

Refrigerate what you don't use after opening. Stored in a closed plastic bag, the dried gourd (which is still pliable, not brittle) will keep for months.

KANTEN (Japanese Gelatin; Agar). This gelatin is processed from sea vegetation, specifically a plant called *tengusa* ("heavenly grass" in Japanese). The gelling properties of this plant, particularly after it has been freeze-dried, are quite remarkable (it will solidify liquid without refrigeration), and it has been known and used in Oriental cuisine for many centuries.

Kanten is usually sold as two sticks of what appears to be brittle cellophane, wrapped in what really is thin cellophane. More recently, powdered *kanten* has come on the market. One stick can usually gell about 1¾ cups of liquid; one packet of powder slightly less (about 1⅔ cups of liquid). A great deal depends upon the chemistry of the specific liquid used.

Store *kanten* in an airtight container on your shelf; it will keep, dried, indefinitely.

KATSUO BUSHI (Dried Bonito Flakes). A tunalike fish called bonito in English and *katsuo* in Japanese is found in fairly temperate waters. The best-known area in Japan for *katsuo* is Tosa, on the Pacific coast of the island of Shikoku. Fresh bonito is an early summer delicacy in Japan; year-round the dried fillets are flaked and used to make stocks and sauces.

Most packages of dried fish flakes in a Japanese grocery combine bonito with other, less expensive fishes, such as mackerel and sardines. The price will tell you. Traditionally, every kitchen kept whole dried fillets, which were then rubbed over a sharp blade attached to a wooden box. The box had a drawer that filled with shavings that could be easily removed. Just as freshly ground coffee beans are far superior to beans ground weeks before, so freshly shaved bonito is far superior to preshaved flakes. Today, though, it's hard to find these boxes, or people who use them. Instead, it's more common to see scissors cutting open individual 5-gram packets of preshaved fish flakes. If you'll be using *katsuo bushi* only occasionally, it's best for you to buy these small packets, wistfully labeled "fresh pack." Five or six of these packets are sold as a unit in either a cardboard box or a large plastic bag. Large bags of flakes, once opened, go rancid rather quickly.

KOMBU (Kelp). The natural taste-enhancing properties of *Laminaria japonica* and *Laminaria ochotensis,* two of many commonly used sea vegetables in Japan, have been known for centuries. These sturdy kelps are used primarily for stock making, though they're cooked and eaten as vegetables, too.

When shopping, ask for *dashi kombu* (kelp for stock making) and let price be your guide; the superior product is more expensive. The whitish, chalklike powder is not an indication of mold or spoilage. The color and thickness of kelp can vary from thick, stony gray to thin green with a reddish cast. All kelp should be stored in an airtight container on a dark shelf, where it will keep indefinitely.

MATCHA (Powdered Ceremonial Green Tea). Made from the budding leaves of the tea plant, dried and crushed to a fine powder, this tea is a gorgeous jade color. *Matcha* is used primarily to make a beverage for special occasions or as part of the ritual tea ceremony. *Matcha* is also used in its native land to flavor some traditional sweets. I've used *matcha* in Western ways to create cross-cultural desserts.

The powdered tea can be purchased at any Oriental grocery; it comes in a small tin canister. Open the vacuum-sealed foil bag inside and transfer the tea to the canister directly. Store the powdered tea in your freezer; it defrosts instantaneously and may be refrozen any number of times. Freezing will help hold its delicate, grassy aroma for many months. Regular green tea leaves, even pulverized, are not a substitute for *matcha*.

MIRIN (Syrupy Rice Wine). With only an 8 percent (by volume) alcohol content, *mirin* is often sold in ordinary supermarkets. It isn't a drinking wine. Instead it's used as a seasoning and glazing agent in cooking other foods.

Store your bottle on a dark, dry shelf. The cap and rim need to be wiped well after each use or else they'll stick badly, as do maple and other syrups.

MISO (Fermented Bean Paste). There are hundreds, if not thousands, of types of *miso* that the Japanese regularly enjoy. Whether mild or pungent, they're all made from the fermentation of soybeans. Generally, *miso* falls into one of two types, dark or light, though there are medium shades (and flavors), too. For the recipes calling for dark bean paste you could use any kind of *aka* (literally, "red") *miso,* though I recommend *Sendai miso,* a regional type. Similarly, for recipes using light paste I recommend *Saikyo miso,* though any *shiro* (literally, "white") *miso* will do.

After opening the plastic package or tub, reseal and store it in the refrigerator for up to 2 months for optimal aroma, though spoilage is rare even after 6 months or more. A white and/or green, moldy growth around the edges or across the surface of the bean paste is a sign of unwanted bacteria. Scrape off the mold and use the remaining bean paste within a day or two.

MISO SHIRU (also called *Omi-otsuké*). Soup thickened with fermented bean paste.

MITSUBA (**Trefoil**). A three-leafed, slender-stalked herb with a subtle yet fresh flavor, *mitsuba* is occasionally available fresh in the spring and fall. Ideally the stalks will curve slightly but gracefully and be a pale green; the leaves should be no larger than 1 inch and a darker, more vibrant shade of green. Avoid yellowed or brown-edged leaves and limp stalks. It's best to select a bunch that still has its roots attached and to trim them off as needed. The leaves and stems are edible after trimming. Wrap *mitsuba* in paper toweling that has been moistened with a drop or two of water, and store it in the vegetable bin of your refrigerator. It should keep well for 5–6 days.

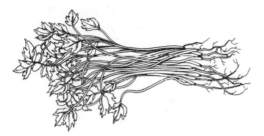

NERI MISO (**Glossy Bean-Paste Sauce**). This is a mixture of fermented bean paste, sugar, and rice wine or syrupy rice wine that's heated, stirring, until glossy and bubbly. It's either used directly on other foods as a glaze or sauce, or added to simmering foods to thicken and season them.

NORI (**Laver, Group of Seaweeds**). This is a generic term for a variety of marine vegetables cultivated and harvested in Japan. It's unfortunate that the derogatory word "weed" has come into such common usage. The Japanese have cultivated and harvested sea vegetables for centuries, and among the many varieties regularly consumed in Japan, *Asakusa nori*—paper-thin sheets of pressed, dried algae—is the most popular here in the United States. Throughout this book I recommend the purchase of *yaki-zushi nori,* which is high-quality *Asakusa nori* that has been pretoasted. It's best to buy flat, unfolded, full-sized (about 7½- by 6½-inch) sheets of pretoasted seaweed. These come in ten-sheet and fifty-sheet packages. Store these (with the antimoisture packet from the original package) in the freezer, in a closed bag or tin, after opening the package. The sheets will defrost instantaneously and may be refrozen any number of times.

OCHA (Green Tea). This is a generic name for green tea leaves that are used to brew a beverage drunk regularly in Japan. There are many grades, and price is the best indication of quality. Store the tea, after opening, inside a canister or other closed container in the freezer. This product is not the same as (nor can it be substituted for) *matcha,* which is a powdered tea.

OROSHI-GANÉ (Metal Grater). The Japanese use a metal grater to grate fresh *wasabi* (horseradish) root, *daikon* (fat white radish), and fresh ginger, mostly. The grater is made from metal (usually gold-toned aluminum) and has many sharp thornlike projections on its surface. Unlike American graters, which must be used over a bowl or plate because the food falls through holes, Japanese graters are flat and have a curved trough at one end to collect the gratings and juice. It's a particularly useful instrument for grating ginger and extracting the juice. Rub a peeled piece of ginger over the thornlike projections in circular motions. Using the stub of ginger remaining in your hand, scrape over the rough surface of the grater to collect all the gratings in one corner of the trough. Gently squeeze the gratings against the metal and the juice will well up in the trough.

Japanese *oroshi-gané* are inexpensive (usually a dollar or two) and often sold in Oriental groceries. I highly recommend one to you if you use ginger juice often. After using, wash it in hot, soapy water and rinse well, or put it in the dishwasher. The Japanese also make ceramic graters in the same or similar shapes. They're fine for grating ginger or radish and easier on the fingers (no cuts from trying to grate too hard or too long), though they chip and crack if not handled with care. The ceramic graters should be washed by hand.

OSHINKO ("New Fragrant Things"). This is the culinary euphemism for pickles in Japan; *tsuké mono* is the literal term. There are a great number of different kinds of commercially pickled vegetables available in Oriental groceries in the United States. A few of the most readily available are:

> *takuan,* a yellow pickled radish
> *shiba-zuké,* a purple pickle of eggplant and gourd
> *yama gobō,* thin, orange, pickled young burdock roots
> *ao-jiso no mi-zuké,* green pickled herb seeds and cucumber or gourd

OTOSHI-BUTA ("Dropped Lid"). A piece of equipment commonly found in Japanese home and restaurant kitchens, the lid falls down into the pot to rest directly on top of the food cooking inside. Purchase a size that's about 1 inch less in diameter than the pot you want to use it with. Usually made from a cedarlike wood, the lids should be washed in warm mild sudsy water and rinsed well with plenty of fresh water. Let the lids dry naturally.

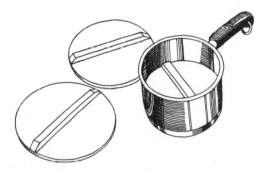

PANKO (Coarse Japanese Bread Crumbs). The Japanese first learned to make bread from the Portuguese and adapted their word for it, *pāo; ko* in Japanese means "flour," "crumb," or "powder." Japanese *panko* have pointed, irregular shapes that make for an unusually crunchy surface when deep fried. There are several brands and varieties available; all are sold in clear plastic bags. I prefer those that have no egg or honey listed in the ingredients. Store *panko* in an airtight container on a dark, dry shelf for up to 6 months.

RICE. The Japanese grow a short-grained rice that they cook in plain water after rinsing off surface starch from the hulled grains. The crushed hulls, called *nuka,* are often used to make a paste for pickling vegetables. Harvested, uncooked rice is called *okomé* in Japanese, while plain cooked rice is called *gohan*. The word for "meal" is also *gohan,* which will tell you just how important rice is to the Japanese; when you've eaten rice, you've had a meal!

Excellent Japanese-style short-grained rice is being grown in California now, and is available in many supermarkets in addition to specialty stores. Ideally, the raw rice should be stored in its original paper bag on a shelf away from heat, light, or dampness. If no shelf in your kitchen fits that description, store the rice in an airtight plastic container. Rice will stay fresh for a year or more so don't be afraid of buying several pounds at once. Most Japanese households consume 25 pounds of rice in a month; a 10-pound bag is probably the right size for an American family with an interest in *sushi* and other rice dishes.

Even though rice is a staple product, the Japanese have always prized the freshly harvested rice crop, called *shin mai,* that comes to market in the fall. In recent years, California has begun to market its new rice crop in America at the same price as the storage crop. (In Japan, one pays a premium for *shin mai.*) Ask the people at your nearest Japanese food store if they have *shin mai* during the months of October and November; if they do, you're in for a treat! See p. 219 for instructions on cooking new rice. Storage procedures remain the same, except that new rice, being more porous, will absorb surrounding odors more readily than the storage crop.

RICE MOLDS. These are called *kata* or *gata* in Japanese. The most commonly found molds are used to shape cooked rice into bundles (*maku no uchi*), fans (*ōgi*), flowers (*hana* or *umé*), or gourds (*hyōtan*). Most molds are packaged in boxes that have pictures of the contents on their covers. Some are wrapped in clear plastic covers that allow you to view the molds. Either way, they're easy to recognize on the store shelf. If you're having difficulty in finding them, ask the clerk at

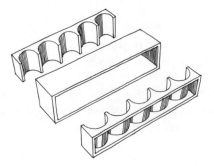

the store; they may be buried in back of other items. Those molds made of wood or plastic should be washed by hand; those of metal can be put in the dishwasher.

 SAKÉ (Japanese Rice Wine). This is a generic name for the alcoholic beverage distilled from steamed rice. It's also known as *nihon shu* (literally, "Japanese wine"). There are two types of *saké: kara kuchi* or dry, and *ama kuchi* or sweet. It depends upon your personal taste for drinking. For cooking purposes, any type or brand of drinking *saké* will do as long as the label doesn't say "cooking wine," which usually indicates a mixture of inferior rice wines and occasionally the addition of sugar or other additives. Price is a good indication of quality. Store, tightly capped, on a dark kitchen shelf.

SANSHŌ (Fragrant Japanese Pepper). The berry of the prickly ash plant is dried and crushed into a delicate and highly aromatic powder that's called *sanshō* or *kona-zanshō*. It's sold in small jars or plastic containers and, once opened, should be stored in the freezer to protect its delicate scent. Occasionally whole *sanshō* berries that have been salted and partially dried are available in clear plastic bags. These are wonderful to add to simmered vegetable, meat, or seafood dishes. Store the berries in a closed container in the freezer.

SARASHI (Muslinlike Cotton Cloth). The Japanese use *sarashi* for many things, from diapers to dishrags. Its fine-woven texture is ideal in the kitchen for straining stocks. The cloth is occasionally sold in Oriental groceries in 10-meter-long bolts, but unless you have several friends who will split the purchase, or a desire for a lifelong individual supply, you'll probably find that lining your strainer with paper coffee filters is best when straining stocks.

SESAME SEEDS (Goma). There are two kinds of sesame seeds used in Japanese cooking: white and black. White sesame (*shiro goma*) comes to market in two forms, hulled and unhulled. The unhulled seeds are a beige color and tend to have a nuttier flavor than the hulled ones. The smooth, cream-colored hulled seeds crush more easily to make a rich paste. Black sesame (*kuro goma*) has medicinal uses (traditionally it's been made into salves and ointments for the skin) as well as culinary ones in Japan. It's the black seeds from which dark, aromatic sesame oil is pressed.

Never purchase preroasted sesame seeds. Always dry-roast the seeds yourself just before using them. Once they've been roasted, their oils come to the surface (that's what makes them so wonderfully aromatic!) and can go rancid quickly thereafter. Store your sesame seeds in a closed container on a dry, cool shelf in your cupboard.

SHAMOJI **(Rice Paddle).** Usually made from bamboo, but occasionally sturdy plastic or ceramic material, *shamoji* are used to scoop up cooked rice from your pot or rice cooker. They come in three sizes (small, medium, and large) and I find them useful tools for sautéing, flipping, and other kitchen tasks besides scooping. Hand washing them and allowing them to dry naturally will preserve them far longer than putting them into the dishwasher.

SHARI **(Rice Seasoned for *Sushi*).** A word used mainly in *sushi* bars.

SHICHIMI TŌGARASHI **(Blend of Seven Spices).** The Japanese use dried chili peppers, usually in powdered form, to season several dishes. Here the powdered pods have been blended with six other herbs and spices (black and white sesame, green laver, dried citron peel, rape seed, and *sanshō* pepper). Sold in small glass jars, it should be stored tightly capped, on a dark, dry shelf.

SHIITAKÉ **(Known as Dark Oak Mushrooms When Fresh, Dark Oriental Mushrooms When Dried).** Fresh *shiitaké* have large bark-colored caps that, depending upon the variety, are smooth or nubbly with lighter-colored striations. A peek under the "umbrella" of either

type reveals white webbing. Both kinds of *shiitaké* are grown in Virginia and are delicious. On the average, both have 1½-inch-wide caps and 1-inch white stems. The Japanese don't eat uncooked *shiitaké,* though they cook them only briefly. The fresh mushrooms should be aromatic and plump; residual dirt clinging to caps or stems is irrelevant. Store the fresh mushrooms in an open plastic bag in your vegetable bin for up to 5 days for maximum flavor and aroma. Dried *shiitaké* are available imported from many Asian countries. Price is an indication of quality; the nubbly thick-capped *donko* variety is the most prized. Store dried mushrooms on a dark shelf in an airtight container, with the antimoisture packet from the original cellophane bag.

SHISO **(Flat-Leafed Japanese Herb).** A distant botanical relative of mint, *shiso* goes by several names in English and Japanese. "Beefsteak-plant leaf" is one English name, "herb leaf" another. In addition to *shiso,* in Japanese the leaves are called *ōba,* meaning "big leaf." Traditionally a summer herb, *shiso* is cultivated year-round in the United States, though the summer months still yield the tastiest leaves. *Shiso* is typically sold on Styrofoam plates covered with clear plastic wrap, each packet containing ten leaves. Keep it refrigerated at home and sprinkle a few drops of water on any unused leaves before resealing

the packet with plastic wrap. The broad-leafed herb will stay fresh for 5–6 days. The first sign of spoilage is the appearance of dark areas on the leaves and/or stems.

SHOKUTAKU TSUKÉMONO KI (Screw-top Pot or Jar for Pickling). Made of sturdy plastic, these modern jars are used in Japan in lieu of traditional heavy weights to make salt-pickled vegetables. These jars aren't suitable for acid (vinegar) pickling solutions. If the lightly pickled vegetables on pp. 254–259 interest you, it would make sense to purchase one of these jars (they're usually priced around ten dollars), since it will simplify matters considerably. Wash your jar in warm sudsy water, rinse well, and let dry naturally.

SHUNGIKU (Edible Chrysanthemum Leaves). Occasionally available in the fall and winter months, these greens have a fresh, herbal bite to them that perks up soups or casseroles. Look for deep green leaves; the smaller ones are usually more tender and less bitter than broad-leafed kinds. Any budding tips should be discarded before using. Chrysanthemum leaves are never eaten raw in Japan; they're always blanched or cooked in some liquid before eating. Store your fresh greens in an open plastic bag in the vegetable bin of your refrigerator; they'll stay fresh for 4–5 days.

SOY SAUCE. Many different types are available, each intended for a slightly different purpose, but for most dishes you'll find regular soy sauce, what the Japanese call *koikuchi shōyu,* suitable. I find the smaller-sized tins the most convenient for my home, but we do use quite a bit of soy sauce. For those who use it only occasionally, the smaller, unbreakable clear bottles are best. Although soy sauce doesn't spoil, its subtle, full-bodied bean aroma does fade after several months. Keep opened bottles tightly capped on a dark shelf in your kitchen.

The different labels on soy sauces can be confusing. The light-colored but intensely flavored *usukuchi shōyu* has its own entry later in this section. The very dark *tamari* soy sauce is mainly used for fish *sashimi* (fresh slices of uncooked fish). The word *tamari* means "filled up" or "accumulated" and refers to the thicker sauce that accumulates at the bottom of large vats of soy sauce. Health food stores often sell *tamari* soy sauce as nutritionally richer than ordinary soy. It's a generally more intense sauce, with a higher concentration of minerals, including sodium. The newer reduced-sodium soy sauces are a product developed in response to the American consumer. I personally feel they're of limited use and questionable flavor; I would prefer to choose recipes that use little or no soy sauce, or dilute regular soy sauce with basic sea stock and/or rice wine to achieve a reduced sodium content. Read the labels carefully, and calculate your own dietary needs.

SU (Rice Vinegar). This mild but fragrant vinegar is used in many Japanese dishes. Many Americans become instant fans of its subtle verve and never return to harsh distilled white vinegar. Several brands are regularly available and each company puts out several kinds of vinegar, so read the labels carefully. The most expensive, and the absolute best, is pure rice vinegar, which is the first pressing from the fermented rice. Ordinary rice vinegar is made from successive pressings. Seasoned rice vinegar for making *sushi* has sugar, salt, and sometimes MSG added to it. Store your vinegar tightly capped on a dark, dry shelf in the kitchen. The vinegar will darken slightly with age and exposure to light or heat.

SUDARÉ. A slatted bamboo mat used primarily for rolling *sushi* and other foods in a Japanese kitchen. Wash your *sudaré* in warm water by hand and let it dry naturally before putting it away.

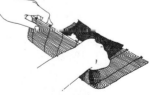

SUSHI (Vinegared Rice Preparations). There's a tremendous variety of vinegared rice dishes collectively known as *sushi*. The introductory comments to Chapter 3, which is devoted to this glorious contribution to international gastronomy, provide a brief history of *sushi* and clarify the nomenclature surrounding it.

SUSHI SU (**Seasoned Rice Vinegar**). Examine all writing on the package carefully to determine if the product labeled "rice vinegar" is this preparation meant for making *sushi,* or an unseasoned vinegar, which would need to be seasoned with sugar and salt before using.

TERIYAKI ("**Glazed Grill**") Although this name has been borrowed from the original Japanese to describe almost anything with a soy-based gravy, the term really means "glazed" *(teri)* and "seared with heat" *(yaki).*

TŌFU (**Bean Curd**). Dried soybeans are crushed and boiled, and the snowy liquid that results is solidified into puddinglike blocks that are usually referred to as bean curd cakes in English. Depending upon such variables as the coagulating agent, the lining and type of mold, time, and pressure, a number of rather different-looking products can result:

Kinugoshi ("silk-strained") bean curd is very soft, delicate, and smooth. It's fragile, like custard, and has, when freshly made, a delightfully nutty aftertaste. It's the bean curd of choice for the *tempura* recipe on p. 183 and the terrine on p. 113.

Momen ("cotton-wrapped") bean curd is firmer and more roughly textured throughout, with a noticeable crosshatch design on the surface; this is from the weave of the *sarashi* cloth that lined the molds. This kind of bean curd is meatier than the "silky" variety and is perfect, after draining off excess liquid, for cubing and floating in soup or for stuffing the fried bean curd pouches on p. 185.

Yaki-dōfu ("grilled" bean curd) is *momen* that has been drained and weighted slightly to remove excess liquid, then grilled. It has obvious grill markings on both top and bottom surfaces of the blocks. *Yaki-dōfu* is the bean curd preferred for most casseroles or stews, where the leisurely, usually untimed cooking wouldn't accommodate the more delicate varieties. The grilling adds a pleasant nuance to the texture and seems to enhance the beanlike flavor. Although no recipe in this book specifically calls for grilled bean curd, it could be added to the seafood stew on p. 175 or the beef and vegetable sauté served over rice on p. 190.

Pressed *tōfu* usually comes in smaller, pillow-shaped blocks of dense "cotton-wrapped" bean curd. They're more common in Chinese and

Korean markets than in Japanese ones, but they're fine for most dishes and especially good for floating in soups.

All types of bean curd are highly perishable and should be refrigerated, sumerged in fresh water, for no more than 2 days. Cloudy water or a thin sticky film on the bean curd indicates spoilage; so does an off odor. Don't freeze *tōfu;* its texture becomes unpleasantly spongy.

TŌGARASHI (**Red Chili Peppers**). The Japanese dry the pepper pods and use them to spice up a number of rice, noodle, vegetable, fish, and meat dishes. The seeds are incendiary and should be avoided unless you have a mouth lined with asbestos. After handling the dried pepper pods, be sure to wash your hands; the natural oils can be particularly irritating to your eyes if accidently rubbed in.

TONKATSU SŌSU (**Dark Spicy Sauce**). This sauce is made from tomatoes and fruit as well as soybeans. Its intriguing, mildly sweet yet spicy flavor is meant to perk up the often subtle taste of breaded fried foods. In fact, its name derives from the pork cutlet (*tonkatsu*) it was originally created to accompany. Buy a small bottle unless you have a large crowd to feed regularly; although the sauce doesn't spoil, its fresh, fruity aroma fades after several months on even a dark, dry shelf. You'll also find this sauce useful alone or in combination with your favorite barbecue sauce as a last-minute glaze on broiled or grilled foods. It's fine for glazing the top of a meatloaf, too.

TSUMAMINA (**Radish Sprouts**). This deliciously sharp, fresh sprout looks pretty on any platter and can liven up an otherwise bland green salad. The Japanese word *tsumamu* means "to pinch" or "pluck," and the suffix *na* refers to edible greens. Because of the close resemblance in sound between the Japanese *tsu* and the English "two," these sprouts

have been marketed in the United States as 2-Mamina. In Japan they're also known as *kaiwaré,* which means "split seashell"; the cleft, clover-like leaf visually reminds the Japanese of an open seashell. These nutritious and delicious sprouts are highly perishable and should be eaten within a day or two of purchase. Look for intensely green leaves (yellowing is a sign of age), and crisp, clean, pale stalks within the roots still attached. Store them loosely wrapped in slightly damp paper toweling, in the vegetable bin of your refrigerator.

UCHIWA (Flat Fan). Although a flat piece of cardboard serves the same purpose, it's not nearly as attractive a kitchen tool. The Japanese fan away steam from freshly cooked rice waiting to be seasoned for *sushi,* and they fan-cool blanched vegetables rather than "refreshing" them in cold water. For these jobs an *uchiwa* is the perfect and lovely tool of choice.

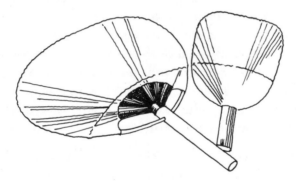

UDON (Thick White Noodles). These wheat-flour and saltwater noodles are available in many forms in Oriental groceries; dried and fresh can both be delicious. Fresh noodles should be kept refrigerated until used, preferably not more than 3 days after purchase. Dried noodles need to stay dry, in a tightly closed canister or other container.

UMÉ-BOSHI (Pickled Plums). These dusty-pink, wrinkled spheres seem innocuous enough sitting on the shelves of a Japanese grocery store in their clear plastic tubs. In reality they possess the most explosively refreshing, mouth-puckering possibilities imaginable. Many Japanese wake up to pickled plums with their breakfast bowl of rice, just as a strong cup of coffee gets many Americans going first thing in the morning. Pickled plums are also thought to have medicinal powers to settle and cure intestinal problems. In this cookbook I've called for the pulp (or *umé niku*) of pickled plums to perk up a miniature hand roll (p. 151). Choose moist, softly wrinkled, large plums that have been tinted with *aka-jiso* leaves (the wrinkled, deep purple leaves should be visible through the package). Cover and refrigerate after opening; the plums will keep for at least 1 year.

UMÉ SHU (**Plum Wine**). Some brands have a slight medicinal, cough-syrupy flavor, others a delicate fruity bouquet. Usually the pale, golden-toned, clear wines are superior to the darker, more opaque ones. In the Pear Ice Cream recipe (p. 278), plum wine is called for to poach the dried pears. Fresh pears poached in plum wine instead of port are delicious, too. In Japan, *umé shu* is a summer drink, served over mountains of crushed ice in squat glasses.

USUKUCHI SHŌYU (**Light Soy Sauce**). This soy sauce is lighter in color but saltier than ordinary *shōyu* or soy sauce. It's favored in the southern and southwestern regions of Japan, where they feel the deeper color of soy stains and muddies the appearance of the food. The natives of the northern and northeastern regions favor the deep, reddish-brown tones of foods cooked in regular soy sauce and think *usukuchi shōyu* an insipid, pallid seasoning. Obviously, there's strong regional prejudice at work here! For most recipes, regular soy sauce is fine (I spent most of my time in Tokyo), though for some, the paler, more delicate amber of light soy sauce is better (my husband's family comes from the south).

Read the labels carefully; the reduced-salt varieties aren't necessarily light in color, and the paler soy sauces aren't necessarily lower in sodium.

WASABI (**Fiery Japanese Horseradish**). This delightfully hot spice is used to highlight many *sushi* and *sashimi* dishes. The *wasabi* root is rather nubbly and usually grows between 3 and 5 inches in length. Fresh roots are hard to find, but if your local Japanese food store has them in the refrigerated case, by all means treat yourself—you'll find herbaceous aroma as well as fire. Choose pale green roots with even coloration and darker ruffly leaves. Dark speckling on the root can be an early sign of spoilage, but look carefully; sometimes it's just clinging earth. Whittle away the leaves and stem, and grate just as much of the root as you need. Cover the rest with clear plastic wrap and refrigerate. The roots should keep well for at least a week. Most often *wasabi* is sold as a powder in tins, or as a paste in tubes. The powdered form is preferable. Buy a small tin unless you use a great deal of the stuff; although the powder doesn't spoil, it often developes a dusty, stale aftertaste within a few months of opening. Re-lid the can well after each use and store on a dark, dry shelf in your cupboard.

YAKI-ZUSHI NORI (**Toasted Paper-thin Seaweed**). These dark, crisp sheets are used primarily at the *sushi* bar, hence their name: *yaki* means "toast," *zushi* is really *sushi* with a slight slur, and *nori* is a general term for many sea vegetables. Many Japanese will buy untoasted sheets called *Asakusa nori* and wave them over their cooking ranges just before using. I've found that it doesn't work well over electric ranges (popular in the United States but almost unheard of in Japan) and will often blow out the pilot light in an American gas range. Placing *nori* sheets in an oven to toast them is a nuisance, and yields uneven results. All these are reasons why I recommend you purchase pretoasted sheets. Keep them fresh in an airtight container in the freezer.

Soups...

*B*asic stocks, *miso*-thickened soups, thick rice and noodle soups, creamy vegetable soups, and clear broths—most meant to herald the start of a fabulous meal, some hearty enough to highlight the menu

In Japan, soups run the gamut from thick and hearty to light and delicate, with something to suit every mood and every meal, even breakfast! Soups are generally drunk directly from individual bowls, with chopsticks helping to reach any solids. In the Japanese scheme of things, soups are either brought to the table along with many small dishes in an informal setting, or served at the conclusion of a formal meal.

Miso shiru, broths thickened with bean paste, are the mainstay of traditional Japanese soups. They're served in every Japanese home first thing in the morning, with hot white rice and assorted pickled vegetables. There are hundreds, perhaps thousands of varieties of *miso* (bean paste) produced throughout the Japanese archipelago, and regional preferences abound—much like local tastes in wines or cheeses in Europe. Generally speaking, the lighter bean pastes are favored in the southwest while the darker ones predominate in the northeast. When a young woman marries in Japan, she's expected to adopt the *miso* soup of her husband's family, forsaking her own mother's recipe if there's a conflict, to display loyalty to her mother-in-law's kitchen!

The Japanese enjoy thick rice and noodle soups, which often become a snack or light meal served by themselves.

Clear Japanese soups are usually reserved for special occasions. They accompany *sushi* and *sashimi* particularly well, since the clean, lean flavors of vinegared rice and fresh fish might be overwhelmed by thicker soups.

The American table has become such an international taste arena that it no longer seems strange to serve classic Japanese soups as part of an American menu. Dark or light *miso* soups will enhance home-style standbys such as meatloaf or fried chicken, and the clear Japanese sea broths present a delicate backdrop to roasted or grilled meats and poultry.

In addition to variations on traditional Japanese themes, I've included three daring, new creamed and pureed vegetable soups. All are original creations intended to accompany the cross-cultural main courses in this book.

I've begun this chapter with a discussion of stocks and basic recipes for making them. None require a great deal of time, skill, or patience to make. I'd like you to get used to making *dashi,* the basic sea stock that's so important in the Japanese kitchen, because it will add a deliciously authentic nuance to all your efforts. You'll find that the Japanese are generally frugal, and the kelp that's left over from making the stocks gets temptingly recycled into a number of side dishes as indicated below.

Browse among the soups in this chapter and choose those that capture your fancy and match your meal; you'll find specific menu recommendations along with the recipes.

Basic Sea Stock

DASHI · Makes 1 quart

This is the master stock for most traditional Japanese soups and many simmered or sauced dishes. The classic version of *dashi* is comprised of two ingredients—*kombu* (a sweet but sturdy kelp) and *katsuo bushi* (dried bonito flakes). Although it takes only a few minutes to make this subtle sea broth well, timing is crucial to success. If you allow the kelp to boil, your stock will become murky and bitter. And if you don't strain the bonito flakes right away, your broth will taste fishy. The Japanese strain their stock through an all-purpose muslinlike fabric called *sarashi.* An old linen napkin or handkerchief, if you have one, is fine, but the disposable paper filters used in coffee makers are probably the most convenient. *Dashi* loses its delicate aroma and subtle flavors when frozen, so it's best to make it fresh when you need it. Any unused stock will keep well for 4 or 5 days in the refrigerator. Early signs of spoilage are clouding and a thick sediment at the bottom of the container.

20 square inches *dashi kombu* (dried kelp for
   stock making; see Note below)
4½ cups cold water
 1 package (5 grams) OR about ⅓ cup loosely
   packed *katsuo bushi* (dried bonito flakes)

Place the kelp in a 2- or 3-quart pot. Add the water and bring to a
boil rapidly over high heat. Remove the pot from the burner and
sprinkle the bonito flakes over the surface of the water. Let the broth
stand for 3 minutes. With chopsticks or tongs, remove the kelp, stir
the flakes until they sink, and pour the broth immediately through a
cloth- or paper-lined strainer or colander.

Note:
Kombu is harvested in the chilly waters off the coast of Hokkaido, Japan's northernmost island. Depending upon the time of year and the
location of the bed where it's harvested, the color, size, and shape of
the kelp varies quite a bit. The type of kelp that's best for making
stocks is called *dashi kombu* and is dried before being packaged. Typically, *dashi kombu* is slate-colored, with a whitish film over much of
its surface. The dried sea vegetable averages about 2 or 3 inches in
width and grows to a length of several feet. Strips of varying lengths
and widths are often packaged together. Since the dried kelp is so light,
it's more practical to measure it in square inches than to weigh it.
Whenever possible, take the required surface area as a single piece,
breaking it only if necessary to fit it into your pot. After making stock,
examine the piece of kelp you used. You'll notice that it's the exposed
and cut or broken edges that have become viscous, while the broad
surfaces are smooth and not a bit slippery.

Get in the habit of saving the kelp after stock making; it can be recycled into many wonderful dishes. Softened kelp can be kept for 1
week to 10 days if you do the following: (1) Rinse the kelp under cold
water immediately after removing it from the stock pot. (2) Drain and
pat dry on paper towels. (3) Store in a closed glass container or plastic
bag. (4) Keep in the vegetable bin of your refrigerator. Recipes such
as Gift-Wrapped Kelp Rolls (p. 116), Simmered Mushrooms and Kelp
(p. 262), and Kelp Squares with Fragrant Pepper (p. 264) make marvelous use of softened kelp.

Enriched Sea Stock

KOI DASHI · Makes 3 cups

This is a zesty sea stock that's commonly used in home kitchens in Japan. It can be substituted in any recipe calling for plain *dashi* stock, and is highly recommended for those who feel the basic sea stock is too subtle for their tastes.

You'll find yourself accumulating a fair number of fresh and softened dried mushroom stems after using the caps in recipes such as Plump Rolls (p. 146), Five-Colored *Sushi* (p. 156), or Japanese Chicken and Vegetable Sauté (p. 188). Save these stems, and other vegetable scraps from cooking, in a sealed plastic bag in the refrigerator for up to 1 week. Then make some of this enriched stock and freeze it for future use. Unlike the more delicate *dashi,* this stock retains its flavor even after being frozen for 1 month.

> 1 **quart *dashi* (basic sea stock, p. 48)**
> 1 **ounce (about 4) stems from *shiitaké* (dark oak or Oriental mushrooms)**
> 2–3 **ounces carrot scraps (peels and end bits)**
> 1 **ounce scallion (white and green parts left over from other uses)**
> 1 **teaspoon soy sauce**

Place all of the ingredients in a pot and bring to a boil over medium-high heat. Reduce the heat to maintain a steady simmer and continue to cook, uncovered, for 15 minutes. Pour the stock through a cloth- or paper-lined strainer or colander, discarding the solids. If the stock isn't for immediate use, allow it to cool to room temperature naturally before chilling. It keeps well for 5 days, refrigerated.

Basic Chicken Stock

TORI-GARA DASHI · *Makes a generous quart*

Since the Japanese have an aversion to animal fats, they prefer to use lean necks and bones when they make stock with a meat base. Still, the Japanese tend to be queasy and want to leach out any residual impurities with salt and a "rinse" of boiling water before cooking the bones. The subtle chickeny infusion that results is used in a number of soups and several simmered dishes.

> 1½ pounds chicken necks and assorted bones
>   OR 1 lean carcass
>
> 1½ teaspoons salt
>   about 2 quarts boiling water
>
>   8 cups cold water
>
> 25 square inches *dashi kombu* (dried kelp for
>   stock making)
>
> ⅛ teaspoon coarsely ground black pepper
>
>   1 leek and 2 scallions OR 4–5 scallions
>
> 1½ teaspoons salt
>
>   1 tablespoon *saké* (Japanese rice wine)
>
>   1 egg white and shell from egg (optional)

Rub the chicken necks and bones with 1½ teaspoons of salt and let them sit on a plate, uncovered, for 5 minutes. Transfer them to a colander and pour half the boiling water over them. With tongs or chopsticks, turn the bones over and rinse again so that all surfaces are exposed to the remaining boiling water. Drain well, and place the bones and necks in a large pot with the cold water and dried kelp. Over high heat, bring the water to a boil. Remove the kelp and save it, if you wish, for use in other recipes, such as Simmered Mushrooms and Kelp (p. 262). Skim off any froth and season the stock with the black pepper. Keep the broth at a simmer.

Cut away the roots and wilted pieces of the leek and scallions. Rinse the leek well to remove any grit or sand. Cut the white and green parts of the vegetables into 2-inch lengths. Add the leek and scallions to the pot and lower the flame to keep the stock gently simmering for 1 hour. Remove the wilted pieces of leek or scallion, add 1½ teaspoons of salt and the rice wine, and continue to cook for 1 more hour.

Pour the stock through a cloth- or paper-lined strainer or colander, discarding the solids. If you want a clear stock, clarify it. To do this, return the strained broth to the pot, making sure that the liquid fills no more than half of it and that there's ample headroom for foam that will form. Bring the chicken stock to a rolling boil and stir in one egg white and the shell from the egg. Keep the stock boiling for 3–4 minutes. Strain the stock again and discard the solids, then allow it to cool completely before storing for future use.

Chilling will help solidify some of the remaining fat and make it easier for you to remove. This stock will stay fresh covered in the refrigerator for up to 1 week; it also freezes well for up to several months. This recipe may easily be doubled.

Light Bean Soup with Slender White Mushrooms and Bean Curd

ENOKIDAKÉ NO MISO SHIRU · Serves 4

Once to be found only in its native Japan, slender creamy-colored *enokidaké* mushrooms are now being grown in California and shipped throughout the United States. Their delicate, almost floral bouquet is beautifully balanced here by the mellow fermented bean paste. The pale blond tones of this soup look good in any colored bowl or tureen.

> 3½ cups *dashi* (basic sea stock, p. 48) OR *koi dashi* (enriched sea stock, p. 50)
> 1 tablespoon soy sauce
> 1 teaspoon *saké* (Japanese rice wine)
> ¼ teaspoon salt

½ block (about 6 ounces) *tōfu* (bean curd), well drained of packing water

1 package (3½ ounces) *enokidaké* (slender creamy-white mushrooms)

2–2½ tablespoons *shiro miso* (light fermented bean paste)

1 slender scallion, trimmed and chopped fine (green and white parts), OR 6–7 stalks *mitsuba* (trefoil)

Put the stock in a pot and season it with the soy sauce, rice wine, and salt. Heat the broth until it barely boils and adjust the heat to maintain a simmer.

Cut the bean curd into ½-inch cubes. Add them to the broth and cook for 1–2 minutes.

Rinse the mushrooms lightly under cold running water, then gently shake dry. Trim off and discard the bottom halves of the stems before adding the mushrooms to the broth. Cook the mushrooms for only 30 seconds or so before ladling out some broth from the pot to a separate bowl that holds the light fermented bean paste.

Stir to dissolve the bean paste into the broth from the pot. Pour the dissolved paste back into the pot and heat through, stirring. Don't let the soup boil. For a hearty taste scatter the chopped scallions across the top of the soup. For a more delicate taste use *mitsuba*. Discard 1 inch from the bottoms of the stalks. Coarsely chop what remains of the stalks and leaves of the *mitsuba* and scatter them across the top of the soup. Serve immediately.

Menu Suggestions: This soup tastes just as good with an American meatloaf or omelet dinner as it does with Japanese classics such as Glaze-Grilled Salmon Steaks (p. 179) or Japanese Chicken and Vegetable Sauté (p. 188).

Dark Bean Soup with Bean Curd and Okra

AKA DASHI · Serves 4

Okra is a much relished and recent addition to the Japanese diet. The Japanese savor the slight viscosity that emerges from the cooked, cut vegetable; it reminds them of their native slippery mushrooms called *naméko*. Americans, who first introduced this vegetable to Japan, are less keen about such textures. So I've blanched the okra whole before slicing and adding it to the soup, to prevent any unpleasant stickiness. Pungent dark bean paste perks up the otherwise subtle broth, and the final dash of fragrant Japanese pepper makes the flavor sparkle.

> 3 cups *dashi* (basic sea stock, p. 48) OR *koi dashi* (enriched sea stock, p. 50)
>
> ¼ teaspoon salt
>
> 2 teaspoons soy sauce
>
> ½ block (about 6 ounces) *tōfu* (bean curd)
>
> 8–10 small fresh okra pods
>
> ½ teaspoon salt
>
> 2½ tablespoons *aka miso* (dark fermented bean paste)
>
> ½ teaspoon *sanshō* (fragrant Japanese pepper)

Heat the stock in a saucepan over medium-low heat and season with ¼ teaspoon of salt and 2 teaspoons of soy sauce.

While the stock is heating, drain the bean curd well, gently pressing out excess liquid. Cut it into small cubes (about ½ inch on a side) and add these to the broth. Cook for 1 minute.

In a small saucepan, bring several cups of water to a rolling boil. Rub the whole okra pods with ½ teaspoon of salt to help remove their fuzz. Then blanch the pods in the boiling water for only 20 to 30 seconds—just long enough to turn the vegetable bright green and barely cooked. Drain the okra pods immediately and allow them to cool at room temperature until you can handle them comfortably. Trim off the stems and pointed tips, discarding these pieces. Slice the pods into ½-inch rounds (star shapes, really) and add these to the simmering bean-curd cubes in the broth.

Place the bean paste in a small separate bowl. Quickly whisk in ¼ cup or so of hot broth from the pot until completely combined. Pour the dissolved bean paste into the soup and stir until fully distributed. Let the soup simmer for 30 seconds more, then serve in individual bowls. Sprinkle a pinch of Japanese pepper over each serving just before bringing to the table.

Menu Suggestions: Serve this soup with a fluffy omelet or with any of the seasoned rice dishes in the Side Dishes chapter, such as Steamed Clams and Rice (p. 222). This dark bean soup would go well with most chicken and fish entrées in this book.

Mussel and Leek Chowder

MIRUGAI NO OMI-OTSUKÉ · Serves 4

Neither mussels nor leeks are native to Japan, but both are enormously popular among those Japanese who live abroad. In this chowder, the "foreign" broth from cooking the mussels enriches a traditional Japanese stock that's later flavored by leeks and thickened with bean paste. All together it makes for a memorable cross-cultural soup.

> 12–15 fresh mussels
> 20 square inches *dashi kombu* (dried kelp for stock making)
> ½ cup water
> 1 tablespoon *saké* (Japanese rice wine)
> 2–2½ cups *dashi* (basic sea stock, p. 48)
> 2 teaspoons soy sauce
> 1 tablespoon *saké* (Japanese rice wine)
> 1 small leek (about 2 ounces), trimmed of roots and tough green stalk
> 2½ tablespoons *shiro miso* (light fermented bean paste)
> 8 stalks flat-leafed Italian parsley, for garnish

With a brush, scrub the mussels well and remove their beards. Place the shells in a 4-quart, wide-mouthed pot with the dried kelp, water, and 1 tablespoon of rice wine. Cover the pot and, over high heat, cook the mussels until the shells open (you can hear them do this), which should take about 2 minutes from the time the water boils. Discard any shells that don't open.

Pour the broth through a cloth- or paper-lined strainer or colander into a 1-quart measuring cup. Add basic sea stock to the broth to make a total of 3 cups of liquid, and season with the soy sauce and 1 tablespoon of rice wine.

Remove the mussels from their steamed open shells, making sure that all traces of beard and grit are removed. If the mussels are larger than 1 inch, cut them in half. Reserve the mussel pieces.

Slit the white end of the leek lengthwise in a deep X and rinse under cold water to remove any sandy soil. Cut across the leek at ¼-inch intervals to chop the vegetable coarsely.

In a 2-quart pot, combine the seasoned broth and leek and cook over medium heat for 2 minutes until the vegetable wilts. Add the mussel pieces to the soup. Dissolve the bean paste in a separate bowl with a bit of broth ladled from the pot, then return all to the pot.

Rinse the flat-leafed parsley under cold water and pat dry with paper towels. Tear off the leaves and chop coarsely. Serve the soup hot, garnishing each bowl with a bit of the chopped parsley.

Menu Suggestions: I like to serve this soup with Herbed Rice (p. 228) and Lemon-Pickled Cabbage (p. 254) at the conclusion of a Japanese-style meal. In a more American mood, I precede a Rustic Japanese-Style Roast Chicken (p. 202) entrée with this zesty seafood soup.

Country-Style Chicken Soup

KASHIWA-JIRU · Serves 4

*B*rimming with tasty bits of chicken, fried bean curd, and vegetables, this filling chowderlike soup is thickened with mellow bean paste. The Japanese would make a light meal of this by adding steamed rice and pickles to the menu; you might translate that to read a hot, crusty peasant loaf and a tossed green salad.

> 1 **large chicken breast, 5–6 ounces with skin and bones removed**
> 1 **teaspoon** *saké* **(Japanese rice wine)**
> **pinch salt**
> 1 **piece** *abura agé* **(fried bean curd), about 2½ by 4½ inches**
> 3½ **cups** *dashi* **(basic sea stock, p. 48)**
> 1 **teaspoon** *mirin* **(syrupy rice wine)**
> 1 **teaspoon** *usukuchi shōyu* **(light soy sauce)**
> 2 **ounces carrot, peeled and cut in 1½- by ¼-inch julienne strips**
> 3 **ounces** *daikon* **(Japanese white radish), peeled and cut like carrots**
> 2½ **tablespoons** *shiro miso* **(light fermented bean paste)**
> 1 **slender scallion, trimmed and chopped fine (green and white parts)**

Holding the knife diagonal to the cutting board, slice the chicken breast across the grain into thin, broad slices. You may find it easier to use partially frozen meat. Stack several of these slices at a time and cut lengthwise to yield fairly uniform strips approximately 1½ inches long and ¼ inch wide. Toss these slices in the rice wine until they're coated, then sprinkle all with a pinch of salt. Bring several cups of water to a boil in a small saucepan. Blanch the chicken in it, stirring to separate the strips, for 10 seconds or just until the surface of the chicken turns white. Remove the strips with a slotted spoon and set aside on a plate.

In the same boiling water, blanch the fried bean curd for 15 seconds or until the slice puffs slightly and a film of oil clearly appears on the water's surface. Drain the bean curd and blot dry on paper towels. Cut the bean curd in half lengthwise, then across into narrow (⅛-inch) strips.

Heat the stock and season with the syrupy rice wine and light soy sauce. Add the fried bean curd and the julienned carrot and radish. Simmer for 5 minutes, then add the chicken and continue to cook for 1 more minute or until heated through.

In a separate bowl, dissolve the light bean paste in a bit of hot broth, then pour this mixture back into the pot. Stir to combine thoroughly. Sprinkle with the scallions and serve the soup hot.

Shrimp, Mushrooms, Poached Egg, and Greens over Thick, White Soup Noodles

NABÉ YAKI UDON · *Serves 4*

This hearty meal-in-a-bowl soup is a perfect antidote to even the coldest of winter days. In Japan, restaurants and many homes have individual *nabé* casseroles made specially for cooking and serving this and similar dishes. These glazed ceramic casseroles can withstand the heat of direct contact with burners. Occasionally I've seen these Japanese casseroles for sale in the United States, though often they're of a larger size that might hold four portions at once. So that everyone can enjoy this fabulous soup, I've given instructions in this recipe for several different kinds of equipment.

broth:
- 7 cups *dashi* (basic sea stock, p. 48)
- 1 teaspoon salt
- 2 tablespoons *usukuchi shōyu* (light soy sauce)
- 2 tablespoons regular soy sauce
- 3 tablespoons *mirin* (syrupy rice wine)

1 tablespoon sugar

1 small onion, peeled and cut in half

1 package (5 grams) OR about ⅓ cup *katsuo bushi* (dried bonito flakes)

noodles: 12–14 ounces fresh, uncooked *udon* (thick white noodles) OR 8–10 ounces dried *udon* (flat white noodles)

toppings: 4 jumbo shrimp

1 tablespoon *saké* (Japanese rice wine)

1 tablespoon cornstarch

2 ounces fresh spinach, with leaves still attached to stems (you'll need two 6-inch lengths of kitchen twine to tie the spinach, too)

½ teaspoon salt in 2 quarts boiling water

4 large whole eggs

2 packages *enokidaké* (slender creamy-white mushrooms), 3½ ounces each

In a 3- or 4-quart saucepan, season the stock with the salt, light and regular soy sauces, syrupy rice wine, and sugar. Stirring occasionally, heat through until the salt and sugar have dissolved. Add the onion and simmer for 5 minutes over medium heat. Remove the pot from the heat, sprinkle the bonito flakes over the soup, and let it stand for 2 minutes. Pour the soup through a cloth- or paper-lined strainer or colander, discarding the solids.

Bring 6 or more quarts of water to a rolling boil in a large stock pot. If you've been lucky enough to find fresh *udon* noodles, add them and cook for 8 minutes after the water returns to a boil or until each noodle is barely tender: firm but with no hard core at the center. The noodles will be briefly cooked again later. Drain and rinse the noodles under cold water and drain again.

If you're using dried noodles, cook them in a very large pot in at least 6 quarts of boiling water until the water returns to a boil. Add 2 cups of cold water and wait for the water to return to a boil a second time. Now cook the noodles for 7–8 more minutes in water that's kept at a constant boil. Test a strand; it should be firmer than the Italian *al dente* since the noodles will later be cooked again, but not so raw as to have a hard core remaining at the center now. Drain the cooked noodles, rinse, and drain again. Set the cooked noodles aside until all the toppings have been readied.

Peel and devein the shrimp. Stir the rice wine and cornstarch until well combined, in a small dish just large enough to hold the shrimp. Add the shrimp and marinate them in the wine and cornstarch mixture for 3–4 minutes while bringing several cups of water to a rolling boil in a small pot. Add the shrimp to the boiling water, stir, and wait 1 minute before straining them through a small colander or strainer. Set aside while you finish making the other toppings.

Rinse the spinach and shake dry. Divide the spinach into two bundles and tie the stems of each with kitchen twine. In a wide-mouthed, shallow pot bring about 2 quarts of water to a boil. Add ½ teaspoon salt and quickly plunge the spinach stems first into the salted water. Stir if necessary to wilt all the leaves and stems, then drain the spinach immediately, refreshing it under cold water. Squeeze the spinach dry, and trim off and discard the very bottoms of the stems with the twine. Slice the spinach into 1-inch lengths and divide into four portions before setting aside.

Break each of the four eggs into its own small bowl, being careful not to puncture the yolks. Cover the eggs and set aside.

Rinse the *enokidaké* mushrooms under cold water and trim off the bottom halves of the stems. Pat the mushrooms dry and divide into four portions.

The Japanese use individual heat-proof casseroles with lids to finish cooking and serving this soup. If you have them, or any 3- to 4-cup capacity containers with lids that can withstand direct heat, follow the procedure described here: Divide the broth among the four containers. Place them on the burners and heat the broth just to a gentle boil. Add the noodles and simmer for 30 seconds, skimming the surface if necessary to remove any excess starch coming from the noodles. Allow the soup to return to a gentle boil, then pour one egg into each casserole and cover. Simmer over medium-low heat. The Japanese like the whites firm but the yolks rather runny; that happens after approximately 3 minutes of poaching. Most Americans prefer a firmer egg, which will take about 2 additional minutes of poaching. Remove the cover from each of the casseroles and, without hiding the egg from view, lay a shrimp, then a portion of mushrooms and a bundle of spinach next to each other and over the noodles and bubbling broth. Replace the covers, then remove the casseroles from the burners and serve at once.

If you don't have individual cooking casseroles, you'll need to poach the eggs separately before assembling the soup. Heat through the seasoned broth and add the cooked noodles. Just as the soup reaches a boil, remove it from the stove. Immediately divide the soup and noodles among four deep soup bowls. Place a poached egg and blanched shrimp on top of the noodles in each bowl, then add some mushrooms and spinach to each serving, gently submerging these last two beneath the piping-hot soup. Serve at once.

Since this soup would be difficult and messy to serve at the table from a large communal pot, I don't recommend making this dish in a single large casserole. Rather, you might take advantage of a microwave oven to heat preassembled individual bowls of soup with their toppings. In that case, divide the cooked noodles among four deep soup bowls. Gently lay a poached egg, a blanched shrimp, a portion of mushrooms, and a bundle of spinach over each bowl of noodles. Pour the seasoned broth over all, being careful not to break the yolk. Cover each bowl with clear plastic wrap and place in a microwave. Set the oven for "boil" for 15 seconds. Remove the plastic wrap and serve at once.

Menu Suggestions: This is truly a full meal all by itself, but if you wanted to serve a salad with it you might slice some ripe tomatoes or try crisp lettuce with ginger vinaigrette dressing (p. 261).

Thick Rice Soup with Chicken, Chives, and Ginger

OJIYA · Serves 4

The word *ojiya*, in Japanese, has motherly overtones; being served it means you're being well cared for. In the wintertime in Japan, this porridgelike dish is made by many a woman for her husband and children, since the soothing soup is thought to relieve all manner of symptoms from overindulgence at an office party to the loss of appetite that often comes with the common cold. In that respect, I guess this thick rice soup is the Japanese equivalent of Western chicken soup, which is thought to have similar restorative powers. I personally crave *Ojiya* soup most when I'm physically fit, and serve it with a large green salad or assorted pickled vegetables. I highly recommend Thick Rice Soup to you on any chilly evening; it's Japanese homey, cozy cooking with a universal appeal. The fact that it provides you with a fine use for cooked rice that might be left over from another meal is an extra bonus.

> 1 quart *tori-gara dashi* (basic chicken stock, p. 51)
>
> 2–2½ cups cooked rice (p. 218); leftovers are perfect
>
> 1½–2 chicken breasts, ¾ pound in all with skin and bones removed
>
> 2 tablespoons *saké* (Japanese rice wine)
>
> ½ teaspoon salt
>
> 1 teaspoon ginger juice (extracted from freshly grated ginger)
>
> 2 tablespoons chopped chives

Heat the chicken stock in a large pot. Place the cooked rice in a strainer and rinse under cold water to separate the grains and remove excess starch. Drain the rice thoroughly before adding it to the chicken stock. Simmer the rice in the stock over low heat for 10 minutes, or until each grain of rice swells to at least twice its original size. Prepare the chicken, ginger juice, and chives while the soup is simmering.

Preheat your broiler. Marinate the chicken breasts in the rice wine for 1–2 minutes. Remove them and sprinkle salt on both sides. Under a hot broiler, cook the salted chicken 3–4 inches from the source of heat for 6–7 minutes. Turn the chicken and cook for another 2–3 minutes. The chicken is done when the surface is very slightly charred in some places and only lightly colored in others. When the chicken is cool enough to handle, shred it with your fingers into thin strips about ¼ inch wide and 1½ inches long. The irregular surface has more taste this way than cut with a knife. Add the chicken strips to the simmering rice soup. Cook for 1 minute.

Grate fresh ginger and squeeze the gratings to release 1 teaspoon of juice. Add it to the pot and stir. Serve immediately in deep bowls and sprinkle with chopped chives.

Oyster and Rice Soup

KAKI ZŌSUI · *Serves 4*

Another thick rice soup, this one with more refined overtones than the previous recipe, for homey chicken-and-rice soup (p. 62). Although this recipe, too, is an excellent way to use leftover cooked rice, the inclusion of fresh, plump oysters is slightly extravagant.

> 1½ cups cooked rice (p. 218); leftovers are perfect
>
> about 1 dozen freshly shucked oysters with their liquor, 6–7 ounces in all without shells
>
> ½ teaspoon salt
>
> 3 cups *dashi* (basic sea stock, p. 50)
>
> 2 tablespoons *saké* (Japanese rice wine)
>
> 2 tablespoons soy sauce
>
> 1 tablespoon chopped fresh chives

Place the cooked rice in a fine-meshed strainer and rinse under cold water until each grain is separated and no longer gummy. Drain the rice well until no water drips from the strainer.

Pour off and reserve any natural juice (liquor) from the oysters. Sprinkle ½ teaspoon of salt on the oysters and toss gently, making sure they're thoroughly coated. Rinse the oysters under cold running water to remove any grit. Pat dry on paper towels. If the oysters are larger than 1½ inches, you might want to cut them in half.

Pour the stock and reserved liquor into a wide-mouthed pot and bring to a boil rapidly. Reduce the heat to maintain a steady simmer, skim off any foam, and add the rice. Stir to separate any lumps.

Add the oysters and cook for 1 minute. Season the broth with rice wine and soy sauce, stir to distribute well, and cook for 2 more minutes. Sprinkle with chives and serve immediately.

Menu Suggestions: In Japan, this rice soup is served with pickled vegetables at the conclusion of a meal. At an American table it might precede a luncheon omelet with a leafy green salad (the one with walnut and *miso* dressing on p. 260 would be nice) or a dinner of roasted poultry or beef.

Shrimp Dumpling Soup with Snow Pea Pods

EBI SHINJO WAN · Serves 6

For centuries, the Japanese have been mincing and mashing shrimp with a knife and a mortar and pestle to create plump, pink dumplings such as these. Here's a modern version produced in the food processor. The broth in which the dumplings nestle is imbued with a subtle ocean aroma from the shrimp poached in it, and is enriched by the addition of some chicken stock. This soup goes magnificently with most of the *sushi* dishes in this book and also makes a fine beginning to a vegetable or egg entrée.

dumplings:	½ pound fresh shrimp, peeled and deveined
	1 teaspoon *saké* (Japanese rice wine)
	pinch salt
	1 slender scallion
	1 teaspoon cornstarch
broth:	1 cup *tori-gara dashi* (basic chicken stock, p. 51)
	4 cups *dashi* (basic sea stock, p. 48)
	1 teaspoon *saké* (Japanese rice wine)
	1 teaspoon *usukuchi shōyu* (light soy sauce)
	¼ teaspoon salt (optional)
	12 fresh snow pea pods, for garnish

Place the shrimp in the bowl of a food processor fitted with the steel blade. Add 1 teaspoon of rice wine and a pinch of salt, and pulse-process to make a fairly smooth paste.

Wash and trim the scallion, then mince it before adding it to the shrimp paste. Pulse-process so that it's well distributed. Sprinkle the cornstarch over the shrimp paste and pulse-process again to combine all the ingredients thoroughly.

In a saucepan, combine the chicken stock and sea stock, and bring to a boil. Season with 1 teaspoon each of rice wine and light soy sauce and, if you think it's needed, a pinch or two of salt. Bring this seasoned broth to a gentle boil.

Moisten your hands with cold water and form eighteen small spheres from the shrimp mixture. Poach these three or four at a time in the seasoned broth, simmering each batch for 1 minute after they float to the surface. Remove them gently with a slotted spoon and set them on a plate. When you've finished poaching all the shrimp dumplings, pour the broth through a cloth- or paper-lined strainer or colander into a quart measure. Add water, or fresh sea stock if you have it, in order to make 1 quart of liquid.

Snap back the stem end of each snow pea pod and pull back along the straight side to remove the string. Blanch the pods in several cups of boiling water just to brighten their color (about 10 seconds). Drain and cool as rapidly as possible under cold water. Pat dry, and trim to resemble leaves, as illustrated.

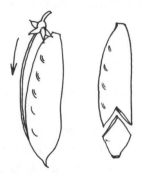

Put the quart of strained broth into a saucepan. Add the shrimp dumplings and heat both thoroughly. Serve three dumplings per bowl with hot broth, garnishing each portion with two decorative snow peas.

Clear Clam Broth with Lemon Peel

USHIO-JIRU · Serves 4–6

Unlike American clam chowders, which are thick and combine a variety of flavors, this clear Japanese soup is accented with only a splash of rice wine, a drop of soy, and a decorative sliver of lemon peel. Native American quahogs found along the eastern seaboard are particularly well suited to this Japanese treatment, though you can use any variety of hard-shell clam with equal success. *Ushio-Jiru* captures the rich yet subtle essence of the clam.

> 15–20 cherrystone OR other hard-shell clams
> 20–25 square inches *dashi kombu* (dried kelp for
>   stock making)

6 cups of cold water
½ teaspoon salt
1 tablespoon *saké* (Japanese rice wine)
1 teaspoon *usukuchi shōyu* (light soy sauce)
peel from ½ large lemon

Scrub the clams with a stiff brush, then soak them in several cups of salted water (it should taste briny, like the ocean) for 45 minutes–1 hour. Stir up and discard the water. Repeat this procedure to get rid of all sand and foreign matter.

Lay the dried kelp in a large, wide-mouthed pot, and pour 6 cups of cold water over it. Place the clams in the pot, cover, and bring to a boil rapidly over high heat. Continue to cook over high heat for 1 minute, or until you hear the clams opening. At most, cook for 3–4 minutes. Then remove the pot from the heat. (Some clams never open and must be discarded. You'll want to serve at least two or three per person, so include a few extra in the pot.) Set aside the steamed clams in their open shells.

Pour the broth from the pot through a cloth- or paper-lined strainer or colander. Discard the kelp (or save for making the recipes on pp. 116, 262, 264). Gently rinse the clams if they seem sandy. Remove half the shell of each clam so that it fits more easily into an individual soup bowl.

Season the reserved broth with the salt, rice wine, and light soy sauce. Keep this broth barely simmering over low heat while you make the decorative lemon peels. Use a sharp, small stainless-steel knife or small scissors when shaping the peel.

In the fall or winter months, shape your lemon peel into pine needles: For each serving cut one or two long, narrow, triangular wedges. Trim them as illustrated.

In the early spring, shape your lemon peel into cherry blossom petals: For each serving, cut three oval shapes, each about ½ inch long and no more than ¼ inch at the widest spot. Trim each as illustrated.

At all other times of the year, a simple flower shape is best: Cut one circle per serving. The circles should be 1 inch in diameter. Trim each one as illustrated.

To serve the soup, place two or three clams in each bowl and pour hot seasoned broth over them. Float the decorative lemon peel on top of the soup. Serve immediately.

Menu Suggestions: The Japanese serve this soup with *sushi* dishes or other seasoned rice dishes, such as Herbed Rice (p. 228) or Autumn Rice with Wild Mushrooms (p. 224). Clear Clam Broth with Lemon Peel is a lovely way to start a meal that will feature roasted poultry, too.

Temple Garden Soup

UMPEN-JIRU · Serves 4

To Americans it may seem odd that elegant cuisine is served at places intended for religious worship, but in Japan the very finest vegetarian food may be found at any number of Buddhist temples that house restaurants within the temple grounds, and some manage restaurants outside the religious precincts as well. Some of these restaurants serve only at midday, while others serve an evening meal in addition.

It was at Muryoan, a Tokyo restaurant affiliated with the Ōbakuzan School of Buddhism, whose main Japanese branch is located in Kyoto, that I first sampled this thick, gingery vegetable soup. The version I present here takes advantage of the recent and increasing availability in the United States of fresh *shiitaké* mushrooms.

> 3 ounces canned bamboo shoots, drained
> ½ small carrot, about 1½ ounces
> 2 ounces fresh *shiitaké* (dark oak mushrooms)
> 1 small white turnip, about 3 ounces
> 1½ ounces fresh snow peas
> 3½ cups *dashi* (basic sea stock, p. 48)
> 1–1½ tablespoons *usukuchi shōyu* (light soy sauce)
> ¼ teaspoon salt
> 1 teaspoon *saké* (Japanese rice wine)
> scant 1 tablespoon ginger juice (extracted from freshly grated ginger)
> 3 tablespoons cornstarch
> 1½ tablespoons cold water

Cut the bamboo shoots in very thin (1⁄16-inch) vertical slices, and if necessary remove any white calcified areas from the "teeth" of the comb-shaped pieces. Peel the carrot and slice it into paper-thin rounds. Or, if you have a decorative flower-shaped cutter, stamp out the rounds to look like flowers.

Remove the stems from the mushrooms and save them for use in enriching stock (p. 50) or discard. Wipe the caps with a damp cloth to remove any dust or soil. Slice the caps into thin julienne strips.

Peel the turnip and slice it into paper-thin rounds. If the diameter exceeds 1½ inches, first cut the turnip in half through the stem, and then cut the halves across into paper-thin half-moon slices.

Snap off the stem end of each snow pea and pull back along the straight side to remove the string. Slice each pod in half sharply on the diagonal.

Bring a small saucepan of water to a rolling boil. First blanch the bamboo shoots for 10–15 seconds, removing them promptly with a slotted spoon. Set aside. In the same boiling water blanch the carrot and turnip for 5–10 seconds and remove them, too, with a slotted spoon, then set aside. Last, remove the saucepan from the heat and toss the snow peas into the hot water. Stir once and immediately drain the snow peas, then refresh them under cold running water. Drain and pat dry before setting aside.

In a 2- or 3-quart saucepan, bring the stock to a simmer, then season with the light soy sauce, salt, and rice wine. Add the bamboo shoots and cook over a low flame for 2–3 minutes. Add the mushroom slices and continue to cook for 1 minute. Skim the broth, if necessary. Add the carrot and turnip slices and cook for 1 minute. Stir in the ginger juice.

Mix the cornstarch and cold water in a small cup to make a smooth paste. Add this to the soup, stirring well. Raise the heat to allow the soup to bubble and thicken. Toss the blanched snow peas into the soup, stir, and serve immediately.

Menu Suggestions: At Muryoan restaurant, this soup is served about halfway through an elegant meal that's incredibly inventive in its use of *tōfu* (bean curd) and other vegetables. If you wish to try a similar vegetarian meal, try pairing Temple Garden Soup with Bean Curd *Tempura* with Spicy Scallion Sauce (p. 183), Herbed rice (p. 228), Simmered Mushrooms and Kelp (p. 262), and a fruit gelatin such as Jellied Orange Wedges (p. 288).

This colorful vegetable soup in its delicate broth could just as easily begin a meal that will feature meat. Lamb Chops with Fresh Wild Japanese Mushrooms (p. 207) or Grilled Veal Chops with *Sanshō* Butter (p. 206) would be a lovely choice.

Ocean Noodle Broth

SAKANA-ZŌMEN · *Serves 8*

Long before the invention of the food processor, frugal Japanese made a version of this soup with scraps left from filleting fish. It was a tedious and time-consuming task to pick bits and pieces of flesh from the fish bones, mince it with knives, then mash it with a mortar and pestle before piping and poaching the "noodles." The results were obviously worth the trouble, since a recipe for this soup dating back to the seventeenth century still exists!

Today, with modern kitchen equipment, the making of these prized ocean noodles has been greatly simplified. Since both the broth and the noodles freeze well, I recommend that you make a full recipe even if you intend to serve only a few portions at a time.

broth:
- 1 whole porgy, about 1 pound (use head and bones for broth, flesh for noodles)
- 1 tablespoon salt
- 2 quarts cold water
- 20–25 square inches *dashi kombu* (dried kelp for stock making)
- 2 slices fresh ginger, each the size of a quarter
- 3 tablespoons *saké* (Japanese rice wine)
- 2 teaspoons salt
- 2 teaspoons *usukuchi shōyu* (light soy sauce)
- 1 large egg (use white and shell to clarify stock; reserve yolk for noodles)

noodles:	flesh from above fish (about ¾ cup, coarsely chopped)
	yolk from above egg
1	teaspoon *saké* (Japanese rice wine)
1	teaspoon ginger juice (extracted from freshly grated ginger)
¼	teaspoon salt
¼	teaspoon *sanshō* (fragrant Japanese pepper)
2	tablespoons *jōshinko* (rice flour)
	about ⅛ cup water
1	small slender zucchini, about 6–7 inches long, for garnish
½	teaspoon salt

Have your fish store fillet the porgy and remove the skin from the fillets. Mention that you'll be using the head and bones in your stock, though you won't be needing the skin. The "meat" will be used in the noodle "dough."

Place the head and bones in a large colander and sprinkle 1 tablespoon of salt over all surfaces. Let the carcass "sweat" for 5–10 minutes. Pour boiling water over the bones and head; turn them over and repeat the boiling water bath. Place the blanched bones and head in a large saucepan with 2 quarts of fresh, cold water (at this stage the bones should be covered by at least ½ inch of water). Place the kelp in the pot and slowly bring to a boil, uncovered, over a low flame (this can take up to 1½ hours). Remove and discard the kelp. Lower the heat if necessary to keep the stock at a gentle simmer. Add the slices of ginger, rice wine, 2 teaspoons of salt, and light soy sauce, and continue to simmer for 10–15 minutes longer. Pour the stock through a cloth- or paper-lined strainer or colander, discarding the solids. Return the broth to a clean pot.

Separate the egg. Cover and set aside the yolk for making the noodles. Lightly beat the white and crush the shell slightly in it. Bring the strained broth to a boil and whisk in the crushed shell and beaten egg white. Continue to cook for 1 minute before pouring the broth again through a cloth- or paper-lined strainer or colander into a 2-quart measuring cup. If you have more than 6 cups of clarified broth, return it to the pot and reduce it by cooking, uncovered, over medium heat. If you have less than 6 cups of clarified stock, add fresh water to make 6 cups.

Carefully pick over the filleted fish, making sure to remove all bones and bits of skin. Chop the flesh into coarse pieces, then place them in the bowl of a food processor fitted with the metal blade. Pulse-process for 10–15 seconds. Add the yolk and 1 teaspoon each of rice wine and ginger juice; add ¼ teaspoon each of salt and Japanese pepper. Continue to pulse-process after each addition to ensure a smooth paste. Sprinkle the rice flour over the fish paste and process again. With the machine turned on, dribble the water through the feed tube. Stop after half of it has been added, to check the consistency; ideally, it should look like a buttercream frosting. With the fish paste, fill a nylon pastry bag fitted with a No. 5 Wilton tip.

Fill a wide pot with water to a depth of 3 inches. Bring to a vigorous boil. Hold the filled pastry bag 18–24 inches above the boiling water. Pipe in about one quarter of the paste in circular motions. Lower the heat and gently poach the noodles for 2–3 minutes (they'll rise to the surface as they cook). Gently remove the noodles with a slotted spoon and transfer them to a bowl of cold water. Drain the noodles to be used immediately. Place the drained noodles at the bottoms of individual soup bowls.

Bring the water in the pot back to a rolling boil and repeat the noodle-making process in three or more batches. Inevitably your arms will tire and begin to fall closer to the level of the hot water, where the steam from the pot "cooks" the fish paste in the tip of the pastry bag. If the tip of the bag should become clogged, use a toothpick to remove the obstruction.

Trim both ends of the zucchini, then cut it in half lengthwise. Cut across at equal intervals to yield eight pieces in all. Gently scrape out any seeds from each piece, then etch and trim the skin of the zucchini pieces so that each resembles a leaf. Blanch the zucchini leaves for 45

seconds in several cups of boiling water to which ½ teaspoon of salt has been added, removing them with a slotted spoon. Pat dry gently.

Rest a single zucchini leaf on top of the noodles in each bowl. Heat the seasoned broth just to the boiling point, then gently ladle ¾ cup of hot fish broth into every bowl. Serve at once.

Note on Freezing the Stock:
Allow the liquid to cool to room temperature before you freeze it. When ready to use the liquid, defrost in the refrigerator, then heat through.

Freezing the Noodles:
Fill a plastic container half full with cold water and lay the noodles in it. That way the noodles will freeze suspended in a solid block. To revive them, allow the noodles to defrost in the refrigerator, then pour off the water. Briefly heat the noodles in a microwave oven (7–8 seconds) or blanch them for 5–10 seconds in boiling water, then remove them carefully with a slotted spoon.

Menu Suggestions: I like to serve this soup with *sushi*—either intricately shaped Camellia *Sushi* (p. 142) and Chrysanthemum *Sushi* (p. 140), or pilaflike Five-Colored *Sushi* (p. 156). I like to think of the *sushi* dishes as the main attraction but might serve Cabbage and Spinach Rolls with Sesame Vinaigrette (p. 242) or Asparagus Salad in Smoky Sauce (p. 248) at the same time. Dessert could be any of the fruit gelatins or ices in this book.

Autumnal Sentiment Soup

AKI NO URUWASHII WAN · Serves 8

From mid-September through late November, large bright-yellow chrysanthemums bloom throughout most of Japan. They're an impressive sight inspiring all sorts of poetic images: Autumnal Sentiment Soup is my personal interpretation of nature's glory. This delicate soup could herald the start of a dinner featuring a simple roasted-meat or grilled-fish entrée.

 3 or 4 slender scallions (green parts only)
 1 package (3½ ounces) *enokidaké* (slender creamy-white mushrooms)
 4 large circles *usutamago yaki* (thin omelet, p. 132)
 2–3 ounces *shungiki* (chrysanthemum leaves) OR fresh chard OR spinach (you'll need eight 4-inch lengths of kitchen twine to tie the greens, too)
 6 cups *tori-gara dashi* (basic chicken stock, p. 51)
 2 teaspoons *saké* (Japanese rice wine)
 2 teaspoons *usukuchi shōyu* (light soy sauce)
 1 package (5 grams) OR about ⅓ cup loosely packed *katsuo bushi* (dried bonito flakes)

Blanch the green parts of the scallions in boiling water just for a few seconds to make them pliable. Drain and cool at once in cold water, then remove them and pat dry. Select eight of the longest and strongest of the green stalks and use one for tying each flower (you should have one or two extra stalks in case a first effort tears).

Briefly rinse the *enokidaké* mushrooms under cold water and shake dry. Divide the mushrooms into eight parts. Don't trim the roots.

Lay the omelets on a dry board and cut them in half; set aside seven halves, keeping a single sheet on the board. Fold the sheet in half, bringing the bottom edge to meet flush with the top. Make many shallow slits on this folded edge. Lay one bunch of *enokidaké* mushrooms so that the knobs are just below the slit edge of the omelet. Roll the omelet snugly around the mushrooms and tie it up with a scallion "string" (use a double knot if possible). Trim off the mushroom stems

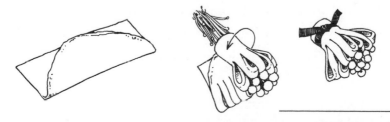

so that they're flush with the bottom edge of the omelet. Stand up the chrysanthemum in the bottom of a shallow bowl (a smooth, dark surface makes a particularly stunning backdrop). Repeat this procedure to make seven more flowers.

Wash the greens carefully and divide them into eight bunches, with the stems of all running in the same direction. Tie the stems of each bunch with kitchen twine. Bring a pot with several quarts of salted water to a rolling boil. With tongs, dip the greens in the water until just wilted and bright green (you may wish to leave chard in the water a bit longer before removing). Remove the greens to a bowl of cold water. Squeeze out all excess water when the greens are cool enough to handle. Trim off the twine and stems, and arrange one bunch of greens in each bowl, swerving to the right of each flower.

Bring the chicken stock to a boil and season with the rice wine and light soy sauce. Remove the stock from the heat and sprinkle the fish flakes over the surface. Let the stock stand for 2–3 minutes before stirring it up and pouring it through a cloth- or paper-lined strainer or colander into a measuring cup. Gently pour or ladle the seasoned stock around the flowers in each bowl so that the petals float, barely suspended in the broth. Serve at once.

Pale Jade Soup

HISUI WAN · Serves 4

Once considered an exotic Oriental vegetable, fresh snow pea pods are increasingly popular and available from supermarkets as well as specialty greengrocers throughout the United States, nearly year-round. With top-quality fresh peas coming to market from March through September and aromatic fresh mint available for only a slightly shorter growing season, this soup takes advantage of the bounty of America's spring and summer.

In this recipe I have barely blanched and pureed the snow pea pods to preserve their vivid greenness and fresh garden flavor, adding them to a subtly seasoned chicken-based broth. I created this soup to serve with broiled and roasted meats and fish.

½ tablespoon butter
2 tablespoons minced scallion (green and white parts)
1 tablespoon *saké* (Japanese rice wine)
2⅔ cups *tori-gara dashi* (basic chicken stock, p. 51)
1 cup (about 4 ounces) freshly shelled peas
3–4 ounces fresh snow peas, strings removed
pinch salt (optional)
1½ tablespoons cornstarch
1 tablespoon cold water
1 tablespoon fresh heavy cream
1 teaspoon finely chopped fresh mint
4 sprigs fresh mint, for garnish (optional)

In a 2- or 3-quart saucepan, melt the butter, add the scallions, and sauté over low heat. When the scallions have wilted, add the rice wine and 1⅔ cups of the chicken stock, and simmer for 10–15 minutes after the soup has come to a boil.

While the stock is simmering, cook the peas for 3 minutes in several cups of boiling salted water. Toss the snow peas into the same pot, stir for 10 seconds, and drain. Place the peas, snow peas, and the remaining cup of chicken stock in a food processor or blender and puree to a smooth consistency.

Pour the pureed pea mixture into the saucepan containing the seasoned chicken broth, and stir to mix thoroughly. Over medium-high heat bring the soup to a gentle simmer, then taste and adjust if necessary with a pinch of salt. In a separate cup, combine the cornstarch and cold water, mixing them into a smooth paste. Dribble the paste into the soup, stirring it constantly, and continue to cook over medium-high heat for 30 seconds until the soup thickens. Stir in the fresh cream and remove the soup from the heat. Sprinkle fresh chopped mint over the soup, stirring it in so that it becomes combined.

Serve immediately, garnishing each portion with a sprig of mint, if you like.

Menu Suggestions: This soup is particularly good served with Sweet and Spicy Grilled Leg of Lamb (p. 211), Steak with *Wasabi* Butter (p. 204), or Glaze-Grilled Salmon Steaks (p. 179).

Tomato and Shiso Bisque

AKANÉ-JIRU · Serves 4

Tomatoes were first introduced to Japan over a hundred years ago by Europeans but didn't really gain any popularity until after World War II. Today, the plump, rosy-red fruit is served mainly in leafy green salads or as a garnish. When cooked in a sauce it's served with Continental food only—tomatoes never appear on a strictly Japanese menu.

I personally adore the combination of fresh tomatoes and a broad-leafed Japanese herb called *shiso.* Experimentation in my Tokyo kitchen several years ago produced this cross-cultural soup. The recent availability in the United States of *shiso* leaves (as well as the seeds to plant in one's own herb garden) makes it possible for me to bring this recipe into my active file once again.

> 6–7 sun-dried tomatoes
> ½ cup water
> 1 tablespoon *saké* (Japanese rice wine)
> ½ tablespoon butter
> ⅓ cup minced onions
> 1 tablespoon flour
> 1 cup *tori-gara dashi* (basic chicken stock, p. 51)

2 cups fresh tomatoes, about 12 ounces
    peeled and seeded
1 tablespoon sugar
2–3 tablespoons fresh heavy cream
10 fresh leaves *shiso* (flat-leafed Japanese herb)

Place the sun-dried tomatoes in a small heat-proof glass or porce-lain-lined saucepan with the water and rice wine. Simmer uncovered over medium heat for 5–6 minutes. Strain the liquid (there should be a scant ¼ cup) and reserve for later in the recipe. Let the sun-dried tomatoes cool until they're comfortable to handle, then remove and discard their paper-thin skins. With a small spoon, try to scrape away as many seeds as possible, leaving just the pulp behind. You should have a generous tablespoon of pulp from six or seven tomatoes.

In a 3-quart, noncorrodible saucepan, melt the butter and sauté the onions over low heat for 2 minutes or until just wilted. Sprinkle the flour over the onions and continue to cook, stirring for 2–3 more minutes (the roux may color slightly). Whisk in the reserved liquid (a scant ¼ cup) from the dried tomatoes and continue to cook, whisking until smooth and slightly thickened. Stir in the basic chicken stock and keep at a simmer while preparing the tomato puree.

In a food processor fitted with the metal blade, pulse-process the fresh tomatoes until evenly but coarsely pureed. Add the pulp from the sun-dried tomatoes and pulse-process again. Add this two-tomato puree to the simmering stock, season with the sugar, and cook for 3–4 minutes. Dribble in the fresh cream, stir to mix, and keep the soup hot but don't let it boil.

Rinse the *shiso* leaves under cold water and pat the leaves dry. Trim off the stems. Reserve four of the smallest, prettiest leaves whole, and roll the remaining six leaves tightly before slicing them into very fine julienne. Toss the shredded herb into the soup and stir to mix.

Serve in individual soup bowls, garnishing each with a whole *shiso* leaf.

Menu Suggestions: I find this thick, rosy bisque quite versatile and serve it with meat, poultry, or fish. I'm particularly fond of pairing it with the Glazed Chicken Roll (p. 196), Cold Steamed Peppered Pork with Mustard Sauce (p. 167), or Braised Ground Veal over Rice (p. 191).

A Bowl of Sunshine

OHISAMA NO WAN · *Serves 4*

This smooth, creamy pumpkin-and-yam soup laced with fresh ginger is named for its bright color and the body-warming glow it produces when consumed. The first time I tasted something similar to this was at the Andoh home in Shikoku, the smallest of Japan's four main islands, before I became an Andoh. My mother-in-law was anxious to make a soup to my western tastes and served a delicious cream-of-yam soup one morning for breakfast! She made it again many years later when Rena (my daughter and one of her favorite grandchildren) and I were visiting her. Rena said the soup reminded her of sunshine, and so it received its "official" name. Since returning to America I've experimented with several variations on the theme and found that native American pumpkins and squashes are wonderful in this sunny soup.

½ tablespoon butter

2 tablespoons minced shallots

1 tablespoon flour

scant ¼ teaspoon salt

pinch white pepper

3 cups *tori-gara dashi* (basic chicken stock, p. 51)

3 slices fresh ginger, peeled, each the size of a quarter

¼ small pumpkin OR 1 small butternut squash, 8–9 ounces peeled and seeded

1 sweet potato OR yam, 6–7 ounces peeled

3–4 tablespoons fresh heavy cream (optional)

In a saucepan, sauté the shallots in the butter over low heat until wilted (about 4 minutes). Sprinkle the flour over them and, stirring all the while with a whisk or wooden spoon, cook the dry roux for 2 minutes (it may color slightly). Season with salt and pepper, then add ½ cup of the chicken stock, whisking it until smooth. Continue to cook, stirring with the whisk, until the mixture thickens considerably. Whisk in 1½ cups more stock and add the ginger. Let the soup simmer while preparing the vegetable puree. The soup should simmer for at least 10 minutes and up to 15; the longer time is for those who adore the gentle fire of fresh ginger. Remove and discard the ginger.

Cut the pumpkin and yam into 1- to 2-inch cubes. Bring several cups of salted water to a boil and cook the pumpkin and yam in it for 5–6 minutes or until just tender (a fork inserted in the vegetables should meet with no resistance). Drain the vegetables and puree until smooth in a blender with the remaining cup of chicken stock.

Add this puree to the simmering gingery broth and stir well to combine. Heat the soup thoroughly over medium heat.

Beat the heavy cream until it holds soft peaks and serve the soup hot with a dollop of whipped cream on top, if you like.

Menu Suggestions: I serve this soup with meat, fish, and poultry entrées such as Lamb Chops with Fresh Wild Japanese Mushrooms (p. 207), Glaze-Grilled Salmon Steaks (p. 179), and *Miso*-Marinated Baked Chicken (p. 193).

Appetizers...

_A_n enticing assortment of finger foods—pristine slices of fresh fish and tidbits of edible poetry that include Seashore Flowers, Misty Fried Shrimp, "Autumn Rains" Spicy Stewed Clams, Glazed Beef and Asparagus Rolls

The recipes in this chapter were inspired by both the elegant, diminutively scaled foods served at formal Japanese meals and the charming finger foods and tidbits usually packed into Japanese box lunches. These Japanese foods adapt particularly well to many American occasions. Some, such as Caviar in Cucumber Baskets, Chicken and Veal Pâté Fans, or Fish and *Tōfu* Terrine, can become spectacular first courses in a sit-down meal. Others, such as Chicken Dumplings or Crisp Vegetables with Sesame Dip, feed large crowds easily. Still others, such as Ginger-Glazed Chicken Wings, Japanese-Style Breaded Fried Oysters, or Gift-Wrapped Kelp Rolls, provide glorious nibbles for a tailgate party or a humble picnic basket.

In addition to the tremendous variety of tastes and textures to sample here, you'll find a new concept in food temperature to explore. While most Americans think of eating foods either chilled or piping hot, the vast majority of these foods are served at room temperature in their native Japan. I think you'll be surprised to discover how tasty steamed Seashore Flowers or Misty Fried Shrimp can remain even after they've cooled down. Or how much more flavorful Amber Aspic Loaf or "Autumn Rains" Spicy Stewed Clams can be when they're no longer icy cold or very hot. Not having to worry about bringing the food to the table hot or cold will simplify your kitchen work, too.

Here follows a collection of twenty enticing appetizers for entertaining or family enjoyment.

Seashore Flowers

HAMABÉ NO HANA · *Makes 2 dozen*

Here a lightly seasoned forcemeat of shrimp and scallops is easily molded into flower shapes before being steamed. Seashore Flowers make a poetically divine appetizer! Serve them alone or in combination with the Batter-Fried Vegetable Bundles (p. 95) or Gift-Wrapped Kelp Rolls (p. 116).

5 ounces carefully rinsed fresh bay OR sea scallops
3 ounces shelled, deveined shrimp
pinch salt
1 tablespoon *saké* (Japanese rice wine)
½ tablespoon cornstarch
½ teaspoon vegetable oil
1 teaspoon drained, very finely minced *beni shōga* (red pickled ginger)
soy sauce for dipping (optional)
flat-leafed Italian parsley OR *mitsuba* (trefoil), for garnish (optional)

Rinse the scallops and pat dry with paper towels. Place the scallops and shrimp in the bowl of a food processor fitted with the steel blade and pulse-process until finely chopped. Add the salt and rice wine, and process until fairly smooth. Sprinkle the cornstarch over the mixture and process until you have a smooth paste.

Lightly oil a heat-proof plate that will fit in your steamer. Wet your hands in cold water and divide the seafood mixture into twenty-four portions. Take each portion and roll it into a compact ball. Flatten the ball between the heels of your hands, then lay it on the oiled plate. Repeat to make two dozen in all. In the center of each circle, place a few bits of minced red ginger. With the blunt end of a toothpick, press these bits lightly into the forcemeat.

Bring the water in the bottom of your steamer to a boil, then adjust the flame so that water simmers steadily and there's a constant flow of steam throughout the top of the steamer. Steam the Seashore Flowers for 10–12 minutes. They'll puff up considerably as they steam, but then resume their original proportions when taken from the steamer. Remove them with a spatula and serve warm or at room temperature, with soy sauce if you like. To enhance the floral effect, garnish your serving platter with flat-leafed parsley or trefoil that has been rinsed, then patted dry.

Note:
Any type of steamer will do for cooking this dish—bamboo or metal, the kind you buy in a housewares store or one that you improvise in your kitchen. If you're going to make your own, I suggest you use a shallow, wide-mouthed pot, one that has a lid that fits snugly. Take two or three small, empty cans (single-serving tuna fish cans are good) and remove both the top and the bottom lids from them. Use these to support a heat-proof dish that's slightly smaller in diameter than your pot.

Chicken Dumplings

TORI DANGO · *Makes 40–50*

When I'm faced with feeding a large crowd, these wonderful meatballs become part of my menu. It's a simple matter to make a large quantity—you could double the recipe for a really large gathering—and they're delicious either piping hot or at room temperature. They can be made hours in advance of your party and frozen for up to 1 month, which makes them ideal for home entertaining. A platter of Crisp Vegetables with Sesame Dip (p. 109) often shares the buffet table with these chicken dumplings.

dumplings:	4–5	ounces onion, about ¼ cup minced
	1	small clove garlic
	½	tablespoon vegetable oil
	¾	pound boneless, skinless breast of chicken
	¾	pound boneless, skinless thigh and/or leg of chicken
	2	tablespoons *shiro miso* (light fermented bean paste)
	1	yolk from large egg
	2	tablespoons all-purpose flour
poaching liquid:	2	quarts water
	1	tablespoon *saké* (Japanese rice wine)
simmering: sauce:	¾	cup soy sauce
	⅓	cup sugar
	¼	cup *saké* (Japanese rice wine)
	2	tablespoons *mirin* (syrupy rice wine)
	2	cups *dashi* (basic sea stock, p. 48) OR water
thickening agent:	3	tablespoons cornstarch
	⅓	cup cold water

Mince the onion and garlic, and sauté in the vegetable oil over low heat for 4–5 minutes. They should be wilted, but not browned. Let the vegetables cool to room temperature.

Place the light and dark chicken meats in a food processor fitted with the steel blade and pulse-process just long enough to chop the meats. Add the light fermented bean paste and egg yolk to the mixture in the processor. Pulse-process to incorporate, and make a fairly smooth paste. Add the minced and sautéed onions and garlic, then sprinkle the flour onto the mixture and process to distribute well.

In a wide-mouthed (9-inch, 4½-quart) pot, combine the poaching-liquid ingredients. Bring to a rolling boil. In another pot of the same dimensions, combine the simmering-sauce ingredients and, over low heat, stir and bring to a simmer.

Moisten your hands with water and form the chicken mixture into forty to fifty spheres, each about 1 inch in diameter. Poach twenty to twenty-five of them at a time (two batches) in the boiling poaching liquid. They'll rise to the surface in about 1½–2 minutes. Remove them with a slotted spoon to the simmering liquid. (While this first batch of chicken balls is simmering, a second batch can be poaching.) Simmer the chicken balls for 5 minutes. Remove these to a separate plate and simmer the second batch of poached chicken balls. (The amount of simmering sauce given here is the minimum required for cooking this recipe. If you're doubling the recipe, though, there's no need to double the simmering sauce, too.)

Mix the cornstarch and cold water to make a smooth paste. Pour this into the remaining simmering liquid, stirring constantly until the sauce thickens. Serve the chicken balls warm or at room temperature, in their sauce.

Note:
If you're making the chicken dumplings in advance and wish to freeze them, do so before the thickening agent has been added to the simmering liquid. Freeze the dumplings in the liquid. Bring them back to room temperature in the sauce before briefly reheating. Proceed to thicken the sauce and serve.

Glazed Beef and Asparagus Rolls

ASUPARA MAKI · Makes about 30

These are a more delicate version of the scallion and beef rolls so popular in Japanese restaurants in America.

½ pound fresh asparagus

1 pound lean sirloin of beef, sliced paper thin and broadly

suet, about 1½ tablespoons melted, OR vegetable oil

1 teaspoon *saké* (Japanese rice wine)

2 scant tablespoons sugar

3 tablespoons soy sauce

1 tablespoon water

Snap off the tough stems of the asparagus; you'll be left with stalks about 4 inches long. Use a single stalk for each roll if the asparagus is ½ inch or more in diameter; use two stalks if they're slender. If you use two stalks, arrange them so that their tips are at opposite ends.

Lay out the slices of beef and try to match with asparagus stalks that are as long as the beef is wide. If the beef should tear, you can patch it up by laying another piece on top of it. Roll the beef snugly around the asparagus and hold it in place by threading a toothpick lengthwise through the meat but not through the asparagus. You should be able to make about ten rolls.

Melt the suet in a heavy skillet, or oil the pan lightly. Heat the skillet, then add the rolls, seam side down, and sear them over high heat. The seams will seal quickly and then you can easily turn the rolls to brown on all sides. After about 1 minute, when the beef has changed color, add the rice wine, then the sugar, soy sauce, and water. Lower the heat slightly and continue to cook for 2 minutes, shaking the pan to keep the rolls moving.

Remove the skillet from the source of heat and remove the toothpicks by first twirling them in place, then pulling them out. If there's a great deal of foamy liquid in the pan at this stage, take the rolls out of the pan and, while you work at removing the toothpicks, let the pan juices simmer to reduce. (You can prepare the rolls up to this point 1 hour before serving. Keep the rolls covered, but at room temperature.)

Return the beef and asparagus rolls to the pan and briefly cook over high heat, shaking the pan constantly to glaze them.

Cut each of the rolls in thirds and serve immediately with fresh toothpicks, or let the sliced pieces cool to room temperature.

Note:
The Japanese typically stack these rolls in pyramidlike groups of three. At New Year's, though, they slice the rolls on the diagonal and stand them up with the sloped edge facing the diner. The sloped configuration reminds the Japanese of their *kado matsu* decoration, which is a pine and bamboo arrangement found at the entrances to most homes from December 28 through January 7 of the following year.

Menu Suggestions: These rolls make a tasty start to a fish entrée, particularly Snapper Steamed with Wild Mushrooms in Parchment (p. 181). The Japanese often include them in a picnic basket with Decorative Rice Bundles (p. 219). The picnic menu might be expanded by adding Lemon-Pickled Cabbage (p. 254), Ginger-Glazed Chicken Wings (p. 100), and perhaps some fresh ripe strawberries.

Skewered Pork Cutlets

KUSHI KATSU · Makes 1 dozen sticks

The Japanese "discovered" the pleasures of breaded fried pork thanks to the Dutch influence in Nagasaki several hundred years ago. More recently, the Japanese redesigned the dish by taking what was essentially a main course and making it over into an appetizer or snack. *Kushi katsu* are now a popular item on many Japanese menus through the United States.

Because the Japanese use special, coarse bread crumbs, the fried pork stays crispy for hours and is quite delicious at room temperature. Bite-size but unskewered nuggets of breaded fried pork find their way into many Japanese lunch boxes.

10–12 ounces lean pork butt

½ large green bell pepper, about 2 ounces with seeds and ribs removed

2 whole scallions

3–4 tablespoons all-purpose flour

1 egg, beaten with 1 tablespoon water

1 cup *panko* (coarse Japanese bread crumbs)

vegetable oil, for deep frying

tonkatsu sōsu (dark spicy sauce), for dipping

Slice the pork into twenty-four pieces, each about ¼ inch thick and 1–1½ inches square. Cut the pepper into six pieces, removing any seeds or ribs. Each piece should be about 1¼ inches square. Trim the scallions and cut them into 1½-inch lengths; you should have about six pieces of white, twelve pieces of green. Toss all the pieces of meat and vegetable in the flour to lightly dust them.

Use short (about 6-inch) bamboo skewers, which can be bought at Oriental groceries or in housewares shops sometimes. On each of six skewers, thread pork and peppers as follows: Begin and end each skewer with a piece of pork, wedging a piece of pepper in between. Each piece of food should be pierced twice by the tip of the skewer.

On each of six short skewers, thread pork and scallions as follows: Begin and end each skewer with a piece of pork wedging three lengths of scallions (the white flanked by the green) in between. Thread the meat so that the tip of the skewer pierces each piece twice.

One at a time, dip the twelve skewers into the egg wash, then immediately into the bread crumbs. Take a wok, a deep metal skillet, or a deep-fat fryer and fill it with at least 2 inches of oil. Heat the oil to approximately 375 degrees. Test the oil by dropping in a few bread crumbs to which some egg wash clings. Ideally the crumbs will drop just below the surface, rise immediately, and sizzle and color slowly on the surface. Deep fry the skewers, two or three at a time, for 2½– 3 minutes. Turn the skewers several times during the frying time. Drain well on paper towels. Serve with the dark spicy sauce.

Menu Suggestions: Pickled Cabbage Salad (p. 256) or Radish and *Shiso* Salad (p. 258) complements the fried pork well.

Misty Fried Shrimp

EBI NO KASUMI AGÉ · *Makes 30*

The poetic name of this dish refers to the illusion of rising white mists created by the deep-fried transparent noodles that cling to the shrimp. This classic Japanese appetizer is one of the most popular party foods in my repertoire. The shrimp are particularly scrumptious when piping hot, if your kitchen can accommodate immediate service of fried foods, but they're crunchy-delicious at room temperature, too.

> 2–3 ounces dried *harusamé* ("spring rain" cellophane noodles) OR Chinese bean thread noodles
>
> 30 large shrimp
>
> ⅓ cup all-purpose flour
>
> ½ teaspoon salt
>
> ¼ teaspoon *sanshō* (fragrant Japanese pepper), optional
>
> 2 egg whites, lightly beaten with ½ teaspoon water
>
> vegetable oil, for deep frying
>
> lemon OR lime wedges

You'll need to cut the brittle noodles into ½-inch lengths, and there are two ways to avoid scattering them all over your kitchen: The first is to use a food processor; the second is to use scissors in a closed bag.

If you choose method one, fit your food processor with the metal blade and pull apart the bunch of noodles as best you can, placing them around the blade to load the bowl evenly. Pulse-process with many short stops and starts. It will make an enormous amount of noise. As the large mass begins to break up, you may want to remove half or even two thirds of the noodle pieces and continue processing in small batches. Because the friction is so great, the bowl may begin to feel a bit warm to the touch. If that happens, let the machine rest for a minute or two, then continue to process until all the pieces are about ½ inch long.

If you choose method two, use the sharpest pair of scissors or kitchen shears you have. Place the noodles inside a large, sturdy, clear plastic bag. Place the hand in which you're holding the scissors inside the bag. Secure the bag to your wrist with string or a rubber band, but be careful not to make your tie uncomfortably tight. Snip away at the noodles, assured that the small pieces won't fly all over your kitchen.

Whichever method you choose to cut your noodles, if you experience difficulty because they seem a bit soggy, place them in a 200-degree oven for about 10 minutes before resuming your cutting efforts. Noodles can be cut weeks in advance and stored in an airtight container on your shelf.

Peel the shrimp, keeping the last section and tail intact. Make a shallow slit down the back of each shrimp and remove the "vein," which is really the intestinal tract. Flip the shrimp over and make two or three shallow diagonal slits across the underbelly. Gently press on these slits to straighten out the curved shrimp and keep them from curling when fried. Rinse the shrimp quickly under cold water, than pat dry.

Season the flour with the salt and Japanese pepper, and lightly dust the shrimp in the mixture. Be sure to dust the tails as well. Dip the shrimp, one at a time, in the beaten egg whites, then roll them in the cut noodle pieces. Each piece of noodle will puff and expand considerably, so don't be concerned by gaps between the brittle pieces before frying. The shrimp can be coated 1–2 hours in advance of frying, and if you plan on doing so, cover them lightly with paper towels, then refrigerate until it's time to fry them.

Heat at least 2 inches of oil in a wok or deep-fat fryer. Test the temperature of the oil with a piece of noodle. Ideally it should sink slightly, rise, and puff, but not color on the surface. The oil should be about 340 degrees. Lay the shrimp gently in the hot oil, two or three at a time. The noodle coating will puff immediately but it will take 1½–2 minutes for the shrimp to cook through. Turn them once after 45 seconds of frying. When done, the flesh of the shrimp peeking through the "misty" noodles should be opaque. Transfer the shrimp to a rack to drain. With a fine-meshed skimmer, clear the oil of any noodle debris from the first batch before continuing. Fry the remaining shrimp, testing the temperature of the oil for each new batch, and skimming the oil afterward.

Serve hot or at room temperature, with lemon or lime wedges on the side.

Menu Suggestions: The shrimp alone are wonderful as a first course preceding roasts or chops. I think the shrimp look particularly attractive when crossed in pairs with the tails at the back, on a piece of simply folded paper. (See p. 300 for folding instructions.)

Batter-Fried Vegetable Bundles

ISOBÉ MAKI TEMPURA · Makes about 40

Tempura is one of the earliest, and most glorious, examples of cross-cultural cuisine. Batter-fried fish was first introduced to Japan by the Portuguese in the seventeenth century. Since that time, the Japanese have altered and perfected their version of the European idea to make what the world now admires as *tempura*.

I've recombined Eastern and Western elements here to create a crisp appetizer. Zucchini is new to the Japanese, and so are American pumpkins, though a squash called *kabocha* that's somewhat like our jack-o'-lanterns is native to Japan. an Oriental touch of ginger livens up the dipping sauce.

dipping sauce: ⅓ cup *dashi* (basic sea stock, p. 48)

    1 teaspoon *mirin* (syrupy rice wine)

    1 teaspoon *usukuchi shōyu* (light soy sauce)

    1 teaspoon ginger juice (extracted from freshly grated ginger)

    2 small zucchini, about 7 ounces in all

    5- to 6-ounce wedge pumpkin, skin and seeds removed

    ½ sheet *yaki-zushi nori* (toasted paper-thin seaweed)

batter:	⅔ cup ice water
	⅔ cup cake (low-gluten) flour
	½ teaspoon baking powder
	¼ teaspoon salt

vegetable oil, for deep frying

Preheat your oven to 200 degrees if you'll be preparing the *tempura* in your kitchen in many batches and bringing it to the table on one tray.

In a small saucepan, mix the sauce ingredients together and heat through.

Wash the zucchini, then slice off about ½ inch from the stem end of each. Using this stem piece, rub the cut surface in circular motions until a thick white foam appears; rinse it away. This is what the Japanese call *aku nuki* or "bitterness removal."

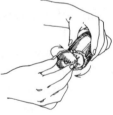

Slice the zucchini into sticks approximately 2–2½ inches long and ¼ inch thick. Cut the pumpkin into sticks of approximately the same length. With scissors, cut the seaweed into about forty strips, each approximately 3 inches long and ¼ inch wide. You can make bundles of each vegetable separately, or combine the two. Each bundle should contain three or four vegetable sticks. Wrap a single band of seaweed around the middle of each bundle of sticks, sealing it with a drop of water and the pressure of your fingertips. These bundles can be made up to 4 hours before frying if stored in the refrigerator on a covered, paper-towel-lined plate. If necessary, just before frying, use 1–2 tablespoons of the flour to toss with the vegetable bundles and dry any surface moisture.

Pour the ice water into a metal bowl, where it will stay chilled longer. Sift all of the remaining flour, baking powder, and salt together in a separate bowl. Sprinkle the flour mixture over the water, stirring to just barely incorporate. Lumps are fine.

Your oil should be at least 2½ inches deep. Even though the Japanese prefer to use a flat-bottomed pot for deep frying, I personally find a Chinese wok the best vessel since it requires less oil to attain the same depth. Heat your oil to about 370 degrees. A test drop of batter should sink ever so slightly, rise immediately, and puff, but not color, on the surface of the oil. Dip the vegetable bundles, one at a time, in the batter to coat them lightly. Deep fry for 1–1½ minutes, turning once or twice to ensure even coloration. The batter should be crisp, but barely beige. Fry four or five bundles at a time. Drain the fried vegetables on a paper-lined rack and keep the first batches warm in a 200-degree oven while you finish up.

Keep the sauce warm on a very low flame, or reheat just before serving. Serve the vegetable bundles immediately, arranged around a bowl with warm dipping sauce.

Menu Suggestions: If your kitchen allows for serving fried foods to a crowd, these vegetable bundles make attractive and tasty hors d'oeuvres with cocktails. These zucchini and pumpkin bundles can also be served as a garnish to Grilled Veal Chops with *Sanshō* Butter (p. 206), *Miso*-Marinated Baked Chicken (p. 193), or slices of Sweet and Spicy Grilled Leg of Lamb (p. 211).

Steamed Clams with Lemon and Soy Sauce

KAI NO SAKA MUSHI · *Serves 4–6*

A simple hot appetizer to start any meal . . .

> about 2 dozen soft-shell clams
> 4 square inches *dashi kombu* (dried kelp for stock making)
> ¼ cup *saké* (Japanese rice wine)
> ½ lemon, cut into wedges
> soy sauce, for dipping

Scrub the shells of the clams to remove any encrustations. Make a salted water solution to cover the clams. (It should taste briny, like the ocean.) Soak the clams in it for about 30 minutes. They should open slightly to "breathe" and expel sand wastes. Pour off the water, rinse the clams in cold water, and repeat the soaking and rinsing.

Place the dried kelp in the bottom of a heavy pot large enough to hold the clams without their touching each other. Add the rice wine, then arrange the clams in a single layer in the pot. Cover and steam over high heat for 3–4 minutes after the rice wine has come to a boil. Any clams that are still unopened should be discarded. Transfer the clams in their shells to individual bowls. Pour the broth from the pot through a cloth- or paper-lined strainer or colander over the clams. Serve immediately with lemon wedges to be squeezed directly on the clams, and soy sauce for dipping on the side. The kelp can be deliciously recycled into the recipes on pp. 116, 262, 264.

Japanese-Style Breaded Fried Oysters

KAKI FURAI · *Makes 2 dozen*

Fried oysters are a favorite picnic item for many Japanese who enjoy foods served at room temperature. The fabulous breaded coating owes its crunch to coarse, pointed crumbs the Japanese call *panko,* and these remain crisp even hours after frying.

> 24 **shucked oysters**
> ¼ **cup** *saké* **(Japanese rice wine)**
> 1½ **tablespoons soy sauce**
> ⅓ **cup all-purpose flour**
> ⅛ **teaspoon salt**
> ⅛ **teaspoon** *sanshō* **(fragrant Japanese pepper)**
> **OR ground white pepper**

2 eggs, beaten with 3 tablespoons cold water
1½ cups *panko* (coarse Japanese bread crumbs)
   vegetable oil, for deep frying
   lemon wedges (optional)
   tonkatsu sōsu (dark spicy sauce), optional

In a small bowl, put the oysters in the rice wine and allow them to marinate for 2–3 minutes. Drain off the rice wine and pour in the soy sauce, tossing the oysters to coat them. Drain off excess liquid and lay the oysters on paper towels to dry.

Combine the flour, salt, and Japanese pepper in a small bowl and dust the oysters, one by one, with the mixture. Dip the oysters one at a time in the egg mixture, then roll them in the bread crumbs, dredging them well.

Heat your oil to about 375 degrees. The oil will need to be at least 2½ inches deep and you may find, as I do, that a Chinese wok is the best implement for this. Test your oil with a few bread crumbs to which some of the egg wash still clings. The crumbs should sizzle gently on the surface, coloring very slowly. Fry the oysters four or five at a time, turning them once, for about 1½ minutes on each side, or until golden brown. Drain on paper towels and serve immediately, or hold for up to 15 minutes in a preheated 200-degree oven. If you wish to serve the oysters at room temperature, let them cool on a paper-lined rack away from drafts. Serve the oysters with lemon wedges or spicy *tonkatsu sōsu*, if you wish.

Menu Suggestions: Breaded fried oysters make a fine first course when meat or poultry is to be served as the entrée. Lamb Chops with Fresh Wild Japanese Mushrooms (p. 207) or the Glazed Chicken Roll (p. 196) would be an especially good choice.

Ginger-Glazed Chicken Wings

TEBA NIKU NO SHŌGA YAKI · Makes 6–8

Served hot or cold these zippy, finger-licking-good chicken wings are a great addition to a buffet or picnic.

    6–8 meaty chicken wings
     ¼ cup soy sauce
      2 tablespoons *saké* (Japanese rice wine)
      2 tablespoons *mirin* (syrupy rice wine)
      1 tablespoon sugar
      1 tablespoon ginger juice (extracted from
          freshly grated ginger)

Rinse and pat dry the chicken wings, then hook the tip of each under its own base to keep it flat and to keep it from opening up when cooking. Place the wings in a glass or ceramic container large enough to accommodate them in a single layer.

In a small saucepan, combine the soy sauce, both the regular and the syrupy rice wines, and the sugar. Stirring until the sugar is completely dissolved, heat the mixture through. Remove the pan from the heat, add the ginger juice, and stir to incorporate. Allow the marinade to cool slightly before pouring it over the chicken wings. Turn the wings several times during the marinating process. Cover the chicken and either refrigerate overnight, or marinate at room temperature for 2 hours.

Preheat your oven to 400 degrees.

I strongly recommend you use a disposable foil broiling pan since cleanup could be messy otherwise. Remove the chicken wings from the marinade and arrange them in a single layer in the foil pan. Cover the pan with aluminum foil and bake for 10–12 minutes. Remove the foil cover and place the chicken wings 3–4 inches from the flame of your broiler and broil for 5 minutes. Dip the wings in the marinade, flip them, and broil for another 5 minutes. Dip the wings in the marinade again and broil for a final 2–3 minutes.

Serve the chicken wings hot, or let them cool to room temperature before covering and chilling to serve cold.

The marinade can be stored, covered in the refrigerator for several weeks, and used two or three more times within a month.

Chicken and Veal Pâté Fans

SUÉHIRO KAMABOKO · *Makes 8*

In Japan, the *suéhiro* or open fan shape signifies increasing happiness or prosperity, and is a popular motif for party food. This gingery pâté is shaped and cut to resemble just such a fan of good fortune, making it an appropriate addition to a party buffet.

¼ **pound ground veal**

veal seasonings:
- 1 **teaspoon soy sauce**
- 1 **teaspoon** *saké* **(Japanese rice wine)**
- 1 **teaspoon sugar**
- 2 **teaspoons peeled, very finely minced fresh ginger**
- ¼ **pound boneless, skinless white-meat chicken**

chicken seasonings:
- ½ **tablespoon sugar**
- ½ **tablespoon soy sauce**
- 1 **egg yolk**
- 1 **tablespoon cornstarch**
- 1–2 **tablespoons oil**
- ¼ **cup** *mirin* **(syrupy rice wine)**
- 2 **tablespoons soy sauce**
- 2 **tablespoons water**
- 1 **tablespoon white sesame seeds**

Place the ground veal in a small pot and season with 1 teaspoon each of soy sauce, rice wine, and sugar. Add the minced ginger and cook over medium heat, stirring to break up the lumps, for 3–4 minutes. When the meat changes color, turn the heat up a bit to reduce the liquid more rapidly. The liquid from the meat may seem cloudy at first, but it will clear as you continue to cook, stirring constantly. Remove the pot from the heat and let the mixture cool slightly.

Cut the chicken into 1- to 2-inch chunks and place them in the bowl of a food processor fitted with the steel blade. Pulse-process to chop the meat finely. Add the sugar, soy sauce, and egg yolk seasonings to the chicken and continue to process to a fairly smooth paste. Sprinkle the cornstarch over the paste and pulse-process to incorporate well.

In a bowl, combine the chicken paste with the cooled, crumbly, cooked veal and stir until both meats are fully integrated. Fold a 12-inch-square piece of heavy-duty aluminum foil in thirds, lengthwise. Lightly oil the top surface of the foil and place the chicken and veal mixture on it. With lightly oiled hands, shape the meat mixture into two neat rectangles, each approximately 2 by 5 inches and ½ inch thick. With scissors, cut the foil to separate the loaves.

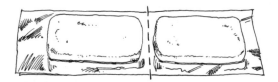

Lightly oil and heat a 7-inch skillet over medium heat and invert one of the pâté loaves into it, peeling off the foil. Sear for 1 minute; then, with the help of a broad, flat spatula, flip the meat over and cook for 1 more minute, before carefully removing this loaf to a flat plate. Repeat this sear-and-flip procedure for the second loaf. (If you have a skillet large enough to accommodate both loaves at once, it will simplify things considerably.)

Return the two seared loaves to the skillet and add the syrupy rice wine, 2 tablespoons of soy sauce, and water. Cover the skillet and cook for 2–3 minutes over medium heat. Flip the pâté loaves over, cover, and cook for another minute. Remove the cover and, shaking the skillet gently, glaze the loaves. Remove the skillet from the heat and al-

low the pâté loaves to cool for 20–30 minutes. The loaves can be made up to this point, covered, and refrigerated for several days. Return them to room temperature before proceeding with the recipe.

Transfer the loaves to a cutting board and slice into eight fan shapes, as illustrated. Insert two wooden toothpicks in the smaller arc of each fan.

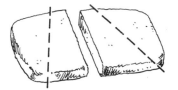

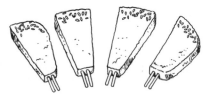

In a clean, dry skillet, roast the sesame seeds over medium-high heat for 20–30 seconds until they just begin to color slightly or a few pop. Shake the pan to keep the seeds in motion. Sprinkle a few roasted seeds on the larger arc of each fan.

Menu Suggestions: I like to contrast the color, flavor, and texture of these fanned pâtés with crisp, tart, white Flower Turnips (p. 265).

Seashore Chicken Swirls

TORI NO ISOBÉ MAKI · *Makes 30*

This is a classic Japanese appetizer meant to be served on its own or in a boxed collection with other bite-size savories, such as Japanese-Style Breaded Fried Oysters (p. 98) or Seashore Flowers (p. 86). This particular version was given to me by Hisako Masubuchi, a dear friend in Tokyo and a fabulous cook.

chicken mixture:

6	ounces boneless, skinless chicken breast
½	medium egg, beaten
1½	tablespoons *shiro miso* (light fermented bean paste)
2	tablespoons finely minced scallions OR chives
1	teaspoon *saké* (Japanese rice wine)
¼	teaspoon salt
¼	teaspoon *usukuchi shōyu* (light soy sauce)
1	tablespoon cornstarch
2	full sheets *yaki-zushi nori* (toasted paper-thin seaweed)
1–2	tablespoons vegetable oil
	soy sauce, for dipping (optional)

Cut the chicken into 1-inch chunks and put them in a food processor fitted with the steel blade. Pulse-process to chop the meat fine. Add the egg and fermented bean paste, and process to incorporate. Add the scallions or chives, rice wine, salt, and light soy sauce and process to a fairly smooth paste. Sprinkle the cornstarch over the mixture and process until combined.

Spread one sheet of seaweed out on a clean, dry surface. Arrange the seaweed so that one of the shorter ends faces you. The rougher-textured side of the seaweed should face up. With a spatula or butter knife, spread half the chicken mixture evenly on the seaweed, leaving a 2-inch border clear on the far side. Gently roll the seaweed away

from you, as you would a jelly roll. Don't roll too snugly, since the seaweed shrinks a bit when sautéed and might open up. Seal the far edge with a drop of water or oil, and let the roll rest, seam side down, for a minute or more. Repeat to make another roll.

Lightly oil a skillet and warm it over medium heat. Sear the rolls, seam side down, then shake the pan to keep the rolls moving. Sauté for 1–2 minutes, shaking frequently. Cover the pan, lower the heat, and cook for 6–7 more minutes. The rolls should be firm when cooked through. Let them cool completely on paper towels. Cut each roll into fifteen slices, exposing the swirl pattern on each piece. Serve at room temperature, with soy sauce for dipping if you wish.

Note:
If you want to make Seashore Chicken Swirls several days in advance of a party, cover the cooled rolls snugly with clear plastic wrap and refrigerate. Slice the rolls while still chilled, but bring the slices back to room temperature before serving.

Pickled Fried Smelts

NAMBAN-ZUKÉ · Makes 1 dozen

*T*his is a classic Japanese delicacy, but one that rarely shows up on the English side of the menu in Japanese restaurants in America. Here's my opportunity to rectify the situation and give you a chance to sample one of those mysterious dishes usually reserved for special customers only. I hope you enjoy it as much as they do.

	12 smelts, about 1½ ounces each
	¼ cup cornstarch
	vegetable oil, for deep frying (a few drops of dark aromatic sesame oil added to corn or soy oil is best)
pickling sauce:	⅔ cup *dashi* (basic sea stock, p. 48)
	¼ cup rice vinegar
	3 tablespoons soy sauce
	3 tablespoons *mirin* (syrupy rice wine)
	3 tablespoons *saké* (Japanese rice wine)
	1½ tablespoons sugar
	1 *tōgarashi* (red chili pepper)
garnish:	1 scallion

The Japanese usually keep the heads and tails of smelts intact, just gutting the belly cavity, but you may be happier removing the heads and tails, along with the guts. Rinse the cleaned fish thoroughly in salted water. (The water should taste briny, like the ocean.) Gently pat the fish dry, inside and out, then dust them in the cornstarch.

In a wok or deep-fat fryer, heat the oil to approximately 375 degrees. Test by dropping a pinch of cornstarch into the oil. It should sink ever so slightly, surface, and disperse immediately, sizzling but not coloring. Deep fry the fish, two or three at a time, for 1½–2 minutes. (Smelts with heads and tails require the longer time.) Drain the fish well on paper towels and transfer them to a ceramic or glass container just large enough to allow the fish to lie submerged in the pickling sauce.

In a small saucepan combine the pickling sauce ingredients, except for the chili pepper. Heat, stirring until the sugar is dissolved. Remove the pan from the stove. Break the pepper pod in half and discard the seeds if you wish to keep the fish just pleasantly spicy. If your tastes run toward the incendiary, keep the seeds as well. Break the pepper pod into several small pieces and stir them into the sauce. Pour the sauce over the fish and, once there's no longer any steam, cover them snugly with clear plastic wrap and refrigerate. Pickle the fish for at least 6 hours and up to 72. (The extended pickling time will "melt" the bones but intensify the piquant taste markedly.)

Just before serving, trim the scallion and chop very fine. Rinse the chopped scallions under cold water and gently squeeze dry.

A single serving is usually two or three fish. Lift the fish from the pickling sauce and place them on small flanged plates, garnishing each with a sprinkling of chopped scallions.

Menu Suggestion: Serve the pickled fish as a first course when you plan on serving Sweet and Spicy Grilled Leg of Lamb (p. 211), Rustic Japanese-Style Roast Chicken (p. 202), or Glazed Chicken Roll (p. 196) as your entrée. A green salad, such as the one dressed with *miso* and walnuts on p. 260, or one with ginger vinaigrette (p. 261), would go well with any of the above. Glazed Zucchini with Sesame (p. 247) would also be a good choice.

The spicy pickled fish are wonderful as part of a brunch menu with fluffy omelets and very un-Japanese bagels and sweet butter!

"Autumn Rains" Spicy Stewed Clams

HAMAGURI NO SHIGURÉ NI · Makes 24–30

I'm not sure why a lusty dish such as this is called by the gentle and poetic name "autumn rains" (*shiguré* in Japanese), but it is. *Shiguré ni* is a classic style of stewing food in an intense gingery soy sauce, and for centuries it has been a common means of food preservation in Japan. Although no longer essential thanks to modern refrigeration, it's still a delicious way to cook clams. Littlenecks are particularly tasty when prepared in the *shiguré ni* fashion, though steamers are fine, too.

24–30 fresh littleneck clams

approximately 9 square inches *dashi kombu* (dried kelp for stock making)

½ cup cold water

¼ cup *saké* (Japanese rice wine)

1 tablespoon sugar

3 tablespoons soy sauce

1 tablespoon ginger juice (extracted from freshly grated ginger)

1 tablespoon *mirin* (syrupy rice wine)

Place the clams in salted water to cover (the water should taste briny, like the ocean) and let them sit there for 30 minutes. If the clams are still alive, as they should be, they'll be tricked into thinking they've returned to their seashore home and begin "breathing"; the shells will open slightly and the clams will excrete sand and other wastes into the water. Stir up the water vigorously, drain, and rinse the clams. Repeat the procedure.

Lay the dried kelp in a pot large enough to accommodate the clams in a single layer, then pour in the cold water and rice wine. Place the clams in the pot, cover, and steam over high heat for about 2 minutes, or until all the shells have opened. (If after 4 minutes some have not opened, they never will, and these should be discarded.) Remove the clams from their shells and rinse them in cold water if they seem sandy or gritty, patting them dry afterward. (The kelp can be saved, if you like, and used in several other recipes. See pp. 116, 262, 264.)

Pour the broth through a cloth- or paper-lined strainer or colander into a small saucepan and add the clam meats. Season with the sugar and cook over medium heat for 5 minutes. The Japanese use a wooden lid that drops down into the pot to lie directly on the simmering food. It's called an *otoshi-buta* and allows the broth to reduce and intensify

while the food's surface is kept moist. If you have one, use it. If not, cook with the pan uncovered, shaking occasionally to swirl the liquid remaining in the pot.

Add the soy sauce and ginger juice, and continue to cook for 10 minutes. Add the syrupy rice wine and cook for a final 2 minutes. The clams will be well glazed and intensely flavorful. Serve warm or at room temperature. If you wish to keep them longer, allow the clams to cool to room temperature before covering and refrigerating up to 1 month.

Menu Suggestions: To make canapés from the stewed clams, serve them whole, or cut in half, on crackers or small toasts lightly spread with sweet butter or cream cheese, or use them in Clam *Sushi* (p. 138).

Crisp Vegetables with Sesame Dip

YASAI NO GOMA MISO SOÉ · Makes about 1 cup thick dip enough to serve with 2–2½ pounds vegetables

With the help of a modern food processor, making this aromatic dip is a simple matter. In Japan, sesame seeds were traditionally ground in a mortar called a *suribachi,* and it took determination and strength to make quantities such as these. This sesame dip is deliciously nutty and aromatic when first made, though it will stay fresh for many weeks if refrigerated. To restore some of the original flavor, should it begin to fade, stir in an extra teaspoon of dark sesame oil.

sesame dip:	½	cup (about 3 ounces) white sesame seeds
	½	cup *shiro miso* (light fermented bean paste)
	2	tablespoons *saké* (Japanese rice wine)
	1½	tablespoons sugar
	1	teaspoon soy sauce
	2	teaspoons *goma abura* (aromatic sesame oil)
	¼–⅓	cup water

In a clean, dry skillet, roast the sesame seeds over medium-high heat for 30–40 seconds until they begin to color slightly or a few pop. Shake the pan to keep the seeds in motion. Transfer the roasted seeds immediately to the bowl of a food processor fitted with the steel blade. Pulse-process until all the seeds have been well cracked.

In a small saucepan, combine the light bean paste, rice wine, and sugar. Stir with a wooden spoon (the Japanese use a *shamoji*) until

smooth. Place the saucepan over low heat and cook, stirring, until glossy. Transfer this mixture to the food processor. Pulse-process to blend well with the cracked sesame seeds. Scrape down the sides of the bowl if necessary.

Add the soy sauce, then the sesame oil, processing each well. With the machine running, dribble the water through the feed tube into the sesame paste. The final sauce should have the consistency of very thick cream.

Menu Suggestions: Barely blanched vegetables such as broccoli, brussels sprouts, and string beans are especially nice with this thick sesame dip; cucumber, celery, cauliflower, and carrot strips are delicious, too. American-grown *hakusai* (Chinese cabbage) is mild and sweet, with crisp white stalks and ruffly pale-green leaves. Trim off the leaves and save them for a salad or to float in a soup. Slice the stalks for dipping into the sesame sauce; 2- or 3-inch-long, 1-inch-wide strips are best. Arrange all your vegetables attractively on a large platter, placing the bowl of dip in the center or off to one side.

Amber Aspic Loaf

KOHAKU KAN · *Makes 2 dozen pieces*

This jellied chicken-and-vegetable loaf is perfect for buffet service or packing in a picnic basket since it doesn't require constant refrigeration. It makes use of *kanten* (agar), which is processed from sea vegetables, not animal protein, and gels firmly without chilling.

> 1 stick *kanten* (Japanese gelatin; agar) OR 1 envelope (4 grams) powdered *kanten*
>
> 2 or 3 small dried *shiitake* (dark Oriental mushrooms)
>
> 2–3 ounces (about ¼ medium-sized) onion
>
> 1 ounce (about 2 inches) carrot
>
> 2–3 ounces boneless, skinless chicken breast
>
> 1 tablespoon vegetable oil
>
> 1 cup *dashi* (basic sea stock, p. 48)
>
> 2 tablespoons *saké* (Japanese rice wine)
>
> 2 tablespoons sugar
>
> 4 tablespoons soy sauce
>
> 5–6 fresh snow peas

Break the stick of *kanten* into several pieces and soak them in cold water for at least 10 minutes. If you're using powdered *kanten*, sprinkle it over 2 tablespoons of cold water and let it stand for at least 5 minutes before using.

Soak the dried mushrooms in 1 cup of warm water for 20 minutes or more. Strain and save the liquid. Remove the stems and save them for enriching stock (p. 50), if you wish, or discard. Rinse the caps to remove any sand or grit, pat dry, and slice into thin julienne strips. Return these strips to the soaking liquid for an extra 2 minutes. Squeeze the mushroom slices to expel excess water, set them aside, and reserve the liquid for cooking.

Slice the onion into thin vertical slices. Peel the carrot and slice it into very thin julienne strips. Slice the chicken breast thinly on the diagonal, then across, into narrow julienne strips.

Heat the oil in a small skillet and sauté the onions over medium heat until slightly translucent. Add the mushrooms, carrot, and chicken and continue to sauté for 1 minute or until the chicken turns white. Add the reserved mushroom liquid and the stock, and season with the rice wine, sugar, and soy sauce. Cook uncovered over medium heat for 5 minutes, skimming the froth occasionally. Reserve both the cooking liquid and the meat and vegetables, separately.

Remove the strings from the snow peas and blanch them for 10 seconds in several cups of boiling salted water. Drain and refresh the snow peas in cold water, then pat dry. Slice the snow peas slightly on the diagonal into thin julienne strips. Add these to the vegetable and chicken mixture.

Pour the reserved cooking liquid through a cloth- or paper-lined strainer into a 2-cup measure. Add water if necessary to make 1¾ cups of liquid. Transfer this liquid to a small saucepan.

Squeeze out all the water from the pieces of *kanten,* and with your hands shred the softened mass into the saucepan. Or add the softened *kanten* powder. Cook the mixture over low heat, stirring constantly until the *kanten* dissolves completely (this could take as long as 10 minutes). Simmer for 2–3 minutes longer before stirring in the chicken and vegetables. Remove the saucepan from the heat.

Gently pour the mixture into a straight-sided glass loaf pan (8½ by 4½ by 2½ inches is ideal). Using a toothpick, pull any bubbles that might have formed on the surface to the edges, where they can be lanced and/or dragged up the sides of the container. You need a glass-like surface. Let the aspic sit at room temperature until all the steam has dissipated, then cover it with clear plastic wrap. The aspic will harden without chilling, though refrigeration will hasten this along. Chill for a least 1 hour and up to 4 days.

When ready to unmold, gently press along the edges with the padded part of your fingertips. This will release the stiff aspic from the smooth glass sides. Place a cutting board or flat tray over the mold and invert it so that the loaf comes out bottom up. Slice the loaf in half lengthwise, then across eleven times, to yield twenty-four pieces in all. A single serving is usually two slices.

Menu Suggestions: Slices of this savory jellied loaf look and taste good when served together with Caviar in Cucumber Baskets (p. 123). A pleasant contrast of textures occurs when smooth, sparkling Amber Aspic Loaf is served with creamy, pale Fish and *Tōfu* Terrine (p. 113).

Fish and Tōfu *Terrine*

KAWARI KAMABOKO · *Serves 6–8*

An appetizer favored by many Japanese, *kamaboko* is a smooth, steamed fish sausage or loaf. Since *kamaboko* can often be rather chewy, its texture is unappealing to many Americans. On the other hand, Western-style pâtés and terrines, which are popular Occidental appetizers, tend to be rather rich and heavy by Japanese standards. This cross-cultural recipe retains the creamy, mousselike texture of standard Western terrines without using a single drop of fat! Made with bean curd and fish, it's liberally seasoned with herbs and spices. Delightful to look at, healthful and delicious to eat, this very different *kamaboko* will quickly become a favorite at your table.

Mixture A:	4–5	ounces drained *kinugoshi tōfu* (silky bean curd; see p. 40 for information about different types of bean curd)
	4	ounces haddock fillet, cut into 1-inch pieces
	½	teaspoon lemon juice
	¼	teaspoon salt
	¼	teaspoon *sanshō* (fragrant Japanese pepper)
	2	tablespoons finely chopped scallion (green part only)
	2	tablespoons finely chopped fresh parsley

Mixture B: 4–5 ounces drained *kinugoshi tōfu* (silky bean curd)

4 ounces haddock fillet, cut into 1-inch pieces

½ teaspoon lemon juice

⅛ teaspoon salt

1 tablespoon finely chopped, drained *amazu shōga* (pink pickled ginger)

½ tablespoon finely chopped scallion (white part only)

tosa *aspic:*   1 envelope unflavored gelatin

2 tablespoons cold water

1 cup *dashi* (basic sea stock, p. 48)

2 teaspoons *mirin* (syrupy rice wine)

2 teaspoons *usukuchi shōyu* (light soy sauce)

1 package (5 grams) OR about ⅓ cup *katsuo bushi* (dried bonito flakes)

10 leaves fresh *shiso* (flat-leafed Japanese herb) OR 25 leaves flat-leafed Italian parsley

Place the bean curd and fish of Mixture A in the bowl of a food processor fitted with the metal blade. Pulse-process until smooth, adding the lemon juice, salt, and Japanese pepper as you blend. Add the scallion greens and parsley, and continue to process to a smooth paste. Spoon this mixture into a smooth-sided glass or ceramic loaf pan (2 by 2 by 6 inches is an ideal size) and spread it evenly with a rubber spatula. On a toweled surface, lightly tap the loaf pan to release any air bubbles that might be trapped inside.

Place the bean curd and fish of Mixture B in the bowl of the processor and pulse-process until smooth. Add the remaining ingredients of Mixture B and continue to process until it's all smooth and pasty. Spoon this mixture over Mixture A in the loaf pan, being careful not to mix the two, while gently pressing with a rubber spatula to smooth this second layer. Again, tap the loaf pan on a toweled surface to release any trapped air.

Place the loaf in a steamer and steam the terrine for 12–15 minutes. Remove the loaf pan and let the terrine cool until there are no longer any large clouds of steam. Pour off all accumulated liquid. Place a flat plate or tray over the loaf pan, turn it upside down, and unmold the terrine onto it. Rinse out the loaf pan and towel it dry; then, with the help of a broad metal spatula, carefully slip the terrine back into the loaf pan, inverting the terrine so that the green layer is on top and the pink on the bottom.

In a small saucepan, sprinkle the unflavored gelatin over the cold water. In another small saucepan, heat the stock and bring to a boil. Season with the syrupy rice wine and soy sauce, and remove the saucepan from the source of heat. Sprinkle the bonito flakes over the seasoned stock and let it sit for 3–4 minutes before pouring it through a cloth- or paper-lined strainer or colander into the softened gelatin. Stir and heat this gelatin until smooth and clear.

Rinse the *shiso* leaves under cold water, shaking them dry. Trim off the stems. Dip each leaf into the liquid aspic and lay them across the top of the terrine in an attractive pattern. If using flat-leafed parsley, follow the same method of decoration. Chill the terrine for 10 minutes or until the leaves seem firmly "glued" on. Pour the remaining aspic over the terrine and chill for at least 2 hours and up to 24.

When ready to serve, insert a thin, sharp knife around the edges of the loaf pan, to release the aspic-coated terrine. Carefully unmold it and transfer it to a clean cutting board. With a sharp knife, slice away excess clear amber aspic from the ends of the loaf and chop this into a very fine dice. Slice the terrine into six to eight pieces and arrange them on individual plates or, in domino fashion, on a single flat serving tray. Garnish the plates or tray with the chopped aspic and serve immediately, or cover and chill until serving time.

Menu Suggestions: This terrine makes a satisfying first course when the menu calls for Western-style steaks or chops, or the cross-cultural kind, such as Steak with *Wasabi* Butter (p. 204) or Lamb Chops with Fresh Wild Japanese Mushrooms (p. 207).

Gift-Wrapped Kelp Rolls

KOMBU MAKI · *Makes 12*

*B*esides being nutritious (kelp is a wonderful source of vitamins and minerals—particularly calcium), these dark, glossy, tied tidbits look intriguing and inviting on an hors d'oeuvre tray. The sophisticated an-iselike flavor of the simmered kelp nicely complements cold meats and poultry, too, which makes Gift-Wrapped Kelp Rolls an exciting and unusual garnish for a buffet platter. Since the rolls can be made from the kelp that's left over from making basic sea stock, they're as frugal as they are fabulous.

> 5 feet *kampyō* (dried gourd ribbon)
> ½ teaspoon salt
> 12 strips softened *dashi kombu* (kelp; leftovers from stock making are perfect), each about 2½ inches long and 1½ inches wide
> 2 cups cold water
> 2 teaspoons rice vinegar
> 1 cup *dashi* (basic sea stock, p. 48)
> 2 tablespoons *saké* (Japanese rice wine)
> 1½ tablespoons sugar
> 3 tablespoons soy sauce
> 1 tablespoon *mirin* (syrupy rice wine)

Soak the gourd in warm water to cover for about 10 minutes. Drain and rub the salt into the gourd, much as you might wash a skein of wool. Rinse the gourd in cold water and let it soak in fresh warm water for another 5 minutes. Drain well and pat dry. Keep the gourd as a long single strip if you can, since it will simplify the job of tying the rolls later.

Take one piece of softened kelp and roll it tightly into a scroll. You'll find it easier if you place the slightly slippery kelp on paper towels as you roll. Tie the roll around its middle with the gourd, finishing with a double knot. Each roll will use about 5 inches of gourd ribbon, but don't cut off the excess until your knot is secure. Then trim the gourd

ribbon so that it extends no farther than the ends of the roll. Repeat this roll-and-tie procedure to make twelve miniature-diploma-like scrolls.

Combine 1 cup of cold water and 1 teaspoon of rice vinegar, in a shallow pan or skillet large enough to hold all twelve rolls in a single layer. When you've brought the acidulated water to a rolling boil, add the kelp rolls. Reduce the heat slightly and cook the rolls for 5 minutes, skimming away any foam that accumulates on the surface. With a slotted spoon, remove the rolls and set aside. Discard the acidulated water, rinse the pan, and bring another cup of cold water and teaspoon of rice vinegar to a boil. Add the kelp rolls, reduce the heat slightly, and cook for another 5 minutes. Drain the rolls and set aside.

Rinse the pan, add the stock and rice wine, and bring this liquid to a simmer. Add the rolls and over low heat, with the pan partially covered, cook for 5–6 minutes. Add the sugar and continue to cook for another 5 minutes. Stir in the soy sauce and simmer for an additional 5 minutes. The liquid will become greatly reduced and very foamy. Add the syrupy rice wine and continue to cook for 1 more minute. You'll notice a glaze forming; swirl the pan to glaze all the rolls well. If at any point in the cooking process the rolls appear to be in danger of scorching, add a few more drops of stock or water and adjust the heat accordingly. If after a total of 15 minutes cooking there's still a great deal of liquid left in the pot, raise the heat to high and cook, shaking the pan, to reduce the liquid to a glaze. Remove the pan from the heat.

Let the kelp rolls cool in their glaze to room temperature. Serve at room temperature, or chilled. The rolls will keep, covered, in the refrigerator for 5–6 days.

Menu Suggestions: Stack the rolls, three at a time, in small pyramids and serve them alongside clusters of steamed Seashore Flowers (p. 86) on an hors d'oeuvre plate. Kelp rolls are fun packed into a picnic with Japanese-Style Breaded Fried Oysters (p. 98) or Misty Fried Shrimp (p. 93).

Sliced Fresh Tuna with Lime and Soy

MAGURO NO SASHIMI · *Serves 4–6*

Though many connoisseurs prefer the marbled and fatty *toro* (the pink meat that comes from the belly of the tuna), I personally adore the lean, ruby-red meat called *akami* that's taken from the dorsal side of the fish. When I was in Hawaii, I discovered the exquisite flavor and texture of *ahi,* a velvety, scarlet-fleshed variety of Pacific tuna. *Ahi* has a delicate flavor compared to the more robust bluefin tuna that's more commonly found on both the east and the west coasts of the United States. Tuna is one of the few fishes that holds up well when frozen fresh, and it's shipped to nearly all Oriental markets with refrigerated sales space. Although Hawaiian *ahi* rarely comes to market along the Atlantic coast, if you should find it at your market, it's well worth the few cents more per pound that it may cost compared to bluefin. *Toro* always sells at a premium price since, like filet mignon, it's only a small strip of meat from a large creature.

For any variety of fresh tuna a simple presentation is best—tender, meaty slices on a chilled glass plate with a zippy lime, horseradish, and soy dipping sauce. This sauce can be served in lime cups to make an elegant garnish.

2–3 small, firm limes

3–4 tablespoons soy sauce

6–8 ounces fresh tuna

  2 teaspoons *wasabi* powder (fiery Japanese horseradish)

1½ teaspoons cold water

It's best to prepare the decorative lime cups before slicing the fish. Barely trim both ends of each lime—just enough to keep the fruit from wobbling when you stand it up. Slice each lime ¾ inch from each cut edge. The two end pieces from each lime will be fashioned into cups; the middle section of each lime can be used for some other purpose. Scoop out the fruit from the end sections, being careful not to poke holes through the skin. I find a grapefruit knife helpful in tracing the inner circumference of the skin but then I use a teaspoon and/or my fingers to scoop out the pulp. Squeeze the pulp from the limes to extract 1 tablespoon of juice. Mix this juice with the soy sauce, cover, and set aside. Turn the lime cups upside down to let them drain while you prepare the fish. A simple dipping sauce made from 1 tablespoon of lime juice and 3–4 tablespoons of soy sauce can be mixed and served later in small dipping dishes, too.

Gently pat the tuna with paper towels to absorb any liquid and place the block of fish on a clean, dry cutting board. With a sharp, long-bladed knife, slice the tuna into ¼-inch-thick slices. Don't saw back and forth with your knife; use smooth drawing strokes. Arrange the slices, domino style, on flat glass plates. In Japan, the numbers 1, 3,

and 4 are inappropriate for serving *sashimi* since each of those numbers represents an unfortunate culinary pun on killing and death. It's best to figure on five, six, or seven slices per person when serving sliced fish.

In a small bowl, mix the horseradish powder with the cold water and stir to make a thick paste. Divide this paste into four to six portions and shape each into a little mound. Place one mound of horseradish in the center of each lime cup, or directly on the plate with the fish. Pour some of the lime and soy mixture that had been set aside into each of the lime cups or divide among individual dipping dishes. Each person stirs horseradish into the dipping mixture to taste. Each slice of fish is briefly swished through the sauce before being eaten.

Menu Suggestions: In Japan *sashimi* is served as one of many small dishes that compose a meal and, although it's usually presented early on in the meal, *sashimi* isn't necessarily the first course. Most Americans will want to serve tuna *sashimi* as an appetizer, to be followed by a main course and perhaps a salad before dessert. Either Snapper Steamed with Wild Mushrooms in Parchment (p. 181) or the Glazed Chicken Roll (p. 196) would be a nice choice for an entrée to follow the fresh fish, and Green Salad with Walnut and Bean Dressing (p. 260) is delicious with any main course. Any of the desserts in the final recipe chapter would finish the meal splendidly.

Fresh Fluke in Smoky Vinaigrette

HIRAMÉ NO TOSA-ZU AÉ · Serves 4–6

*I*f you're lucky enough to have a source for impeccably fresh fluke, or any other delicate white-fleshed fish, you can enjoy this subtly flavored fish salad as an appetizer. I've suggested two ways of slicing the fish, depending upon your knife skills; both are lovely.

tosa-zu dressing:	⅔ cup *dashi* (basic sea stock, p. 48)
	1 tablespoon *usukuchi shōyu* (light soy sauce)
	1 teaspoon soy sauce
	1 teaspoon *mirin* (syrupy rice wine)
	1 package (5 grams) OR about ⅓ cup *katsuo bushi* (dried bonito flakes)
	¼ cup rice vinegar
	10 ounces fresh fillet of fluke, sea bream, OR snapper
	4–6 leaves fresh red-tipped lettuce
garnish:	2–3 teaspoons finely chopped chives OR scallion greens

In a small saucepan, combine the stock, two soys, and syrupy rice wine. Heat this mixture until it just begins to simmer. Sprinkle the bonito flakes over the seasoned stock. Remove the saucepan from the heat and let the stock steep for 3 minutes before pouring it through a cloth- or paper-lined strainer or colander. With the back of a spoon, press on the solids to extract all the liquid from the bonito flakes. Let the seasoned stock cool to room temperature, then add the rice vinegar to complete making the smoky vinaigrette. Cover the dressing and chill for at least 30 minutes before serving. You may prepare this step ahead of time. The dressing keeps for up to 1 week in the refrigerator.

Rinse the fillet under cold water and pat dry completely. Lay the fillet on your cutting board and, with a long-bladed, very sharp knife, slice the fish into broad, thin, diagonal slices. Your knife should be held at a 45-degree angle to your board and the blade should be pulled smoothly through the fish, not sawed back and forth. If you succeed in producing eight or ten gorgeous slices (and you will—with a bit of practice), you can arrange them to look like a rose. If the slices should fall apart or not measure at least 4 inches in length and 1½ inches in width, finish cutting by making narrow julienne slices from what you do have.

Rinse the lettuce leaves under cold water and shake them free of excess moisture (a few remaining "dew drops" are fine). Place the leaves on your serving plates.

Set aside 2–3 tablespoons full of the chilled smoky vinaigrette. If you're going to make roses, let your broad flat slices marinate in the remainder of the dressing for 5 minutes. If you're using julienne strips, toss them in the remainder of the dressing, draining after a minute.

To make roses from your slices, roll the fish as illustrated. Place two flowers on each lettuce leaf. With a blunt point, open up the center of the flowers just enough to allow a few bits of chive or scallion green to nestle in each. If you're serving the fish in julienne shreds, toss them with the chives or scallion greens, then mound them on the leaves. In either case, moisten the fish with a few drops of the reserved smoky vinaigrette dressing just as you get ready to bring the plates to the table.

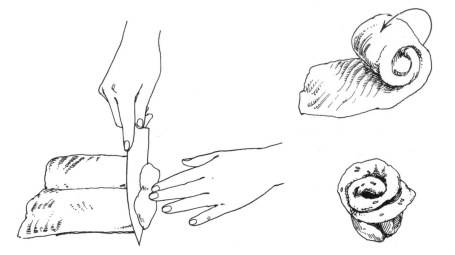

Note:

If you're purchasing your fish, do so at a reputable establishment and mention that you want to use the fillets uncooked. Serve the fish the same day you buy it.

If you're making use of a personal catch, the fish should be gutted and iced immediately upon taking it from the water, and filleted and refrigerated shortly thereafter. The fish you catch for your own *sashimi* should be no more than 6 hours out of the water when you start to prepare this dish. If, when filleting, you discover any larvae or tracks in the flesh that might indicate the presence of parasites, don't use the fish for *sashimi*.

Menu Suggestions: This light and delicate appetizer could precede almost any main course, though I think it's particularly lovely before a meal of roasted or broiled meat, such as Sweet and Spicy Grilled Leg of Lamb (p. 211) or Grilled Veal Chops with *Sanshō* Butter (p. 206).

Caviar in Cucumber Baskets

KYŪRI NO IKURA-ZUMÉ · Makes 6

These charming, elegant little hors d'oeuvres are meant to be consumed in just a bite or two.

> 1 unwaxed cucumber, about 5–6 ounces
> 2 ounces *ikura* (salmon roe)
> 1 teaspoon *usukuchi shōyu* (light soy sauce)
> 1 teaspoon *wasabi* powder (fiery Japanese horseradish)
> 1 teaspoon cold water

Wash the cucumber well and slice off about ½ inch from the stem (darker green) end. Using this stem piece, rub the cut surface in circular motions until a thick white foam appears; rinse it away. This is what the Japanese call *aku nuki* or "bitterness removal." Trim off the flowering (lighter-color) end, then cut the cucumber into six even pieces, each about ¾ inch.

If you like, you can create a design on the cucumber pieces. Using a zester or other narrow chiseling instrument (wood- or linoleum-block tools are perfect for this job), remove a shallow strip of dark green skin about ¼ inch from the edge of each piece.

With a melon baller, hollow out each cucumber basket. Scoop out as much of the seeded portion as you can but be careful not to poke through the walls of your baskets. Turn the baskets upside down to drain off any excess liquid. (The baskets can be made up to this point, covered with clear plastic wrap, and refrigerated for up to 4 hours.)

In a small bowl toss the caviar with the light soy sauce and let it marinate for a few moments before draining.

In another small bowl or dish, mix the horseradish powder with an equal quantity of cold water and stir to make a paste. Place a dab of the horseradish paste on the inside of each cucumber basket. Fill the baskets with the red caviar and serve at once. Or cover with clear plastic wrap and refrigerate for 30–60 minutes.

Menu Suggestions: At a buffet or cocktail party, arrange alternating rows of green cucumber baskets filled with bright caviar and circles of Seashore Chicken Swirls (p. 104) displaying their dark and light whirlpool patterns. Or for a sit-down meal create individual appetizer dishes, each with one cucumber basket, a trio of Gift-Wrapped Kelp Rolls (p. 116), and two Seashore Flowers resting on flat-leafed parsley (p. 86).

Sushi...

*T*he basics of *sushi* making—cooking and seasoning the rice, making paper-thin omelets—plus ten delectable vinegared rice recipes, some rolled, some molded, and some tossed, to serve as snacks, appetizers, or entrées

*J*ust as pizza and pita bread have found their way into American cooking, there's little doubt that *sushi* is the next to enter the American diet on a grand scale. It has already found a large and eager audience, particularly in the big cities on the east and west coasts. The *sushi* bars that began as a gastronomic refuge for the homesick Japanese businessman abroad have been taken over by his sophisticated American associates: Now it's Americans who crave these vinegared rice delicacies, wanting to make them at home.

Some *sushi* dishes are best served as appetizers or snacks, others as main courses. But to make any *sushi* recipe successfully, you have to know how to cook and season the rice that's essential to all of them. There are also certain recipes and techniques that apply to many *sushi* dishes, the explanations of which become tedious and cumbersome if repeated often. I've placed these basic building blocks at the beginning of the chapter to help you with the more elaborate assemblages that follow. But first, a brief history of *sushi*. . . .

A look at the changes in the written characters for the word *sushi* provides a capsule history of the dish. In the earliest Japanese documents, the character *su,* meaning acidity, was used to describe any pleasantly sour food that resulted from fermentation. There are records of gifts of *sushi* to the imperial and other powerful families dating from as early as the eighth century. In those records *sushi* was written with a single ideograph that combined the symbols for "fish," and "create" or "make." The *sushi* was a tart food made from the natural fermentation of salted (preserved) fish and seafood.

By the beginning of the seventeenth century, *sushi* was being written in a new way. The "create" was replaced by "deliciousness," indicating that a seasoned vinegar was being used to flavor the fish tartly rather than relying upon the natural fermentation process.

By the nineteenth century, seasoned rice appeared beneath slices of fresh fish. These "new" creations were reserved for special occasions, and so *sushi* began to be written with two ideographs: one for "felicity" and the other for "management."

Today you'll find the word *sushi* can be written in three ways: the ancient "made from fish," the auspicious "happily managed," and the phonetic *su* and *shi* from the Japanese syllabary (an alphabetlike writing system with no inherent meanings implied). This last became popular as the variety of vegetarian vinegared-rice dishes burgeoned. In the broadest sense of the word, *sushi* refers to delicacies made with vinegared rice, and encompasses a wonderful variety of dishes.

Sushi can be molded into any number of shapes, and frequently the shape or method of molding gives the dish its name. For example, the name of the very popular *nigiri-zushi* means "compact *sushi*" and describes the dense nuggets of seasoned rice on which slices of fresh (often uncooked) fish lie. *Hako-zushi,* which means "box *sushi*," indicates that the seasoned rice has been molded into a square or rectangular shape with the aid of a special lidded box. These kinds of *sushi* are often layered, then cut into a number of thin slices. Sometimes a damp cloth is used to mold the rice into the desired shape; other times wooden, plastic, or metal molds called *kata* are employed.

Maki-zushi ("rolled *sushi*") is usually made with the aid of a bamboo-slatted mat called a *sudaré*. Rolls can contain many different ingredients and a great deal of rice wound up in a large sheet of seaweed (*futo maki*) or can be a single ingredient—such as cucumber or simmered gourd—rolled with a little rice in a half sheet of seaweed (*hoso maki*). Some rolls are made with the rice outside (these are called *ura maki* or "inside-out rolls") and require both a *sudaré* mat and a damp cloth to help shape them. Other rolls, called *te maki* or "hand rolls," enclose a bit of rice with any ingredient you fancy wound into a cylinder or cornucopia with just a flick of the wrist.

Chirashi-zushi, mazé-zushi, or *bara-zushi* is a scattered, pilaflike dish that typically combines many finely cut or chopped ingredients with the basic vinegared rice. The surface is sometimes decorated with additional sliced fish, shellfish, or vegetables. Shredded thin omelet is a popular topping for many of these *sushi* dishes. In Tokyo, you'll also find *chirashi-zushi* that are individual portions of plain seasoned rice, topped with slices of fresh fish.

I've collected ten spectacular *sushi* dishes for you to make, some more complex than others. All are suitable for home entertaining and enjoyment, to be served as appetizers, snacks, or main courses in your home.

PICNIC LUNCH • Larger box, clockwise from left: *Misty Fried Shrimp (p. 93), Japanese–Style Breaded Fried Oysters (p. 98), Decorative Rice Bundles (p. 219), broccoli (with separate sesame dip—p. 110).* Smaller box, clockwise from left: *rice with yellow pickled radish, Kelp Squares with Fragrant Pepper (p. 264), snow pea "leaves," Chicken Dumplings (p. 87)*

SASHIMI PLATTER • *Fresh lean tuna with lime,* wasabi *horseradish, and soy sauce (p. 136); radish sprout garnish tied with* nori *seaweed*

DESSERT • *Felicity Swirls of marzipan and candied ginger (p. 292), Pine Needle sugar candies of green tea and cocoa (p. 276)*

SALMON DINNER • Clockwise from left: *Autumn Rice with Wild Mushrooms* (p. 224), *Green Salad with Walnut and Bean Dressing* (p. 260), *A Bowl of Sunshine* (p. 80), *Glaze-Grilled Salmon Steak with garnish of fresh* shiso *herb leaf* (p. 179), *Flower Turnip with black sesame seeds* (p. 265)

CLAM SUSHI • *Clam* Sushi *with snow peas (p. 138)*

APPETIZER TRAY • Clockwise from upper left: *Caviar in Cucumber Baskets (p. 123), pink pickled ginger,* wasabi *horseradish, Seashore Flowers (p. 86), Pressed Salmon* Sushi Tart *(p. 153), Seashore Chicken Swirls (p. 104), Gift-Wrapped Kelp Rolls (p. 116)*

DUCK SALAD LUNCH • Clockwise from upper left: *rice molded into a gourd shape and garnished with toasted sesame seeds, fresh* shiso *herb leaf and half-moon slices of yellow pickled radish, Pale Jade Soup (p. 76), Soy-Braised Duck Salad (p. 169)*

JELLIED ORANGE WEDGES • (*p. 288*)

The Basics of Sushi Making

Let's start with the most basic of basics, the seasoned rice on which all *sushi* recipes depend. The commonplace name for this food is *sushi meshi,* but in the lingo of the *sushi* bar it's known as *shari.* If you want to impress the *ita-maé* (literally, "[the one who stands] in front of the cutting board," i.e., the chef) and others within earshot, you'll refer to the rice as *shari,* the soy sauce as *murasaki* (literally, "purple"; soy sauce is otherwise known as *shōyu*), the powerful horseradish as *namida* ("tears"), and the sprightly pickled ginger as *gari* ("crunchy"). Tea, which is elsewhere referred to as *ocha,* is known in the *sushi* bar as *agari* or "up" (as in "drink up").

The standard recipe for *shari* yields 3 cups of seasoned rice, and you'll find this just the right amount for making most of the *sushi* recipes in this chapter. Occasionally a recipe will ask for half that much, or perhaps double the quantity. For the standard recipe a 2-quart pot is ideal; for a half recipe a 1½-quart pot yields better results. If you're increasing the yield beyond the standard, adjust your pot size accordingly. Of course an electric rice cooker with thermostatic control eliminates many problems, and I highly recommend it to the serious *sushi* or rice eater. Most rice cookers come with a Japanese measuring cup enclosed, and the markings on the side of the pot correspond to that measuring cup.

The seasoned vinegar (*sushi su* or *awasé-zu*) used in *sushi* is commercially prepared by several large food companies. It simplifies matters to have a bottle on hand, especially since the commercial product is produced under sterile conditions, which means there's no necessity to store it in the refrigerator after opening it. But if you can't stand to have yet another bottle on your shelf, or you wish to alter the proportions of seasonings to suit your own needs and tastes, I've included a basic formula for the seasoned vinegar at the end of the *shari* recipe.

Rice Seasoned for Sushi

SHARI · Makes 3 cups

> 1½ cups raw rice (Japanese-style short-grained)
> 1¾ cups cold water
> ¼ cup *sushi su* (seasoned rice vinegar)

Place the rice in a bowl and cover it with cold water. Stir vigorously to wash it clean of excess starch. Strain the rice and repeat the washing procedure with fresh cold water. Continue to rinse-and-swish with fresh cold water until the rinsing water runs clear. This will probably take three or four rinses. Drain well after the final rinse.

Place the rice in a sturdy, straight-sided 2- or 3-quart pot. Measure in 1¾ cups of fresh cold water. (If during the autumn months you're lucky enough to obtain *shin mai,* which is newly harvested rice, cook it with equal quantities of cold water.) Ideally, let the rice sit in its cooking water for 10 minutes before cooking. That way, the grains of rice have a chance to absorb some of the water before cooking, making for more-tender cooked rice. If you're pressed for time, add ½ teaspoon more water. Cover the pot with a tight-fitting lid.

Over high heat, bring the water in the pot to a rolling boil. It's best not to remove the lid to check on the rice's progress. Instead, rely on other clues; you can hear the bubbling noises and see the lid begin to dance. This should take about 5 minutes. Reduce the heat and continue to cook until the water is absorbed (about 5 minutes longer); you may hear a low hissing sound. Increase the heat to high again for 30 seconds to dry off the rice. Remove the pot, still tightly covered, and let the rice stand for at least 10 and up to 30 minutes.

Transfer the cooked rice to a large bowl. The Japanese use a wooden tub called a *handai* or *sushi oké,* which is ideal. But a wide-mouthed glass or ceramic bowl is fine, especially if it has a wide flat bottom (avoid metal since it tends to retain heat). Toss the rice while fanning to cool it without condensation forming. The Japanese use a flat lacquered fan called an *uchiwa,* but a piece of cardboard is just as useful. Use a wooden spoon to toss the rice (the Japanese use a paddlelike one called a *shamoji*).

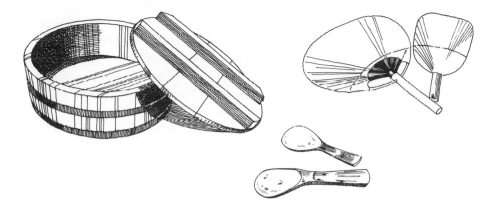

When there are no more clouds of steam rising from the rice, begin to toss it with the seasoned vinegar. Start with just a tablespoonful. Using gentle folding and tossing motions, gradually season the rice with the rest of the vinegar. Sample a bit; if it seems just right, add an extra sprinkle for good measure. As the rice cools, some of the vinegar evaporates and leaves the rice milder than when you first tasted it.

Cover the seasoned rice with a damp cloth until ready to use. It will keep well at room temperature for 4–6 hours. DO NOT REFRIGERATE IT as the rice will become crusty, hard, and thoroughly unpleasant. The seasoned vinegar acts as a preservative, protecting the rice from spoilage.

Note on the seasoned vinegar:
Japanese rice vinegar is mild and delicate. In fact, I suspect that once you try it you'll be so enamored of its mellow tartness that you'll find yourself using it for nearly every recipe in your repertoire. If you must, you could substitute ordinary distilled white vinegar, but I suggest you dilute it with a few drops of cold water for every cup since its taste is harsh. The basic formula for making seasoned vinegar is:

> 4 **parts vinegar**
> 1 **part sugar**
> ¼ **part salt**

(Many commercial brands add monosodium glutamate to their formulas.)

Combine the ingredients in a saucepan and heat over a low flame, stirring, just until the sugar and salt melt. Allow the mixture to cool to room temperature, unlidded, before using. Any leftover seasoned vinegar should be stored in a covered glass or ceramic container and refrigerated if you anticipate that more than 1 or 2 days will pass by before using it again.

Thin Omelet

USUTAMAGO YAKI · *Makes 5–6 large circles (8-inch diameter), 8–10 small circles (4- to 5-inch diameter)*

*H*ere's a basic recipe for making paper-thin omelets. The Japanese use these crepelike egg sheets in a variety of ways and you'll find numerous recipes in this book that call for them. Learning how to flip the omelets with a single chopstick may take a few tries, but once you've mastered the technique, you'll find it a marvelous and useful skill.

> 3 jumbo OR 4 extra-large eggs
> 2 teaspoons *saké* (Japanese rice wine)
> 1 teaspoon sugar
> ⅛ teaspoon salt
> 1 teaspoon cornstarch (optional)
> 1 tablespoon cold water (optional)
> vegetable oil, for seasoning pan (optional)

Break the eggs into a bowl and remove the white squiggly clumps of albumen that often cling to the yolk; if left intact they make unattractive white streaks in an otherwise smooth, yellow sheet. Season the eggs with the rice wine, sugar, and salt. Beat just enough to break the viscous texture of the whites but try not to incorporate air as you do this. If the egg mixture gets very foamy (containing air), allow it to sit until smooth.

If you plan to use the egg sheet whole in a decorative manner, such as in Clam *Sushi* (p. 138), it's best to strengthen the omelet with the addition of a thin cornstarch paste. If, however, you're going to shred the sheets to make thin julienne strips, as in Five-Colored *Sushi* (p. 156), you need not bother. If you choose to include cornstarch, mix it with the cold water to make a thin paste, then stir this into the egg mixture to combine it well.

If you'll be using an ordinary skillet, you'll have to season it with a thin layer of oil and re-oil your pan between sheets. Instead, I recommend the use of a nonstick surface such as Teflon or SilverStone. An 8-inch skillet is best for making the larger circles; to make the small circles, I often use the bottom of a shallow saucepan. Heat your skillet or pan over medium heat.

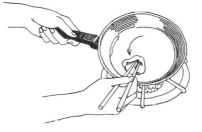

Pour about 3–3½ tablespoons full of the egg mixture into the skillet to make the larger circles about half that for the smaller ones. Measure the egg before pouring so that it's added to the pan all at once. Swirl this mixture to cover the surface of the skillet evenly. Keep it over medium heat until the edges seem to dry a bit. Remove the skillet from the source of heat and let the egg sheet cook with retained heat for another 20–30 seconds before flipping it over.

The Japanese use a single chopstick to help flip their sheets of omelet. Trace completely around the circumference of the omelet with the tip of your chopstick. Then, holding the skillet in one hand and the chopstick in the other, tilt the pan so that your hands face each other. Insert the tip of your chopstick just under the edge of the omelet, and alternate twirling motions with back-and-forth strokes, to work your way across to the other side of the pan. Lift the omelet, draped over the chopstick, and lay it back in the pan, inverted. Allow the other side to dry off (at most 30 seconds' additional exposure to heat), then

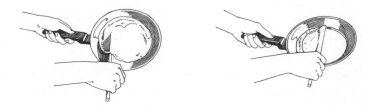

flip it out of the skillet. Continue to make the omelets, in the same manner, stacking them as you go. Thin omelets such as these will keep for 5 days, covered and refrigerated.

California Rolls

KARIFORUNIA MAKI · *Makes 3 rolls, yielding 18 pieces*

The California Roll was one of the first recipes to surface and gain general acceptance in a new era of Japanese cuisine abroad. It represents one of the clearest, and most delicious, examples of the current trend to blend American foodstuffs with Japanese technique. This American *sushi* has recently been transplanted to Japan's urban centers of gastronomy, where it has been greeted with pleasure.

There are many versions of this classic-in-the-making, and I offer my personal favorite.

   ½ small ripe avocado
    1 tablespoon lemon juice
    3 or 4 seafood sticks (commercially made to simulate crab legs) OR 2–3 ounces fresh crab meat
    2 teaspoons *wasabi* powder (fiery Japanese horseradish)
    2 teaspoons water
    4 sheets *yaki-zushi nori* (toasted paper-thin seaweed)
    3 cups *shari* (rice seasoned for *sushi,* p. 130)
      soy sauce, for dipping

Peel the avocado and cut into six slices, lengthwise. Toss the avocado strips in a few drops of the lemon juice to help hold the color, and set aside.

Gently hand-shred the seafood sticks (they'll form long strips easily), *or* pick over the fresh crab meat discarding cartilage. Toss the seafood shreds or crab in the remaining lemon juice and let it stand for 5 minutes before draining.

In a small bowl, mix the horseradish powder with the water, stirring well to make a paste.

Cut one sheet of the seaweed into thirds; each roll will use one of these strips plus a full sheet.

Take one full sheet of seaweed and lay it on a *sudaré* (slatted bamboo mat) so that the shorter edges of the seaweed run parallel to the slats of the mat. The shinier side of the seaweed should face down. Dampen your hands lightly with water and spread 1 cup of seasoned rice evenly over the seaweed, leaving a border of 2 inches on the far side. Lay one of the three extra strips across the middle of the rice.

Using one third of the horseradish paste, paint a stripe across the extra strip of seaweed. Take one third of the seafood-stick shreds and lay them evenly across the seaweed. Take two strips of avocado and lay them evenly on top of the seafood shreds.

Place your thumbs under the mat and your forefingers on top of the seaweed in the lower right and left corners. Lift slightly and roll snugly to close the fillings. If necessary, help seal the roll with a few grains of rice on the far edge. Lay the roll seam side down on a clean, dry, flat surface.

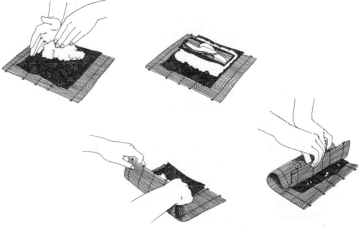

Make two more seafood and avocado rolls in the same manner as the first.

To slice the rolls, use a sharp, damp knife (I like to keep a damp cloth next to my cutting board and draw the blade of my knife over it before and after each slice). Each roll should be cut in half, then the halves into three pieces each yielding eighteen pieces in all. Serve with soy sauce on the side, for dipping.

Menu Suggestions: Two or three pieces of California Roll can be served as a first course to almost any meal, though I think it's best when you're serving fish for your main course. For lunch or a light dinner, the California Roll pairs nicely with any of the other rolled *sushi* recipes in this chapter.

Inside-Out "Fire Brand" Tuna Rolls

TEKKA URA MAKI · Makes 4 rolls, yielding 2 dozen pieces

Since the red of the tuna's flesh is supposed to look like steel being forged to make a samurai sword, *tekka maki* has always enjoyed something of a macho image in Japan. Typically, in restaurants, it's the bits and pieces trimmed from tuna *sashimi* that are used in making these rolls. At home, you might want to practice your knife skills in making *sashimi* (p. 118), keeping this recipe in mind as a fine way to use the less-than-glorious-looking slices that might result from first efforts. Even after your swordsmanship improves, you'll want to remember this dish for its technique of "inside-out" rolling.

> 2 sheets *yaki-zushi nori* (toasted paper-thin seaweed)
> 2 cups *shari* (rice seasoned for *sushi,* p. 130)
> 1½ tablespoons *wasabi* powder (fiery Japanese horseradish)

2–3 ounces lean, raw tuna (scraps are fine)
2–3 tablespoons *kuro goma* (black sesame seeds)
 soy sauce, for dipping

Lay half a sheet of seaweed, rough side facing up, on a clean, dry surface. With hands moistened in water, spread ¼ cup of seasoned rice evenly over the seaweed.

Wet an uncolored muslin or linen cloth (approximately 6 by 8 inches) in cold water and wring it out well. Flip the rice-covered seaweed onto this cloth, with the rice facing down.

Mix the horseradish powder with an equal amount of cold water and stir to make a paste. Paint a line across the seaweed with some of this paste.

If the tuna is a block of meat, cut it into ¼-inch-thick strips and lay one quarter of them across the center of the seaweed. If you're using odd bits and pieces, cut them into narrow strips and lay them across the seaweed to create a similar effect.

For ease in rolling, carefully transfer the cloth (with rice, seaweed, and fish on it) onto a *sudaré* (slatted bamboo mat). Roll the *sushi* snugly, remove the mat, then peel back the damp cloth.

In a dry skillet, toast the black sesame seeds for a few seconds. Sprinkle one quarter of them on your cutting board and quickly roll the *sushi* in them. With a sharp knife wiped on a damp cloth, cut the

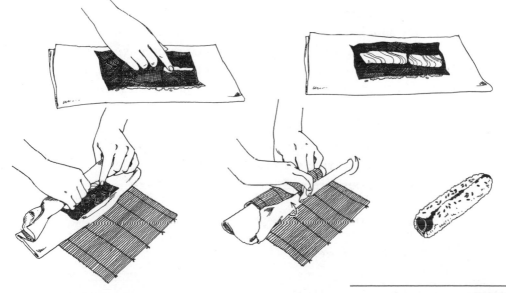

roll in half, then each half into three pieces. Repeat the rolling and cutting procedure to made twenty-four pieces in all. Serve some of them facing up to show off the spiral effect of the filling, others on their sides to show the black seeds against the white rice. Serve with soy sauce for dipping.

Menu Suggestions: Several pieces of inside-out roll make an attractive appetizer, or rolls cut into eight or ten pieces each (instead of the more usual six) yield lots of bite-size, sophisticated cocktail hors d'oeuvres, particularly wonderful when served with champagne or other sparkling wine. These tuna rolls nicely complement Clam *Sushi* (p. 138) and could make an attractive presentation with them at lunch or on a dinner buffet table.

Clam Sushi

HAMAGURI-ZUSHI · *Makes 30 pieces*

This gorgeous *sushi* will elicit a "Wow!" from even the most jaded epicure. Although it requires a fair amount of time to make all the component parts, most of them can be made days ahead. The assembly is relatively simple and can also be accomplished in advance of your guests' arrival. A platter of Clam *Sushi* makes an impressive display on a buffet table or, served in pairs, the morsels become a spectacular first course. Place the *sushi* on dark, unpatterned dishes for a truly dramatic effect.

½ cup *shiguré ni* stewed clam meats (p. 107)

3 cups *shari* (rice seasoned for *sushi,* p. 130)

1 tablespoon drained, finely minced *amazu shōga* (pink pickled ginger)

30 small circles *usutamago yaki* (thin omelet, p. 132)

30 fresh snow peas

Place the stewed clam meats in the bowl of a food processor fitted with the steel blade. Pulse-process the clams until very finely minced. Toss the minced clams into the seasoned rice, then toss in the pink pickled ginger, too. Gently mix until all are evenly distributed.

With hands or spoon moistened with water, divide the rice into thirty even portions. Using either your hands or a dampened but well-wrung-out cloth, compact the rice in each portion to make a 1- to 1½-inch patty. Keep the patties covered with a damp cloth while working. They can be kept covered at room temperature for 2–3 hours.

Trim the circles of omelet, if necessary, to remove dry, brittle edges. Take a single circle of omelet and place a patty of rice off-center on it. Fold the omelet in half, then in half again, enclosing the rice in a triangular wedge-shaped cover. Repeat to make twenty-nine more.

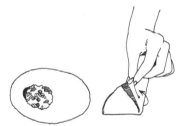

To create a pattern similar to clam shells on the omelet cover, each piece of *sushi* will need to be seared with a hot metal skewer. Hold the tip of a metal skewer directly over a low gas flame, or place it directly on an electric coil set to high. When very hot, remove the skewer from the source of heat and rest it against the omelet. The sugar in the omelet will caramelize, leaving a reddish-brown mark. Usually

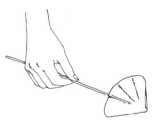

enough heat is retained in the skewer to make two or three lines before reheating. Each piece of *sushi* will require three lines. Continue until you've marked all thirty pieces of *sushi*. (This procedure will probably take 15–20 minutes and can be done up to 2 hours in advance of serving.) Place the *sushi* on your serving platter and cover snugly with clear plastic wrap until ready to serve. Keep the platter at room temperature, away from excessive heat or cold.

Remove the strings from the snow peas. Bring a pot of salted water to a rolling boil and blanch the snow peas for 10 seconds. Drain immediately and refresh the snow peas under cold water. Drain again and pat dry. Arrange two or three snow pea pods, points facing up, in a fanlike bunch. This can be prepared up to 1½ hours before serving.

To garnish a large platter, wedge these bunches of snow pea pods at random between the "clams" to simulate tufts of sea grasses that might be found on a sandy beach. If serving two Clam *Sushi* as a single portion, you may prefer to decorate individual plates with a scattering of snow peas cut into thin, diagonal julienne strips.

Chrysanthemum Sushi

KIKU-ZUSHI · *Makes 25 pieces*

Chrysanthemums are a favorite autumn motif in Japanese culinary aesthetics and these bite-size vegetarian *sushi* are shaped to resemble the fall flower. They make a stunning first course when served on red lacquered plates—or combine them with Camellia *Sushi* (p. 142) on a dark, unpatterned tray or platter.

> 2–3 tablespoons drained, finely minced *amazu shōga* (pink pickled ginger)
>
> 3 cups *shari* (rice seasoned for *sushi*, p. 130)
>
> 1–2 tablespoons white sesame seeds
>
> 10 large circles *usutamago yaki* (thin omelet, p. 132)
>
> 25 leaves fresh *shiso* (flat-leafed Japanese herb), OR 25 fresh snow peas, for garnish
>
> 3–4 tablespoons drained, finely minced *beni shōga* (red pickled ginger)
>
> soy sauce, for dipping

Toss the pink pickled ginger into the seasoned rice and mix gently, but thoroughly.

In a clean, dry skillet, roast the sesame seeds over medium-high heat for about 30 seconds until they begin to color slightly or a few pop. Shake the pan to keep the seeds in motion. Sprinkle the roasted seeds over the rice and gently fold them in.

With damp hands, divide the rice into twenty-five portions. Using hands moistened in cold water or a cloth dampened with water and then well wrung out, mold each portion into a sphere. Flatten slightly.

Cut the thin omelets into very fine julienne strips, about 1½ inches long and ¹⁄₁₆ inch wide. Divide these into twenty-five portions and arrange the strips of a single portion over each flattened sphere of rice to look like petals of a chrysanthemum. The *sushi* can be made up to this point and covered snugly with clear plastic wrap 2–3 hours before serving. Keep away from extremes of heat or cold.

Shiso leaves tend to wilt after about an hour of sitting out on a tray, so just before serving, rinse the leaves and shake free of excess water. Trim away the bottom stem of each *shiso* leaf. Lay the leaves about 2 inches apart on your serving tray or platter. Place one "flower" on the trimmed edge of each leaf. Press the center of each flower with the thicker end of a chopstick, making a slight indentation. Fill this hollow with a few pieces of red pickled ginger. Serve with soy sauce, for dipping.

Note:

For longer buffet presentation, use snow peas to create a leaf effect. Remove the strings and blanch the pods in boiling salted water for 10 seconds. Strain and refresh the snow pea pods under cold water, then pat dry. Slice each snow pea pod in half, on the diagonal. Arrange so that the points face up, as illustrated.

Camellia Sushi

TSUBAKI-ZUSHI · Makes 25 pieces

Inspired by a classic Japanese winter floral motif—the camellia—I first developed this recipe for a December class taught in New York City. My students wanted a spectacular-looking and -tasting *sushi* to serve as a first course or offer as part of a buffet for holiday entertaining. The ability to prepare this salmon *sushi* in advance of their guests' arrival was an important consideration.

> 3 cups *shari* (rice seasoned for *sushi,* p. 130)
>
> 1½ tablespoons *wasabi* powder (fiery Japanese horseradish)
>
> 1½ tablespoons cold water
>
> 6–7 ounces very thin, broadly sliced, smoked salmon (very lightly salted, rosy-toned salmon is best)
>
> 2 yolks from hard-boiled eggs
>
> 25 leaves fresh *shiso* (flat-leafed Japanese herb) OR 25 fresh snow peas, for garnish
>
> soy sauce, for dipping

With hands moistened in cold water, divide the seasoned rice into twenty-five portions and shape each into a compact sphere. You could mold the rice with a cloth dampened in water and then wrung out, if you find that easier. Flatten each sphere slightly.

Mix the horseradish powder with an equal amount of cold water and stir to make a paste. Dab some of this paste on top of each rice sphere.

Cut the salmon into twenty-five pieces and drape one slice over each sphere (scraps can be pieced together, if necessary). With dampened hands, compact the spheres well and, with your thumb, indent the center of each piece on the salmon side.

Force the egg yolks through a fine mesh strainer. Fill each indented *sushi* with some of this sieved yolk.

Rinse the *shiso* leaves and shake off excess water. Lay them on your serving platter, placing a single camellia-shaped *sushi* on top of each. Or remove the strings from the snow peas and blanch them for 10 seconds in boiling salted water. Drain and plunge the snow peas into cold water to stop the cooking process. Pat the snow peas dry and slice each in half, on the diagonal. Arrange the two halves so that the points face in the same direction, fanning open the pair slightly. Lay these on your platter in lieu of the *shiso* leaves. Serve at once, with soy sauce for dipping.

Note:

Camellia *Sushi* can be made up to 3 hours in advance of serving. Shape, drape, and indent all spheres and cover tightly with clear plastic wrap. Keep the *sushi* at room temperature, away from excessive heat or cold. Sieve the egg and place it in a covered bowl, in the refrigerator. Blanch and slice the snow peas and arrange them on a platter. Cover with plastic wrap and set aside in a cool spot or refrigerate. *Shiso* leaves wilt quickly and are therefore not a good choice for long, standing buffets. But you can rinse the leaves hours ahead of your party and keep them wrapped in damp paper towels until ready to serve. Fill the *sushi* with the sieved egg yolk just before serving.

Menu Suggestions: Serve Camellia *Sushi* alone or in combination with Chrysanthemum *Sushi* (p. 140) on dark, smooth plates to make a particularly dramatic presentation.

Rainbow Rolls

OSHINKO MAKI · *Makes 3 rolls, yielding 18 pieces*

Oshinko literally means "new fragrant things," referring to the pleasantly heady aroma of many Japanese pickled vegetables. Vibrant colors such as gold, heliotrope, and chartreuse are typical of these crisp and pungent pickled vegetables. Many tasty varieties are commercially prepared and readily available in vacuum-sealed bags in Oriental groceries. The Japanese serve some kind of pickled vegetable with steamed rice at nearly every meal, and they enjoy brightly colored pickles in *sushi* dishes as well. I've developed this recipe to show you how to use these "ready-made" rainbow-hued fillings to make a simple rolled *sushi*.

> 1 tablespoon white sesame seeds
>
> 3–4 ounces *takuan* (yellow pickled radish) OR 6 thin sticks *yama gobō* (orange pickled burdock root)
>
> 1–2 ounces *ao-jiso no mi-zuké* (green pickled herb seeds and cucumber)
>
> 4 ounces *shiba-zuké* (purple pickled eggplant and gourd)
>
> 2–3 ounces *amazu shōga* (pink pickled ginger)
>
> 4 sheets *yaki-zushi nori* (toasted paper-thin seaweed)
>
> 3 cups *shari* (rice seasoned for *sushi*, p. 130)

In a clean, dry skillet, roast the sesame seeds over medium-high heat for 30–40 seconds until they begin to color slightly or a few pop. Shake the pan to keep the seeds in motion. Set aside.

Prepare the pickled vegetables: Rinse the yellow pickled radish under cold water and pat dry on paper towels (the color of this and other pickles may bleed a bit, so avoid cloth). Either slice the pickle in long, very thin julienne shreds, or into ¼-inch-thick sticks, preferably 6 inches long. If you're using the pickled burdock, rinse and pat dry on paper towels. Drain the pickled herb seeds and cucumber of all excess liquid. Rinse the purple pickled eggplant and gourd under cold water and pat dry on paper towels. Slice the thicker pieces into strips no wider than ⅛ inch. Drain the pink ginger and chop coarsely.

Cut one sheet of seaweed into three broad strips.

Lay one sheet of seaweed on a *sudaré* (slatted bamboo mat), rough side up, with one of the shorter sides closest to you. With hands dampened in cold water, take one third of the seasoned rice and spread it evenly over two thirds of the seaweed, leaving a broad border on the far side. Sprinkle one third of the toasted sesame seeds across the center of the rice, then place one of the three strips of seaweed over the seeds.

Arrange one third of the pickled vegetables on the seaweed in bands of bright color: the yellow *takuan* or orange *gobō,* green herb seeds and cucumber, purple eggplant and gourd, pink pickled ginger. Roll the *sushi* snugly away from you and let it sit, seam side down, for a few moments before slicing it with a sharp knife into six pieces. Moisten the blade of your knife between slices by wiping it on a damp cloth.

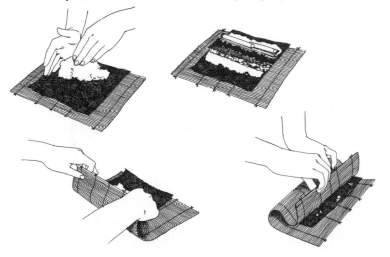

Repeat the assembling and rolling procedures to make two more rolls, yielding eighteen slices in all. Arrange the slices in rows, domino style, on a large unpatterned platter. Serve with soy sauce for dipping, if you like.

Note:
Though the seaweed will lose its crispness if the rolls aren't served at once, this type of *sushi* is fine if left unrefrigerated for up to 3 hours. The flavors marry well, and paradoxically the slight chewiness of the wrapping seems to enhance the dish.

Menu Suggestions: This is a favorite picnic lunch in its native Japan and would make an attractive and delicious alternative to the more conventional sandwiches packed along for most American outings. Rainbow Roll *sushi* is a good choice for indoor buffets and luncheons, too, expecially when served with wedges of Pressed Salmon *Sushi* Tart (p. 153). You could add a soup (Shrimp Dumpling Soup with Snow Pea Pods, p. 64, or Clear Clam Broth with Lemon Peel, p. 66, are two fine choices) and an assortment of fruit with Fresh Ginger Cookies (p. 284) for dessert.

Plump Rolls

FUTO MAKI-ZUSHI · Makes 3 rolls, yielding 18 pieces

Thick rolls of *sushi* brimming with a variety of vegetables and egg are particularly popular in the southwestern part of Japan, where they're often packed along on picnics, or appear on family tables when friends or relatives come to visit.

The fillings are simple to make: mushrooms that can be simmered days ahead, egg strips that can be salvaged from omelet-making practice sessions, purchased pickled ginger that merely gets drained, and greens that require only a quick dip in boiling water.

> 5 or 6 dried *shiitaké* (dark Oriental mushrooms)
> 1 tablespoon *saké* (Japanese rice wine)
> 1½ tablespoons sugar
> 2½ tablespoons soy sauce
> about 4 dozen sprigs *mitsuba* (trefoil) OR 2 dozen sprigs flat-leafed Italian parsley
> 4–5 cups *shari* (rice seasoned for *sushi*, p. 130)
> 3 full sheets *yaki-zushi nori* (toasted paper-thin seaweed)

½ cup drained, julienned *beni shōga* (red pickled ginger)

⅔ cup egg shreds (scraps from thin omelet, p. 132, are fine)

Soak the dried mushrooms in 1¼ cups warm water for 15–20 minutes. Remove the mushrooms and strain the soaking liquid into a shallow pot, reserving it for later use. Remove the stems from the softened mushrooms and save them for enriching stock (p. 50), if you wish, or discard. Rinse the caps under fresh cold water, making sure that no grit clings to the underside. Slice the mushroom caps into thin julienne strips and return them to the strained and reserved soaking liquid.

Over medium heat, bring the mushrooms and liquid to a boil, then adjust the heat to maintain a steady simmer. Add the rice wine and cook for 5 minutes. Add the sugar and cook for another 5 minutes. Add the soy sauce and cook for a final 5 minutes. While cooking, it's best to use a Japanese *otoshi-buta* or "dropped lid," if you have one, since it keeps the mushrooms moist while they simmer in fairly little liquid but at the same time allows that cooking liquid to reduce and intensify. If you haven't got a dropped lid, use slightly lower heat and stir frequently while the mushrooms cook.

Allow the mushrooms to cool to room temperature in the pot in which they were cooked, then transfer them to a covered container for longer storage. The mushrooms keep well, refrigerated, for 5–6 days. Drain the mushrooms of excess liquid just before using.

Rinse the trefoil or parsley carefully under cold water. Divide the greens into three bunches, keeping all the sprigs running in the same direction. Tie the bunches around the stems with string. Bring several cups of salted water to a rolling boil and quickly dip the bunches of greens in it. Drain immediately, running cold water over the greens to stop the cooking process. Squeeze out all excess water and pat the greens dry. Trim, discarding the string and root ends.

With damp hands, divide the seasoned rice into three portions and shape each into a roughly oblong mass. Set aside, covered by a damp cloth.

Lay one sheet of seaweed, rough side up, with one of the shorter edges facing you, on a *sudaré* (slatted bamboo mat). With damp hands, spread one portion of rice across the bottom two thirds of the seaweed. You'll be making a colorful striped pattern across the rice with the fillings.

First, take one bundle of greens and arrange half of it with the leaves pointing to the right and the other half with the leaves pointing left. Lay these greens near you in a horizontal stripe across the rice. Drain the red ginger on paper towels and arrange one third of the julienne strips in the next stripe across the rice, just beyond the greens. Then, arrange one third of the mushrooms (drain on paper towels if they seem excessively moist) in a band beyond the ginger. Finally, make a stripe on the far side from one third of the egg shreds.

Lifting the mat, begin to roll the *sushi* away from you. Flip up and over, snugly enclosing the fillings. Continue to roll, lifting the mat and pushing the *sushi* away from you at the same time. When you get to the far end, press a few grains of rice on the edge of the seaweed before completing the roll, to seal the edge.

Repeat with the remaining ingredients to make two more Plump Rolls. With a sharp knife wiped on a damp cloth between cuts, slice

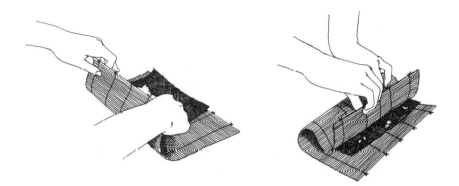

each roll in half, crosswise, and then each half in three slices, yielding eighteen pieces in all. Serve at room temperature with soy sauce for dipping, if you like.

Menu Suggestions: These Plump Rolls make a satisfying vegetarian lunch or dinner when served with a *miso*-thickened broth such as Light Bean Soup with Slender White Mushrooms and Bean Curd (p. 52) or Dark Bean Soup with Bean Curd and Okra (p. 54). If you're looking to expand the menu further, add Batter-Fried Vegetable Bundles (p. 95) or Gift-Wrapped Kelp Rolls (p. 116).

Miniature Hand Rolls with Three Fillings

TE MAKI-ZUSHI · *Makes 2 dozen rolls*

The amiable yet sophisticated atmosphere of American *sushi* bars seems to add a nuance of flavor to the already acknowledged eating pleasures that await you there. Hand rolls, those personalized tidbits wound and bound on command with a flick of the wrist, have become particularly popular recently. Most people like to experiment with lots of unusual combinations but find the large hand rolls quite filling. I've redesigned these, scaling them down to miniature cornucopias, and listed three of my personal favorites in fillings. For additional fillings you could take ideas from other *sushi* recipes in this book, or look in your refrigerator and see what you have. Combinations of various herbs and spices, bits of fruit and vegetables, fish, seafood, and fish roes make wonderful fillings.

6 sheets *yaki-zushi nori* (toasted paper-thin seaweed)

1½ cups *shari* (rice seasoned for *sushi,* p. 130)

herbed plum filling:

1 tablespoon *umé niku* (plum paste) OR 5–6 *umé-boshi* (pickled plums)

4 leaves fresh *shiso* (flat-leafed Japanese herb) OR 1½ dozen leaves fresh mint

1½ inches unwaxed cucumber

crisp and smoky filling:

1 package (5 grams) OR about ⅓ cup *katsuo bushi* (dried bonito flakes)

1 scant tablespoon soy sauce

40–50 stalks *tsumamina* (radish sprouts) OR ¼ cup fresh alfalfa sprouts

1 teaspoon white sesame seeds

broiled salmon-skin filling:

6–7 inches skin from smoked salmon

1 teaspoon *wasabi* powder (fiery Japanese horseradish)

1 teaspoon cold water

1½ tablespoons finely chopped scallion (green part only)

soy sauce, for dipping

Cut each of the sheets of seaweed in quarters and stack them, rough side up, in a dry spot near your work surface. With damp hands, divide the rice into twenty-four portions and gently compact each into a small nugget. Place a damp cloth over the rice to keep it from drying out.

Next, prepare whatever fillings you'll want to use and set them out on plates or in bowls near your work surface.

HERBED PLUM FILLING

If you were unable to purchase plum paste and could only find the pickled plums whole, remove the pits and mash the plum meat to make a paste. Lick your finger; the plum should be pleasantly astringent. If it's too salty or sour for your taste, add a pinch of sugar if necessary (the commercially prepared paste eliminates the skins, resulting in a more mellow taste than that of the mashed whole pickled fruit).

Rinse the *shiso* leaves under cold water and shake off excess moisture. Trim away the bottom stems and slice the leaves in half, lengthwise. Each roll will use a half leaf and a dab of plum paste. If you were unable to find fresh *shiso* leaves but have access to fresh mint, use two or three small mint leaves in each roll instead of the larger *shiso*.

Cut the cucumber into very thin slices slightly on the diagonal, then across into fine julienne strips. Use one eighth of these threadlike cucumber shreds for each roll.

CRISP AND SMOKY FILLING

In a small bowl, toss the bonito flakes with the soy sauce until barely moistened.

Rinse the radish sprouts under cold water, shaking off excess moisture. Trim and discard the roots. If you're using alfalfa sprouts instead, rinse and shake dry; no trimming is necessary.

In a clean, dry skillet, roast the sesame seeds over medium-high heat for 30–40 seconds until they begin to color slightly or a few pop. Shake the pan to keep the seeds in motion. Transfer the roasted seeds to a cutting board and mince them (as you would parsley) just to crack the seeds and release their aroma. Set the cracked seeds aside.

Each roll will use one eighth of the fish flakes, a few stalks of the radish sprouts (or a small clump of alfalfa sprouts), and a sprinkling of sesame seeds.

BROILED SALMON-SKIN FILLING

Preheat the oven to broil. Place the salmon, skin side up, in a disposable foil pan, preferably one with ridges so the oil can drip down and away from the skin. Broil 2–3 inches from the heat until the skin begins to blister and brown (about 2 minutes). If the skin comes from unsalted salmon, you may wish to sprinkle it with a pinch of salt before broiling it. Drain the broiled skin on paper towels, then cut the skin crosswise into eight strips.

Mix the horseradish powder with an equal quantity of cold water and stir to make a paste.

Soak the scallion in cold water for 3–4 minutes, then drain and pat dry.

Each roll will use a strip of broiled salmon skin, a dab of horseradish, and a few scallion bits.

ASSEMBLING AND ROLLING THE ROLLS

To make herbed plum rolls, take a single small piece of seaweed and place it on a dry board. Dampen your fingers with cold water before pressing a nugget of rice into the upper quadrant of the seaweed. Moistening your fingers with cold water keeps the rice from sticking to them. Spread a bit of plum paste on the rice and lay the *shiso* or mint leaves on top of that, with the pointed herb leaves facing up. Place a few threadlike cucumber shreds on top of the herb leaves. Lift the lower corner of the seaweed up to cover about half the filling. Holding down the first fold gently with one finger, fold over one side, rolling snugly toward the other side to form a cone shape. To help seal the roll, place a grain of cooked rice in the corner and press.

If you've decided upon crisp and smoky filling, make the rolls in a similar fashion. Take a sheet of seaweed and, with fingers dampened with cold water, press a nugget of rice to it in the upper quadrant. Scatter some sesame seeds on each portion of rice before placing one eighth of the seasoned fish flakes over that. Add some sprouts (with the green buds facing up for the radish variety) and lift the lower corner of seaweed up to cover about half the filling. With one finger, gently hold down this first fold at the same time as you wind and roll to form a cone shape. Seal the roll with a grain of cooked rice.

If you're making rolls with broiled salmon-skin filling, take a sheet of seaweed and, with dampened fingers, press a nugget of rice in the upper quadrant. Spread a dab of the horseradish paste on the rice, lay down the strip of salmon skin, then place some bits of scallion over that before winding and sealing each roll.

Serve the miniature cornucopias with soy sauce for dipping.

Menu Suggestions: Miniature Hand Rolls make splendid hors d'oeuvres at a cocktail party and can be made an hour or so before company arrives. Roll and cover them with clear plastic wrap but don't refrigerate.

Or set up a do-it-yourself mini–*sushi* bar on a buffet table. Make ahead a platter of cooked rice nuggets and cover with a damp cloth and clear plastic wrap. Don't refrigerate. Remove the cover just before bringing the rice out to the buffet. Have a tray ready with stacks of small crisp seaweed squares and plates or bowls filled with colorful and tasty fillings. Have a bowl of cold water for hands and several damp cloths ready to wipe sticky fingers. Give a quick demonstration of rolling techniques to your guests, then let them roll their own. Provide soy sauce for dipping.

Pressed Salmon Sushi *Tart*

DAISETSU OSHI-ZUSHI · Makes 12 wedges

Salmon caught in the chilly rivers of Hokkaidō, Japan's northernmost island, is utterly delicious and the natives there take great pride in their salmon cookery. Box lunches made from local produce and seafood are sold to travelers in many train stations throughout Japan, and the station of Asahigawa, Hokkaidō, is famous for its pressed salmon *sushi,* called *Daisetsu Oshi-Zushi.* The name derives from the station's location at the foot of Mount Daisetsu, which means "Big Snows."

Lightly salted lox is very similar in taste and texture to the Japanese *shaké* (salmon), and although the original prototype of this *sushi* dish is made in a special wooden box lined with bamboo leaves, a shallow, round tart plate with a removable bottom makes a marvelous substitute for the original mold.

I've added dill, a Western herb, to the original Japanese sea herb flakes, since it goes so well with salmon and rice. Unlike other kinds of fish *sushi,* made from raw ingredients, this dish must be prepared several hours in advance of serving.

> 4 ounces thinly sliced lox (lightly salted smoked salmon), the broadest slices possible
>
> 1 teaspoon fresh lemon juice
>
> 1 teaspoon *wasabi* powder (fiery Japanese horseradish)
>
> 1 teaspoon cold water
>
> 2 cups *shari* (rice seasoned for *sushi,* p. 130)
>
> 1 tablespoon chopped fresh dill
>
> ½ teaspoon *ao nori* (sea herb flakes)
>
> 2 teaspoons *kuro goma* (black sesame seeds)
>
> soy sauce, for dipping (optional)

Remove the bottom flat circle of metal from a shallow 6-inch tart plate and set aside. Line the rim of the round tart plate with clear plastic wrap so that it extends well beyond the edges of the plate.

With a pastry brush, paint one side of the slices of smoked salmon lightly with the lemon juice. Fit these slices, painted side down, into the lined tart plate so that the entire 6-inch circle within the rim is covered with a thin, even layer of salmon. Piece together scraps if necessary.

Mix the horseradish powder with the cold water and stir to make a paste. Spread this paste thinly but evenly over the salmon with your fingertips or a brush.

Dampen your hands in cold water and scoop up half the seasoned rice and press it into the salmon-lined tart plate, making an even layer from it. Dampen the flat metal disk (the bottom of the tart plate that you previously removed and set aside) in cold water and use it to evenly press down and compact this layer of rice. Typically, the rice will be compressed to half its original height. Remove the metal disk.

Mix the chopped dill with the sea herb flakes and scatter this mixture evenly across the flattened surface of rice. Using the remaining rice, fill the tart plate with it and compact it evenly, as you did the first layer. Remove the flat metal disk and cover the rice with clear plastic wrap. Replace the flat metal disk and place weights on top of it. Books, bricks, even potatoes are fine; you should have at least 5 pounds of pressure but no more than 10. Make sure that the first weight you place on the metal disk is small and flat; most paperback books are perfect for this job. Let the *sushi* tart rest at room temperature for at least 1 hour and up to 3.

In a clean, dry skillet, roast the sesame seeds over medium-high heat for 30–40 seconds until a few pop. Shake the pan to keep the seeds in motion. Set aside.

When ready to serve the *sushi,* remove the weights and invert the filled tart plate. Remove the rim of the tart plate and peel off the clear plastic wrap. Decorate the outer rim of the *sushi* with the black sesame seeds. With a sharp knife, cut the *sushi* "tart" into twelve wedges. Wipe the blade of your knife on a damp kitchen towel between slices to keep the rice from sticking to it. Slip a metal spatula dampened with cold water under each wedge of *sushi* (leave the clear plastic wrap behind) to transfer the pieces to your serving platter. Provide soy sauce for dipping, if you like.

Menu Suggestions: Serve the Pressed Salmon *Sushi* Tart at the start of a dinner of broiled or roasted meat; Steak with *Wasabi* Butter (p. 204) or Grilled Veal Chops with *Sanshō* Butter (p. 206) would be a particularly good choice. An attractive buffet or cocktail tray might combine wedges of *sushi* tart with Chicken Dumplings (p. 87) served on skewers, and blocks of Amber Aspic Loaf (p. 111).

Five-Colored Sushi

GO SHOKU CHIRASHI-ZUSHI · *Serves 4–6*

Nearly all the components of Five-Colored *Sushi* can be made days ahead and the dish assembled at your leisure several hours before serving it. The final arrangement of multicolored garnishes in a vivid geometric design creates an impressive centerpiece for any luncheon or buffet dinner.

garnishes:
3–4 ounces shelled fresh OR quick-frozen peas

2 sheets *yaki-zushi nori* (toasted paper-thin seaweed)

6 large circles *usutamago yaki* (thin omelet, p. 132, finely shredded)

1 cup Sweet and Sour Turnip Strips (p. 268), well drained

1 cup drained, julienned *beni shōga* (red pickled ginger)

2 large smoked chubs, about 8 ounces in all, OR 1 piece smoked whitefish, 6–8 ounces

1 teaspoon *usukuchi shōyu* (light soy sauce)

1½ tablespoons white sesame seeds

3–5 cups *shari* (rice seasoned for *sushi*, p. 130)

In a small saucepan bring several cups of salted water to a rolling boil. Cook the fresh peas for 1½ minutes, then drain and let them cool to room temperature naturally. If using frozen peas, just place them in a strainer and pour boiling water over them. Drain well and set aside. This can be done an hour or so before serving time.

Cut the seaweed with scissors into very thin threads about 1 inch long. Cover these snugly with clear plastic wrap and set aside. These can be made up to several hours in advance.

The egg shreds can be made and refrigerated many days in advance of serving, while the pickled turnip shreds keep well for weeks and the red ginger for months, if refrigerated.

Have all five *sushi* garnishes ready and waiting on separate plates: the green peas, the black seaweed threads, the yellow egg shreds, the shredded white pickled turnip, and the julienne strips of red pickled ginger.

Remove all bones and skin from the smoked fish, flaking the flesh as you go; you should have about 1 cup. Place the flaked fish in a small bowl with the light soy sauce and toss until it's well mixed and the fish has absorbed all the liquid.

In a clean, dry skillet, roast the sesame seeds over medium-high heat for 30–40 seconds until they begin to color slightly or a few pop. Shake the pan to keep the seeds in motion. Stir the roasted seeds into the seasoned smoked fish until well distributed. Gently fold the fish and sesame mixture into the seasoned rice.

Scatter the rice mixture so that it lightly covers a large plate or tray (12–20 inches in diameter). Don't let it mound higher than 1½ inches.

The seasoned rice mixture can be made 3–4 hours in advance of serving, as long as you cover it snugly with clear plastic wrap and keep it at room temperature, away from extremes of hot or cold.

Just before you serve, garnish your *sushi*. There are two geometric patterns you can choose from: The first creates a multicolored striped effect, the second a wedged pattern. To create either you'll need long cooking chopsticks, or other narrow straight guidelines, dampened with cold water so they don't stick to the rice.

To make the stripes lay four guidelines, slightly on the diagonal and at equal intervals, over the lightly mounded rice mixture. I like to start filling in the first stripe with white pickled turnip shreds, then fill the next row with green peas. I place yellow egg shreds in the center aisle,

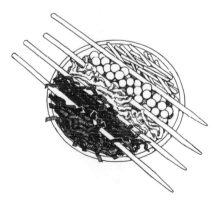

then red pickled ginger, and finally black seaweed in the remaining row. When the stripes have been created, remove the chopsticks and touch up the border areas, if necessary.

To make a wedged pattern, place two very long chopsticks over the rice to make an X. Fill the top and bottom wedges with turnip shreds and egg shreds, respectively. Fill the right quadrant with green peas and the left with red pickled ginger. Remove the guidelines, smooth the borders, and mound the black seaweed in the very center, where the four colors merge. Serve at room temperature.

Menu Suggestions: This pilaflike *sushi* makes a wonderful luncheon or dinner entrée, especially when preceded by a clear soup such as Clear Clam Broth with Lemon Peel (p. 66) or Shrimp Dumpling Soup with Snow Pea Pods (p. 64).

Main Dishes...

Generous portions of stunningly presented cold meats and seafood, piping-hot stews and casseroles, succulent roasts and glazed grills, savory fish and vegetarian choices to feature at your table

There's no single focal point, or "main" course, in a Japanese meal. Rather, a number of smaller dishes, each with just a bit of meat or fish, combine to create the menu. Traditional Japanese and American concepts of meat—the quantity consumed and the role played by it in the meal—differ tremendously. The Japanese typically figure that ⅓ pound of meat will feed four, even five people, while Americans estimate ¼ pound or more per individual serving. Poultry provides the bulk of meat in the Japanese diet, with pork and occasionally beef being eaten as well. Despite the relative proximity of Australia and New Zealand, lamb is virtually unknown to the general populace in Japan. Veal is rarely seen in Japanese markets since all calves are bred to beef-yielding maturity.

Recent dietary trends on both sides of the Pacific, though, have made each country's cuisine more appealing to the other. Health-conscious Americans are cutting back on red-meat consumption and contemporary Japanese households are eating more and more varied kinds of meat than ever before. Great numbers of Japanese are traveling and living abroad, where they explore Western cuisines firsthand. At the same time Japanese restaurants in America continue to proliferate as more Americans become enamored of Japanese food.

The recipes in this chapter reflect American expectations in heartiness, yet rely heavily upon Japanese kitchen techniques and seasonings to create their cross-cultural identity. The chapter begins with cold salads of beef, chicken, pork, duck, and lobster, each exquisitely presented in accordance with Japanese culinary aesthetics. Light but satisfying, beautifully inviting and definitely delicious, these meat platters combine the best of both gastronomic worlds.

Fish, other seafood, and *tōfu* (bean curd) provide most of the protein in the traditional Japanese diet. For Americans wanting to explore these possibilities at their own tables, I've presented treasures from the sea, such as crispy, gingery fried crabs and glazed salmon steaks, as well as vegetarian options, such as bean curd *tempura* with a scallion sauce.

Too many Americans think that all Japanese food is synonymous with Spartan portions and stark, stagy appearances. In reality the Japanese enjoy copious quantities of lusty, unfussy food, too. I want you to have a chance to sample this informal fare in your own home, so I've included a few stews and casseroles and several *domburi* dishes, which are bowls of rice with assorted savory toppings.

The chapter concludes with larger and more generous cuts of meat prepared with an eclectic mixture of Oriental and Continental techniques. The *miso*-glazed baked chicken, steaks and chops with Japanese herb butters, and grilled meats with Japanese sauces were inspired by the trend toward culinary internationalism.

Wasabi *Beef Rolls with Green Beans*

GYŪNIKU NO HIYA MORI · *Serves 4*

This platter of rolled cold beef is perfect on a hot summer evening or any warm-weather luncheon menu. No serious cooking is called for—already roasted beef can be purchased at almost any food market—and the zippy *wasabi* (Japanese horseradish) mayonnaise on beef and potatoes is sure to revive even the most heat-sapped appetites.

> 6–8 ounces fresh green beans
> 6–8 ounces thinly sliced, rare roast beef
> 2–3 tablespoons *wasabi* mayonnaise (p. 241)
> 2 teaspoons *kuro goma* (black sesame seeds)
> ⅛ teaspoon freshly ground black pepper
> 2½–3 cups Potato Salad with *Wasabi* Mayonnaise (p. 240)

You'll use three or four beans per beef roll and there will be four rolls for each serving. Select the longest and best beans, trimming them to even lengths (about 3½–4 inches). Bring several cups of salted water to a rolling boil and blanch the beans in it for 1 minute, or until bright green and barely tender.

Fold each slice of beef top and bottom to even off the edges and make a band about 2½–3 inches wide. Wrap a 3½- to 4-inch length of this band around three or four green beans. Make sixteen rolls in all, four for each serving. On each individual dinner plate, arrange the rolls in a horizontal row, slightly in front of center, with the seams down.

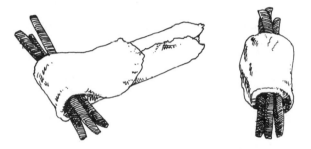

Either pipe or spoon the mayonnaise across the middle of the beef and green bean rolls.

In a clean, dry skillet, roast the sesame seeds over medium-high heat for 30–40 seconds until a few pop. Shake the pan to keep the seeds in motion. Save a few whole seeds for garnishing later but crack the rest coarsely by mincing with a knife or adding to a pepper mill that has only a few peppercorns in it. Mix the cracked sesame with the black pepper and sprinkle this mixture over the mayonnaise.

Divide the potato salad into four portions and mound one behind the beef and green bean rolls on each plate. Top each mound with a few whole, roasted black sesame seeds. Serve at room temperature, or chill the plates for 15 minutes in the refrigerator before serving.

Gingery Japanese-Style Chicken Salad

TORI NO SHŌGA MAYO AÉ · Serves 4

Chicken salad seems to be part of the American way of life; it's a
luncheon standby and a picnic favorite. Here I've created my own version redolent of fresh ginger and accented with toasted macadamia nuts.
I owe the presentation of the salad to Japanese culinary aesthetics, using shredded *daikon* radish and cucumber "mountains" as garnishes.
But you could Americanize your presentation and mound the chicken
on crisp lettuce leaves.

	2 large whole chicken breasts, about 1¼ pounds each with skin and bones intact
poaching liquid:	1½ cups *dashi* (basic sea stock, p. 48) OR water
	1 tablespoon *saké* (Japanese rice wine)
	2 or 3 pieces fresh ginger peel, each about 1 inch square
	¼ cup (about 2½ ounces) macadamia nuts
	¾ pound *daikon* (Japanese white radish)
	1 teaspoon salt
	2 small unwaxed cucumbers, about ½ pound in all
ginger dressing:	1 yolk from jumbo egg, at room temperature
	2 teaspoons dry mustard
	¼ teaspoon salt
	pinch sugar
	⅓ cup vegetable oil
	1 teaspoon rice vinegar
	1–2 teaspoons ginger juice (extracted from freshly grated ginger)

It's best to poach and shred, then cover and refrigerate the chicken
before toasting the nuts and making the vegetable garnishes and the

ginger dressing. The cooked chicken should have a chance to chill for at least 30 minutes, but you can keep it refrigerated up to 3 days if that suits your schedule best.

Place the chicken breasts on your cutting board, skin side up. Press down firmly on the breastbone, cracking to flatten the meat somewhat. Combine the ingredients for the poaching liquid in a shallow pot just wide enough to accommodate both chicken breasts snugly. Add the peels from the ginger that will be grated and squeezed later for the dressing. Lay the chicken breasts in the liquid and cover. Over low heat, gradually bring the liquid to a simmer. Cook the chicken for 25 minutes, then remove the pot from the source of heat. Let the chicken cool until it's comfortable to handle. Remove and discard the skin and bones. Strain and save the poaching liquid, if you like, for use in soups like Thick Rice Soup with Chicken, Chives, and Ginger (p. 62) or Shrimp Dumpling Soup with Snow Pea Pods (p. 64). Shred the meat by hand, with the grain. These hand-shredded, rough-textured pieces present more surface area to absorb the delicious dressing and are preferable to knife-sliced strips. The hand-shredded pieces should be approximately 1½ inches long and ⅛ inch wide. Cover snugly with clear plastic wrap and refrigerate.

Cut each whole macadamia nut in half, then place them in a clean, dry skillet over medium-high heat. Shake the pan frequently to ensure even coloration, toasting the nuts for about 1 minute until they're a golden-brown color.

Peel the radish and save the peels for use in the sauté on p. 253, if you wish, or discard. Slice the vegetable into very thin pieces. Stack several of these at a time and cut across them to create thin, threadlike julienne strips. Place the strips of radish in a bowl and salt them. Let the radish sit for 5 minutes, then squeeze to extract as much liquid as possible. Discard this brine, rinse the now wilted radish under fresh cold water, and squeeze again to get rid of excess liquid. Cover and chill the shredded radish for at least 30 minutes and up to 4–5 hours, if you want to make this well in advance of serving time.

Wash the cucumbers well and slice off about ½ inch from the stem (darker green) end of each. Using this stem piece, rub the cut surface in circular motions until a thick white foam appears; rinse it away. This is what the Japanese call *aku nuki* or "bitterness removal." Trim the other (light-colored) end of the cucumber. Cut each cucumber in half,

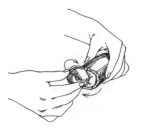

to produce four short (about 2-inch) cylinders. Each of these will be further cut into two mountain shapes. Insert a knife, lengthwise, into one of the cylinders. Keep that knife in place while using a second knife to slash the cucumber on the diagonal. Keeping the first knife in place, flip the cucumber cylinder over and with the second knife make another diagonal slash. Remove the knives and pull the cucumber mountains apart. Repeat to make eight mountains in all. Cucumber mountains are at their crunchy best when cut no more than 1 hour before serving.

To make the ginger dressing, beat the egg yolk in a bowl with a whisk until creamy and smooth. Add the dry mustard and continue to beat to make a stiff paste. Beat in the salt and sugar (the mixture is probably clinging to your whisk by now, and you may be having trouble incorporating any new substances). Dribble the oil in, drop by drop, beating as you go to make a smooth, thick mayonnaise. Incorporate half the oil in this fashion before you begin to alternate drops of rice vinegar with the oil as you beat. Finally, dribble in the ginger juice and beat to mix well; the ginger will have a loosening effect on the dressing and thin the mayonnaise considerably.

Dress the shredded chicken with the ginger mayonnaise, then toss in the toasted macadamia nuts, too. Divide this mixture into four portions and coax each into a mountainlike shape, to be placed just to the right and slightly forward of the center of one of four flat dinner plates. Divide the radish into four portions and, again, shape each into a peak. Place this mound to the left of and just behind the chicken. Arrange two cucumber mountains just in front and slightly to the right of the chicken. Serve immediately.

Note:
Fresh ginger's refreshing fire fades considerably with time. For optimal flavor, and spice, make the dressing less than 2 hours before serving.

Cold Steamed Peppered Pork with Mustard Sauce

BUTA NIKU NO KARASHI SU MISO KAKÉ · *Serves 6–8*

This dish is particularly well suited to hot weather dining since both the meat and the sauce can be made in the cool of one evening, refrigerated, and then served several days thereafter. Although the cold pork is especially inviting in the summer months, it could join a buffet of cold sandwich meats in any season.

> 2 pounds pork loin OR lean pork shoulder
> 1 teaspoon salt
> ½ teaspoon *sanshō* (fragrant Japanese pepper)

mustard sauce:
> ⅓ cup *shiro miso* (light fermented bean paste)
> 1 tablespoon sugar
> 2 tablespoons rice vinegar
> 1 teaspoon soy sauce
> 1 teaspoon prepared mustard
> 1 tablespoon water

Rub all the surfaces of the meat with the salt and Japanese pepper, then tie the pork with kitchen twine so that it keeps its shape throughout the cooking. Place the pork in a steamer with at least 1½ inches of water in the bottom section. Bring the water to a boil, then adjust the heat to medium to keep a steady flow of steam. After 10 minutes, check the water level. If it has been reduced by half, you'll need to add hot water every 15 minutes. The pork must steam for a total of 45 minutes or until the internal temperature reaches 170 degrees. It's best to check this with a meat thermometer.

After steaming the pork, remove it from the heat and let it cool, covered with a damp cloth, at room temperature. When the cloth is no longer hot and no clouds of steam are visible, wrap the pork snugly in clear plastic wrap and refrigerate for at least 2 hours to chill it. The cooked pork will keep, refrigerated, for several days.

Combine the sauce ingredients in a small noncorrodible saucepan and stir well. Heat the sauce over a low flame until bubbly and glossy. Chill the sauce for at least 15 minutes, or refrigerate up to 1 week in a covered glass jar.

Remove the twine from the pork, cut it in ⅛-inch-thick slices, and arrange these, domino style, on a platter. Stir the sauce and thin it slightly, if necessary, with a drop or two of water. Serve the sauce separately, or drizzled across the sliced meat.

Menu Suggestions: I like to serve this sliced pork dish with a crisp vegetable salad. Green Salad with Walnut and Bean Dressing (p. 260) could be one choice; Radish and *Shiso* Salad (p. 258) or Pickled Cabbage Salad (p. 256) might be others.

Soy-Braised Duck Salad

KAMO NO SHŌYU NI · *Serves 4*

Duck and other waterfowl were hunted and eaten occasionally by the nobility in feudal Japan. Some of the ancient recipes, such as this succulent soy-braised duck, remain part of the contemporary culinary repertoire. I've modernized this classic dish even further by making it the main attraction of the meal (a slice or two are normally relegated to appetizer status in Japan) and presenting it with crisp, raw vegetables. This dish is usually served at room temperature, though it's just as delicious hot or cold.

	4½	**pound duckling**
		ice water
marinade:	¼	cup *saké* (Japanese rice wine)
	3	tablespoons *mirin* (syrupy rice wine)
	2	tablespoons *usukuchi shōyu* (light soy sauce)
	⅓–½	cup *dashi* (basic sea stock, p. 48)
garnish:	2	small unwaxed cucumbers
	4	large leaves *hakusai* (Chinese cabbage), inner white leaves preferred
	1	bunch (about 3 ounces) *tsumamina* (radish sprouts), optional

Have your butcher bone the duckling so that you have a full breast, split lengthwise and with the skin intact, and both thighs (with lower legs), butterflied so as to lie flat. These pieces should also have their skin intact. You should have four pieces of meat weighing a total of about 2 pounds. Trim away excess fat. Melt some pieces to render about 1 tablespoon of fat in a heavy skillet. Pour off this fat and save it to sauté the duck later.

Prick the skin of the duck meat all over with the sharp tines of a fork. Over low heat, sauté the duck meat, skin side down, in the melted fat for 2 minutes or until lightly colored. Immediately remove the meat and plunge it into ice water; the excess fat will congeal and float to the surface, facilitating removal. Strain the fat from the skillet through a fine-meshed strainer and save it, covered, in the refrigerator.

Remove the meat from the cold water and pat dry with paper towels. Place the meat, skin side up, in a glass or ceramic container just large enough to accommodate the four pieces in a single layer. Combine the marinade ingredients and pour them over the meat. Turn the meat several times during the marinating process if the liquid doesn't rise to cover the meat. Cover and marinate a minimum of 2 hours at room temperature, or up to 24 hours in the refrigerator.

Lift the meat from the marinade and pat dry. Reserve the marinade. In a skillet just large enough for the four pieces of meat, heat the duck fat saved from the first sautéing. Over low heat sauté the meat, skin side down, for 2 minutes. Flip the meat and continue to sauté for 2 minutes more. Blot up or pour off all excess fat before adding the reserved marinade to the skillet. Add ⅓ cup of the stock, cover the skillet, and bring to a simmer, then braise the duck over medium heat for about 8 minutes.

Flip the meat so that the skin faces down again and check the amount of liquid in the skillet. If the braising liquid is already reduced by more than half, add the remaining stock to the skillet now. If not, keep the extra stock on hand in case you need it later. Cook, covered, for another 5 minutes if you like the duck pink, 8–10 minutes if you prefer it a bit better done. (Unlike currently fashionable rare duck dishes, this recipe produces succulent and tender meat that's well cooked. When it's pierced, the juices should be rosy and clear, and the internal temperature about 160 degrees.)

Pour off the pan juices and remove excess fat from them. (I find pulling strips of paper towel over the surface of the juices the easiest way, though chilling and lifting off solid fat is fine if you have the time.) Ideally the juices have reduced to a thick sauce. If the sauce is still rather watery, simmer uncovered over low heat until it thickens naturally to a glazelike consistency, then set aside.

Wash the cucumbers well and slice off about ½ inch from the stem (darker green) end of each. Using this stem piece, rub the cut surface in circular motions until a thick white foam appears; rinse it away. This is what the Japanese call *aku nuki* or "bitterness removal." Trim the opposite end of the cucumber, then cut it into thin slices slightly on

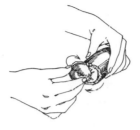

the diagonal. Stack several of these slices at a time and cut across into narrow julienne strips. The strips will be tipped in dark green, while the centers will be pale. Soak the cut cucumbers in ice water for 5 minutes while preparing the cabbage, then drain well.

Rinse the cabbage leaves under cold water, then pat dry. Trim away any wilted edges. Slice the cabbage leaves in half, lengthwise, then across into $1/16$-inch-wide slices.

If you want to add a bit of zest to your garnishes, include the crisp but spicy radish sprouts. Rinse them under cold water, shake off the excess, and trim away the roots.

On each individual plate, place one quarter of the shredded cabbage just to the left of center. Mound one quarter of the drained cucumbers just to the right of center. Lay a small clump of radish sprouts in the middle. Slice the duck meat slightly on the diagonal and lay the slices, domino style, against the bed of cabbage, cucumbers, and radish sprouts. Serve extra sauce either dribbled across the sliced meat or in a separate dish.

Menu Suggestions: I like to serve Pale Jade Soup (p. 76) with this duck dish. Temple Garden Soup (p. 69) would also make a fine first course. Herbed Rice (p. 228) is a delightful side dish to serve either warm or at room temperature in a separate rice bowl. Plain rice (p. 218) molded into some fanciful shape and garnished with sesame seeds makes a nice side dish, too.

Lobster Salad with Two Sauces

ISÉ EBI NO SARADA · Serves 2

Homarus americanus, the lobsters that are native to the American North Atlantic coast, look quite different from the spiny, clawless creatures known as *isé ebi* that crawl along the Japanese coastline. Japanese *isé ebi* are incredibly expensive and contain very little, though usually sweet, meat. Their shells turn bright red as our lobsters' do when cooked, and since red is the color of felicity in Japan, *isé ebi* are served at weddings and on other auspicious occasions.

Most Japanese professional and home cooks living in the New England area are immediately captivated by our hefty and comparatively low-priced *Homarus americanus.* Whenever a friend or relative visits from Japan, a lobster dinner makes it a memorable affair. I serve the lobster with two sauces, one a tart soy and the other a creamy but spicy mayonnaise. If you have some *wasabi* mayonnaise (p. 241) left over from another day, by all means use it. The version given here, though, makes use of a whole lime—juice and rind—and yields just enough for two portions.

2	live lobsters, 1–1½ pounds each
7	quarts water
1	tablespoon salt
2	tablespoons *saké* (Japanese rice wine)

lemon-soy sauce:

1	small blemish-free lemon
3–4	tablespoons soy sauce
1	small blemish-free lime
¼	cup *wasabi* mayonnaise (p. 241) OR:
2–2½	teaspoons juice from above lime
	yolk from egg, at room temperature
	pinch salt
2	teaspoons *wasabi* powder (fiery Japanese horseradish)
3	tablespoons vegetable oil

garnish: 1 ounce (small bunch) *tsumamina* (radish sprouts)
3 colossal pitted black olives

Everyone agrees that when shopping for lobsters, you should choose the liveliest creatures you can find and cook them soon. There's some controversy, though, on the subject of whether lobsters should be killed just prior to plunging them into boiling water, or whether the plunge itself is sufficient. The Japanese believe that the sudden hot bath tightens the flesh of their native *isé ebi,* a crustacean more similar to crayfish than to our *Homarus americanus.* The Japanese insert a sharp metal skewer just where the head meets the body to "relax" the lobster before cooking it. If you're squeamish, or if your lobsters are so active as to make holding them while skewering them a problem, I think the boiling water alone is just fine.

Bring 6 quarts of water, the salt, and the rice wine to a rolling boil in a deep pot large enough to comfortably hold one of the lobsters. Plunge the lobster into the boiling water and cook for 10 minutes. With tongs, remove the lobster to a colander to cool. Add another quart of fresh water to your pot and allow it to come to a rolling boil again before repeating the cooking process for the next lobster.

When both lobsters have been cooked and are cool enough to handle comfortably, extract the meat from the claws, legs, and body. I find it easiest to use a nutcracker or hammer to crack the claws and legs. I shred this meat by hand, checking to remove bits of cartilage and shell. I use kitchen shears to cut down both sides of the tail in order to remove the meat in a single piece. Slice this tail meat evenly into pieces about ¼ inch thick. I personally don't care for the look of lobster meat arranged on the plate to resemble the original crustacean's shape. For each lobster, I prefer to gently mound the odd pieces of claw and leg meat in the center of a large dinner plate. Cover the mound with sliced pieces of tail meat, laid domino style. At this point, the meat can be covered with clear plastic wrap and refrigerated for several hours.

Slice the lemon in half through its middle at the thickest part. With the help of a grapefruit knife, carefully remove the fruit from the rinds. Squeeze the fruit and save 3 tablespoons of juice to mix with 3–4 tablespoons of soy sauce. Trim the stem and flower ends of the lemon just enough to keep them from rocking back and forth. Divide the lemon juice and soy mixture between the two lemon cups and place one on each of the two plates of cooked lobster, to the right and just in front of the mounded meat.

Cut the lime in half through its middle at the thickest part and, with the help of a grapefruit knife, remove the fruit. If you're making the mayonnaise fresh from this recipe, rather than using some left over from another use, squeeze the fruit and reserve the juice, discarding the pulp. Save the rinds and trim off just enough from the stem and flower ends of each to keep it from rocking. In a bowl, combine the egg yolk, salt, 1 teaspoon of lime juice, and horseradish powder. Beat until creamy and smooth. Dribble in a few drops of vegetable oil, continuing to beat the mixture. Add more oil, a few drops at a time, beating vigorously as the mixture thickens. After half the oil has been added, whisk in 1 teaspoon of lime juice. Beat in the remaining oil. Thin the mayonnaise to the consistency of lightly whipped cream with a few more drops of lime juice, if necessary. If you're using leftover mayonnaise, it's still prettiest when served in lime cups as described here. Divide the *wasabi* mayonnaise and fill both lime cups with it. Place one of these on each dinner plate, to the right of and slightly behind the lemon-soy sauce.

Rinse the radish sprouts under cold water and shake them dry. Divide the sprouts into six bundles. Slice the pitted olives to make three rings from each. Slip the rooted ends of one bundle of radish sprouts through a single ring and trim off the roots. Repeat to make six ringed bundles in all. Use three bundles to garnish each plate, placing them to the left of the mounded lobster meat. Chill the plates for 5–10 minutes before serving.

Menu Suggestions: I like to start my lobster meal with either Tomato and *Shiso* Bisque (p. 78) or a few pieces of vegetable *sushi*, such as Rainbow Rolls (p. 144) or Plump Rolls (p. 146).

Japanese Seafood Stew with Cellophane Noodles

YOSÉ NABÉ · Serves 4–6

Every nation with a coastline seems to have its own bouillabaisse or seafood stew, and the Japanese are no exception. *Yosé nabé* means "gathering pot" and it's a soul-satisfying meeting of fish, shellfish, and vegetables in a bubbling broth. Use your most attractive casserole for the quick kitchen cooking and bring it to the table piping hot.

12 large shrimp

10 ounces fillet of snapper, grouper, monkfish, OR tilefish

4 ounces fresh *shiitaké* (dark oak mushrooms) OR other fresh mushrooms

1 Cabbage and Spinach Roll (p. 242) without dressing OR 4 ounces fresh kale

2 ounces *harusamé* ("spring rain" cellophane noodles)

4 scallions

12 slices carrot, ¼ inch thick

broth:

2½ cups *dashi* (basic sea stock, p. 48)

3 tablespoons *mirin* (syrupy rice wine)

⅓ cup *usukuchi shōyu* (light soy sauce)

Peel and devein the shrimp, leaving the tail section intact. Cut the fish fillets into bite-sized pieces. Remove the stems from the mushrooms and save the stems for enriching stock (p. 50), if you wish, or discard. Wipe the caps with a damp cloth, being sure to remove all gritty material. Slice any large mushrooms into halves or quarters, holding your knife at a 45-degree angle to your board.

Slice the undressed Cabbage and Spinach Roll into twelve pieces. Or rinse the fresh kale well under cold water, then tie the stems together with kitchen twine. Bring a pot of lightly salted water to a rolling boil and place the kale bundle in it for 10 seconds. Drain immediately and rinse the kale under cold water to stop the cooking process. Squeeze out all excess water, trim away the tied stems, and cut the kale bundles into 2-inch lengths.

Soak the cellophane noodles in warm water for 20 minutes, then drain and, if you like, cut the noodles into 4-inch lengths. Rinse the scallions under cold water, and trim them before cutting into 2-inch lengths, on the diagonal.

If you have a flower- or maple-leaf-shaped vegetable cutter, use it to trim the carrot rounds. The five-petaled plum blossom is a common motif in the winter months, while the maple leaf is usually reserved for the fall. Or leave the carrots in rounds.

Combine the broth ingredients in an attractive ready-to-serve casserole and bring to a boil. Adjust the heat to maintain a steady simmer adding the scallions, carrots, and fresh kale, if you're using it. Cook the vegetables for 3–4 minutes. Add the fresh *shiitaké* or other mushrooms. Next add the pieces of fish fillets, one at a time. Cook for 1 minute, skimming away any froth from the surface. Add the shrimp, and cook for 30 seconds before removing the pot from the source of heat. Add the cellophane noodles and fit the pieces of Cabbage and Spinach Roll into the pot, submerging them beneath the bubbling liquid. Cover the casserole and bring to the table immediately.

The table is best set with shallow bowls (or deeply flanged plates), chopsticks, and spoons (for drinking the broth, if you don't want to drink directly from your bowl or plate as the Japanese do). All the diners help themselves to bits from the communal pot. A ladle might be helpful in dishing out the broth.

Menu Suggestions: This stew is a meal in itself, though the Japanese always have rice and an assortment of pickled vegetables on the table when it's served. Americans might be more interested in filling out the menu with dessert, perhaps Green Tea Ice Cream (p. 279) and Fresh Ginger Cookies (p. 284).

Tatsuta *Deep-Fried Soft-Shell Crabs with Ginger*

KANI NO TATSUTA AGÉ · *Serves 4*

The Japanese technique of deep frying foods that have been marinated in soy sauce, then dredged in cornstarch, is called *tatsuta agé* after Princess Tatsuta, a legendary figure said to have been fond of red maples. The burnished red color of the fried foods is thought to resemble the autumnal foliage as it begins to turn. This style of frying is particularly popular with bits of chicken and small whole fish, such as sand dabs.

I first sampled soft-shell crabs served *tatsuta* style at Restaurant Nippon in New York. Mr. Kuraoka, manager of the restaurant, is a firm believer in using regional American ingredients in cooking Japanese food. I've added ginger to my marinade, which I think helps bring out the sweetness of the crab. These crunchy crustaceans are culinary bliss!

> 8 small soft-shell crabs
> ¼ cup soy sauce
> 2 tablespoons *saké* (Japanese rice wine)
> 1 tablespoon ginger juice (extracted from freshly grated ginger)
> ½–⅔ cup cornstarch
> vegetable oil, for deep frying
> 1 lemon OR lime, cut in wedges

Rinse the crabs well under cold running water and pat dry. Cut each in half between the eyes, so that each piece has legs and body attached.

In a shallow glass or ceramic bowl, mix the soy sauce, rice wine, and ginger juice. Allow the crabs to marinate in this mixture, covered, for at least 15 minutes but no more than 2 hours. Turn the crabs several times if the marinade doesn't cover all surfaces.

Remove the crabs from the marinade and pat dry on paper towels. The marinade can be reused within a day or two if covered and refrigerated in the interim. Toss the crabs in the cornstarch to cover each piece lightly but well. Allow the dredged crabs to sit for at least 5 and up to 20 minutes before frying. The cornstarch will change to a brown color as it absorbs some of the marinade, making it more flavorful when fried.

You'll need a depth of at least 1½ inches for your oil when deep frying; 2–3 inches would be even better. Heat the oil to about 375 degrees. Test the oil by dropping a pinch of the cornstarch into it; it's preferable to use a sample that has marinade clinging to it. Ideally the sample will drop ever so slightly beneath the surface of the oil and rise immediately to sizzle gently. Start by frying two or three pieces of crab at a time. Using tongs or long cooking chopsticks, gently slide the crabs into the oil, top down. They may splatter a bit as the oil bubbles around the crabs—all the more reason for using the longest chopsticks you can comfortably control. Fry for 1 minute, then flip the crabs and fry for another 30 seconds. As the frying proceeds, the oil will become less bubbly and active. Remove the crabs to paper towels to absorb excess oil. Fry the rest of the crabs in the same way, two or three pieces at a time, until all are done. If you wish to keep the already fried crab pieces warm in a preheated 200-degree oven, that's fine for up to 10 minutes. After that they'll dry out.

The Japanese present fried foods such as these on folded paper, much as Americans place cookies or candies on paper doilies. If you want to follow the Japanese example, the specially treated papers are available at most Oriental groceries and I've included a diagram to guide you in forming the standard simple fold. The smoother side should

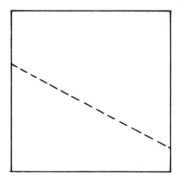
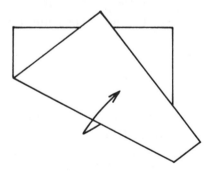

face down at the start. Place a folded sheet on each flat dinner plate and arrange the crabs either in a mound in the center, or aligned to re-form the crab shapes. Serve with lemon or lime wedges on the side.

Menu Suggestions: I like to begin the meal with either Pale Jade Soup (p. 76) or Temple Garden Soup (p. 69), then serve either warm Herbed Rice (p. 228) or Homemade Cold Herb Noodles (p. 236) with the fried crabs. Glazed Zucchini with Sesame (p. 247) or Eggplant and Green Pepper Sauté (p. 244) makes a delicious vegetable accompaniment, while Cantaloupe Sherbet (p. 281) would make an ambrosial conclusion to the meal.

Glaze-Grilled Salmon Steaks

SHAKÉ NO TERIYAKI · Serves 4

The word *teriyaki* has become synonymous with Japanese-style cooking on restaurant menus throughout America. The word is often tagged to chicken or steak that's served with some sort of soy sauce gravy. In fact, *teri* means "to shine" and *yaki* means "to sear with heat." True *teriyaki* foods are grilled or broiled, then sealed with a shiny soy glaze to keep in the juices of the cooking fish or meat. The succulent salmon steaks here are a fine example of *teriyaki* cooking at its best.

sauce:

   3 tablespoons soy sauce

   3 tablespoons *mirin* (syrupy rice wine)

  ½ tablespoon sugar

   2 teaspoons ginger juice (extracted from freshly grated ginger)

  ¼ teaspoon salt

   4 small salmon steaks, about 5–6 ounces each, OR 1-pound side of fresh salmon, cut into 4 pieces

In a small saucepan, combine the soy sauce, syrupy rice wine, and sugar. Cooking over low heat and, stirring constantly, wait until the sugar is totally dissolved before adding the ginger juice. Continue to simmer the sauce—it will become quite foamy—stirring occasionally for 3–4 more minutes. This glaze can be made a week or so in advance and stored, covered, in the refrigerator.

Preheat your broiler or, if you're cooking outside, make sure that your coals are fairly hot before you begin to grill over them. Salt the salmon steaks lightly on all surfaces. If you're broiling the fish at home, I highly recommend the use of disposable foil pans; if you're grilling out of doors, have a broad metal spatula ready to help flip the fish.

Broil or grill the fish for 2–3 minutes, then turn it over and continue to cook for 2 more minutes. (If you're using a side of salmon, place the skin side near the source of heat first.) Brush the flesh with the glazing sauce and grill or broil for 1–2 minutes. Turn the fish over with the help of a broad metal spatula and brush the skin or other side of flesh with the glazing sauce. Broil or grill for 1–2 minutes. Do a final painting of the flesh with the glazing sauce and complete the cooking with another minute of exposure to high heat. Serve hot or at room temperature, with a few drops of additional sauce dribbled on the salmon, if you like.

Note:
The gingery glazing sauce prepared in this recipe is wonderful with chicken or steak, too. The glaze should always be applied during the last 5–6 minutes of broiling or grilling.

Menu Suggestions: The meal might start with either an appetizer of *sushi* or a clear soup such as Clear Clam Broth with Lemon Peel (p. 66). The gingery pumpkin and yam soup on p. 80 makes a nice beginning, too. Glazed-grilled foods look and taste good when garnished with Flower Turnips (p. 265). The Lemon-Pickled Cabbage (p. 254) tastes fine with soy-glazed foods, too. Leafy salads are always welcome and I particularly like the one on p. 260 with a *miso* and walnut dressing. Dessert could be almost anything, though I'm especially fond of Jellied Orange Wedges (p. 288).

Snapper Steamed with Wild Mushrooms in Parchment

KAMI TSUTSUMI NO SAKA MUSHI · *Serves 4*

The Japanese often use various natural products to wrap food in before cooking it. Dried bamboo leaves and broad, softened kelp are two of the most popular, each imparting its own fragrant nuance to the dishes in which it's used. Since neither bamboo leaves nor broad kelp is readily available to the American home cook, I've adapted the steaming technique here to make use of cooking parchment. To add a subtle aroma to the final presentation, I line the paper with fresh slices of lime. The recent and increasing availability of fresh *shiitaké* mushrooms in North America has encouraged me to keep them a part of this recipe. If you can't find them when you wish to make this dish, substitute fresh button or other wild fresh mushrooms for the *shiitaké*.

Snapper is called *tai* in Japanese, and this fish is served on special occasions since it provides a culinary pun on the word *omedetai* or "congratulatory." On a less formal table, scrod or sea trout might be a more economical choice.

> 4 red snapper fillets, 4 ounces each
> 2 tablespoons *saké* (Japanese rice wine)
> 1 small lime, bright green and blemish-free
> ½ teaspoon salt
> 4 ounces fresh *shiitaké* (dark oak mushrooms)
> soy sauce (optional)

Check the fish for scales or bones that might have been overlooked at your fish store. Remove any that you find, rinse the pieces of fish under cold water, and then pat dry on paper toweling. In a shallow glass or ceramic container, marinate the fish in the rice wine for 5 minutes.

Cut four sheets of cooking parchment into 12- to 14-inch squares. Cut the lime in half, through the stem, and lay the cut side against the board. Slice thin (about ⅛-inch) half-moons from one part of the lime, and divide these into four equal portions. Cut the other half of the lime into four wedges, lengthwise, and set aside for a final garnish.

In the center of each of the four papers, lay a portion of lime slices. (It's most attractive if you arrange the slices so that they overlap each other slightly.) Lay one slice of fish, skin side down, over each row of lime slices. Sprinkle a pinch of salt over each portion of fish.

With a clean but damp sponge, carefully wipe the fresh mushrooms to remove any soil or foreign matter. Remove the stems and save them for enriching stock (p. 50), if you wish, or discard. Then cut the caps into narrow (about ⅛-inch) slices. Using one quarter of the mushroom slices for each portion, scatter them over the fish. Sprinkle again with a pinch of salt.

To seal each packet, bring the bottom and top edges of paper together over the middle of the fish. Fold the paper over twice to snugly enclose the food. Fold and crease the paper just to the right and left of the fish. Open either side just enough to slip the other side into it. Carefully turn the package over and place it in a flat steamer. Repeat to seal the remaining three packets.

Steam the packets over vigorously boiling water for 7 minutes.

To serve, either bring the packets on plates to the table and pierce the paper just before eating, or carefully remove the pieces of fish from their paper casings and transfer them, skin side up, to individual plates. A broad spatula slipped under the mushrooms will help keep the fish intact. Serve with extra lime wedges and soy sauce, if desired.

Menu Suggestions: This delicate steamed fish goes well with many dishes. You might want to start your meal with a soup, in which case a *miso*-thickened broth (pp. 52, 54) would be nice. So would a creamy vegetable soup, such as A Bowl of Sunshine (p. 80) made with pumpkins and yams, or Pale Jade Soup (p. 76) made from garden-fresh peas and snow pea pods. Asparagus Salad in Smoky Sauce (p. 248) or Cabbage and Spinach Rolls with Sesame Vinaigrette (p. 242) would be welcome additions to the menu.

Bean Curd Tempura
with Spicy Scallion Sauce

AGÉ DASHI-DŌFU · *Serves 2*

The Japanese affectionately refer to bean curd (*tōfu*) as "the meat of the field" (*hataké no niku*), and here it's prepared like *tempura*. Dipped in a light batter and deep fried, the bean curd is served piping hot with a spicy sauce and is often considered a main, or at least major, course in a Japanese meal. Single squares could be made into appetizers if you prefer. If you plan to serve the fried bean curd as a main course at lunch or as a light dinner, this recipe will serve two.

12- to 16-ounce block fresh *tōfu* (bean curd, preferably silky *kinugoshi* (see p. 40 for details on different types of bean curd)

sauce:
- 1 cup *dashi* (basic sea stock, p. 48)
- 1 scant tablespoon soy sauce
- 2½ tablespoons *usukuchi shōyu* (light soy sauce)
- 1½ tablespoons *mirin* (syrupy rice wine)
- 1 teaspoon sugar

condiments:
- 2–3 ounces *daikon* (Japanese white radish)
- ¼ teaspoon *shichimi tōgarashi* (blend of 7 spices)
- 1½ tablespoons finely chopped scallion (green part only)

batter:
- ⅓ cup ice water
- ½ cup cake flour
- pinch salt
- vegetable oil, for deep frying

You'll need to weight your bean curd for several hours overnight in the refrigerator to improve its flavor, and to make frying it less hazardous. Drain the bean curd and wrap it in muslin or other plain cloth. Place the wrapped bean curd on a plate or board and arrange it so that this surface stays on a 45-degree angle; I usually set mine to lean against the side of a large bowl or pot. Place another flat plate or board on top of the bean curd, then about 5 pounds of pressure. (Books or potatoes are fine; wrap them in plastic bags to keep them dry.)

Unwrap the bean curd and pat dry with paper towels. It should appear considerably compressed and weigh several ounces less than when you started, and there should be quite a puddle of liquid in the bowl after the weighting process is complete. Slice the block in half lengthwise, then across three times to yield eight pieces in all. Gently pat dry all newly exposed surfaces. (If you weighted your bean curd overnight in the refrigerator, bring the pieces to room temperature before frying.)

Combine the stock, soy sauces, syrupy rice wine, and sugar in a small saucepan. Stir and heat until bubbling. Remove the sauce from the heat but keep warm.

Peel and grate the radish. Drain off excess liquid before mixing the grated radish with the seven-spice blend. Soak the scallions in cold water for 1 minute, then drain, squeezing lightly to get rid of all excess moisture. Set aside both the radish and the scallions.

Mix the batter just before frying; pour the ice water into a bowl and sift the flour and salt over it. Stir until barely mixed; a few lumps are fine. You'll need several inches of oil for deep frying; a wok or deep skillet is best. Heat your oil to about 375 degrees. A test drop of batter should sink slightly, rise immediately, and puff and sizzle on the surface. Coat each piece of bean curd thoroughly and deep fry two or three pieces at a time, until a pale crisp crust has formed (about 1½ minutes). Turn the pieces once during frying to ensure even coloration. The bean curd is a precooked food so you don't have to be concerned with "cooking" it again by frying. Drain the fried bean curd on a rack.

Assemble the dishes: Place four blocks of fried bean curd in each of two shallow bowls or deeply flanged plates. Arrange the fried bean curd so that the pieces lay in a single layer. Place a mound of the spicy radish mixture and a sprinkling of scallions in the center of each serving. Ladle the previously made warm sauce over the bean curd. Serve immediately.

Menu Suggestions: If bean curd is your main dish, try a "meaty" soup for starters; either the Shrimp Dumpling Soup with Snow Pea Pods (p. 64) or Ocean Noodle Broth (p. 71) would be wonderful. Autumn Rice with Wild Mushrooms (p. 224) or Steamed Clams and Rice (p. 222) could add more volume to your meal. Any of the vegetable side dishes, such as Eggplant and Green Pepper Sauté (p. 244) or Cabbage and Spinach Rolls with Sesame Vinaigrette (p. 242), would be welcome.

Bean Curd and Vegetable Bundles

SHŌJIN FUKU-BUKURO · *Serves 2*

The Japanese enjoy bean curd prepared in a multitude of ways. This particular dish combines two types: Pouches of fried bean curd are stuffed with a *tōfu* and vegetable mixture, then simmered in a sweetened soy broth. This is home-style Japanese cooking at its coziest and nutritious best.

6- to 7-ounce block firm *tōfu* (bean curd); *mo-men-dōfu* is best (see p. 40 for information on different types of bean curd)

5–6 feet *kampyō* (dried gourd ribbons), optional
    pinch salt

3 or 4 small dried *shiitaké* (dark Oriental mushrooms), about ¼ ounce

1½ tablespoons finely minced carrot

1 tablespoon finely minced *gobō* (burdock root) OR parsnip

3 pieces *abura agé* (fried bean curd), each about 2½ by 4½ inches

simmering broth:

½ cup mushroom liquid

1 cup *dashi* (basic sea stock, p. 48)

1 tablespoon sugar

2 tablespoons soy sauce

1 tablespoon *saké* (Japanese rice wine)

You'll need to weight your bean curd for a few hours to improve the flavor. Follow the instructions on p. 183 to do this. You can close your pockets with toothpicks, or, if you wish to make them elaborate looking (as well as enrich their taste), you can tie them with ribbons made of gourd. Soak the gourd in warm water to cover for 10 minutes, then drain, squeezing out excess moisture. Take a pinch of salt and rub it in the gourd to soften the fibers. Rinse away the salt with cold water. Bring a small saucepan of water to a boil and blanch the gourd ribbons for 5 minutes, then drain.

Soak the dried mushrooms in warm water to cover for about 20 minutes or until soft enough to easily slice with a knife. Strain and reserve ½ cup of the soaking liquid. Remove the stems from the mushrooms and save the stems for enriching stock (p. 50), if you wish, or discard. Rinse the caps under fresh warm water, making sure to remove any sand or dirt that may be clinging to them. Squeeze out excess liquid, mince the mushroom caps, and combine them with the carrot and burdock or parsnip pieces in a bowl along with the firm bean curd.

Bring several cups of water to a boil in a small pot and, one slice at a time, blanch the fried bean curd for 10–15 seconds. This blanching accomplishes two things: It rinses off excess oil and it helps the air trapped inside to expand, allowing greater ease in creating pockets later. Cut each slice in half to make six pieces, each about 2½ inches square. Hold a single square of blanched fried bean curd on your open palm with the cut edge toward your fingertips. With your other hand open, slap down on the fried bean curd, forcing the air out. With your fingertips, carefully pry open the pocket. Use this slap-and-pry technique to open the remaining five pockets. As you work, keep the opened pockets under a damp cloth to keep them from drying out.

Divide the bean-curd and vegetable mixture into six portions and stuff each fried bean-curd pocket with a single portion of this mixture. If you're using gourd ribbons to tie each pocket closed, gather the cut edges together and encircle them once. Each pocket should be finished with either a bow tie or a double knot. If you're using toothpicks to close the pockets, fold the open edges like an envelope and thread a toothpick through to seal.

In a shallow pot just wide enough to hold all six pockets in a single layer, combine the simmering broth ingredients. Bring to a boil, stirring, until the sugar is melted. Remove the pot from the heat temporarily to place the pockets, tied or sealed edges up, in the hot liquid. Cook the pockets for 5 minutes, then turn them upside down and continue to simmer for 5 more minutes. The Japanese use a wooden lid, called an *otoshi-buta* or "dropped lid," that rests on the food itself. This forces the simmering liquid to cook both top and bottom surfaces at once. The simmering liquid reduces and intensifies in flavor while keeping the surface of the cooking foods moist. If you can't find a dropped lid, cook the pockets with an ordinary cover partially askew over slightly higher heat, so that the liquid is simmering vigorously.

Serve the pockets hot in a shallow bowl or flanged plate with just enough simmering liquid to keep them moist. Three pockets make a single main-course serving.

Menu Suggestions: These vegetarian pockets are best served with steaming-hot white rice and a zesty vegetable side dish such as Steamed Radish with Pungent Bean Sauce (p. 50) or Eggplant and Green Pepper Sauté (p. 244). Dessert might be rich, smooth Pear Ice Cream (p. 278) and maybe even some Green Tea Cookies, too (p. 285).

Japanese Chicken and Vegetable Sauté

IRI-DORI · Serves 4

This is a popular dish in many Japanese homes, and I feel sure it will become a favorite in your house, too. Serve it as you would a stew, with hot white rice or crusty bread, and perhaps a green salad on the side.

3/4 pound boneless, skinless, white meat
   chicken
  6 dried *shiitaké* (dark Oriental mushrooms),
   about 1/2 ounce in all
4–5 ounces drained canned bamboo shoots
  3 ounces peeled, trimmed carrots
1/2 tablespoon vegetable oil
  1 tablespoon *saké* (Japanese rice wine)
  2 tablespoons sugar
  3 tablespoons soy sauce
  2 teaspoons cornstarch
  2 teaspoons cold water

Cut the chicken into pieces that are about 1 inch square. Quickly blanch the chicken in boiling water until the surface of each piece turns white. Set aside.

Soak the mushrooms in 3/4 cup of warm water for 20 minutes. Remove the stems and save them for enriching stock (p. 50), if you wish, or discard. Then cut the softened caps into quarters. Resoak these in the mushroom liquid for another 2–3 minutes, then remove the caps, lightly pressing out all liquid. Strain the mushroom liquid and add water, if necessary, to make 1/2 cup.

Cut the bamboo shoots into 1/2-inch dice. Cut the carrots into 1-inch lengths, then slice each of these in half on the diagonal.

Over high heat, heat the oil in a skillet and sauté the vegetables in the oil for a few seconds until each piece glistens. Add the reserved and strained mushroom liquid, then the blanched chicken, and reduce the heat slightly. Season with the rice wine, sugar, and soy sauce, stir, and continue to cook uncovered for 4–5 minutes. The liquid will be quite foamy. Continue to stir occasionally as the liquid thickens and reduces.

In a small cup, mix the cornstarch with the cold water to make a smooth paste. Add this paste to the simmering chicken and vegetables, stirring constantly and vigorously to ensure even distribution. Once the sauce thickens and clings to the chicken and vegetables, remove the skillet from the heat and serve.

Braised Beef and Vegetables over Rice

GYŪNIKU DOMBURI · Serves 4

Domburi means "big bowl," referring to both the deep ceramic dish and to the heaping portion of rice topped with sauced meat, fish, and vegetables that's served in it. As the history of *domburi* goes back several hundred years, it might be considered Japan's first contribution to the fast-food industry. Centuries ago, the busy merchants of Edo (today's Tokyo) were so preoccupied with making deals that they hadn't time for a proper meal. They would stop at a roadside stand and slurp a bowl of noodles and broth, or devour an extra-large bowl of rice topped with cooked bits of fish, vegetables, and sauce. Toward the end of the nineteenth century, the Meiji Restoration industrialized much of Japan, and an increasingly busy yet frugal-minded middle class became devotees of *domburi* dishes. Workers, too, found this style of food filling, unfussy, and inexpensive, while home cooks took advantage of leftovers from the previous evening's meal to make their rice toppings.

The *domburi* dish I've chosen here is made from thinly sliced beef and will appeal to even the heartiest of American appetites. *Domburi* dishes such as this, and the ground veal version following, are a perfect way to make use of leftover rice.

1 piece beef suet, about 1 inch square, OR 1½ tablespoons vegetable oil

12 ounces paper-thin beef sirloin (see Note below)

6 scallions, trimmed and cut in 1½-inch lengths

½ pound fresh bean sprouts, well drained

1 tablespoon sugar

2 tablespoons *saké* (Japanese rice wine)

3 tablespoons soy sauce

3 cups cooked rice, still warm (p. 218); reheated leftovers are fine

Melt the suet or heat the oil in a heavy skillet. Sear half the meat at a time, pushing those pieces that are partially cooked to the side of the skillet to make room for the uncooked beef. Cook the meat just until it begins to change color, then push it all aside to make room for the scallions. In the same pan, sauté the scallions for 20 seconds, push these aside, and then add the bean sprouts. Reduce the heat slightly; sprinkle the sugar over the beef and vegetables; pour in the rice wine and soy sauce. Cook, stirring the beef and vegetables each separately once or twice, for 1 minute.

Divide the warm rice among four deeply flanged dishes or soup bowls. Arrange some beef, scallions, and bean sprouts over each portion of the rice. If there's a great deal of liquid left in the skillet, continue to boil to reduce the amount to about 2 tablespoons. Spoon this remaining "gravy" over the four portions and serve at once.

Note:
Well-marbled sirloin is the tastiest choice for this dish, but any tender cut, such as boneless rib or fillet, will do. Partially freezing the meat will facilitate thin slicing.

Menu Suggestions: A *miso*-thickened soup, such as the one with slender white mushrooms on p. 52, would make a wonderful start to a *domburi* meal. The Japanese often serve pickled vegetables on the side, and Lemon-Pickled Cabbage (p. 254) might be a nice choice, though crisp sticks of cucumber, celery, and carrot would go well with this hearty dish, too.

Braised Ground Veal over Rice

SOBORO DON · *Serves 4*

Soboro means "fine-crumb" and refers to the texture of the ground meat, while *don* or *domburi* tells you that the food is being served over steamed white rice. Hearty, unfussy food like *domburi* dishes are popular menu items in casual eateries and in homes throughout Japan.

In Japan, *soboro* is usually made from ground, raw chicken, which is the most common item in the meat case of any supermarket there. Here in the United States, it's nearly impossible to find and a nuisance to make. In trying to capture the homey satisfaction of the original dish, I experimented with several ideas before choosing ground veal. I found the addition of ginger juice perked up the veal, making the *soboro* richly colored, moist, and intensely flavorful. This appealing main course is simple to prepare and can be made in less than 15 minutes.

1 **pound ground veal**

1 **tablespoon sugar**

2 **tablespoons *saké* (Japanese rice wine)**

3 **tablespoons soy sauce**

½ **teaspoon ginger juice (extracted from freshly grated ginger)**

3 **cups hot cooked rice (p. 218); reheated leftovers are fine**

8 **fresh snow peas (optional)**

In a 9-inch skillet, combine the meat with the sugar, rice wine, and soy sauce. Stir slightly to mix well. Over medium heat, cook the mixture, stirring constantly to break up large lumps of meat. At first the liquid will be plentiful and quite cloudy; it will begin to clear after 4–5 minutes. Add the ginger juice and stir well. Continue to cook, uncovered, for 4–5 more minutes until nearly all the liquid has reduced.

Divide the rice among four deep dishes. Spread one quarter of the meat mixture over each portion of rice, covering it so as not to leave any white peeking through.

If you like, string the snow peas and blanch for a few seconds in boiling salted water. On each snow pea, trim and discard a small V-shaped wedge from one end to make a leaf pattern. Arrange two snow pea "leaves" in the center of each portion of braised meat.

Menu Suggestions: In my cross-cultural household, I serve a creamy vegetable soup such as the Tomato and *Shiso* Bisque (p. 78) when I make veal *soboro*. A green salad (like the one on p. 260 with *miso* and walnuts) or Cabbage and Spinach Rolls with Sesame Vinaigrette (p. 242) rounds out the meal nicely.

Miso-*Marinated Baked Chicken*

TORI NIKU NO MISO-ZUKÉ YAKI · *Serves 4*

The Japanese have long been aware of the tenderizing and preserving properties of fermented bean paste on fish and seafood. If fact *miso*-marinated fish was a staple in most households before refrigeration became possible or popular. Fresh fillets of fish, which would otherwise spoil within a few hours without chilling, can be preserved buried in fermented bean paste for up to 3 days. Even after the advent of home refrigeration, the Japanese continue to "pickle" fish in *miso* because of the marvelous aroma and savory rich taste of the fish when grilled.

Here I've combined the ancient technique of *miso* marinating and added the relatively new (to the Japanese, that is) method of oven baking to create a chicken dish that's sure to win fans on both sides of the Pacific. Dark meat, such as thighs, is tastier, though breasts could be prepared the same way. Baking the *miso*-marinated chicken produces delicious pan juices, which reduce further to create a glorious, rich mahogany gravy that's wonderful over a bed of plain rice, noodles, or mashed potatoes. The chicken is delicious cold, too.

2–2¼ cups *shiro miso* (light fermented bean paste)

¼ cup *mirin* (syrupy rice wine)

4 meaty chicken thighs, bones removed but skin intact, about 1 pound in all

1 teaspoon soy sauce (optional)

¼ teaspoon *sanshō* (fragrant Japanese pepper) OR white pepper

In a glass or ceramic dish that's large enough to hold the chicken pieces in a double layer (I find a loaf pan measuring 8½ by 4½ by 1½ inches just right), mix the bean paste and syrupy rice wine thoroughly. Scoop out two thirds of the mixture, transferring it temporarily to any noncorrodible surface, such as glass or porcelain. Smooth out the remaining third of the mixture.

Rinse the chicken pieces under cold water and pat dry. Lay two of the pieces, skin side up, over the smoothed *miso* mixture. Make sure that the meat is spread out so that all surfaces come in equal contact with the marinade. Spread some of the reserved *miso* marinade over the chicken. Lay the remaining pieces of chicken, skin side up, over this new layer of *miso*. Bury the chicken under the remaining *miso* marinade. Cover with clear plastic wrap and marinate for a minimum of 3 hours at room temperature, or refrigerate for up to 3 days.

Set your oven for 350 degrees. Pour off any accumulated liquid and scrape off the *miso* marinade, saving it for future use (it may be used four or five times, for up to 1 month, if refrigerated).

I like to use the disposable foil broiling pans when making this recipe. Lay the chicken in the pan in a single layer, skin side up. Cover the pan snugly with aluminum foil, shiny surface down. Bake for 30 minutes.

Remove the foil "lid" and pour off and save the accumulated pan juices; they will become your gravy. Chill to help remove any fat, or spoon or blot the fat away. Taste and season the gravy with the soy sauce, if necessary. Keep the gravy warm.

Line the pan with the "lid" foil and place the chicken, skin side down, in a single layer on the shiny foil. Place the chicken under the broiler for 1 minute. Flip the chicken and sprinkle with the fragrant pepper.

Broil for another minute or until the skin is bubbly, blistery, and richly colored. Watch the chicken carefully; it burns easily. Serve hot with gravy, or cold.

Menu Suggestions: A bowl of Temple Garden Soup (p. 69) is a particularly tasty way to start a meal when *Miso*-Marinated Baked Chicken is the main attraction. Glazed Zucchini with Sesame (p. 247) makes a nice vegetable accompaniment to the tender baked chicken.

"Tortoiseshell" Pork and Radish Stew

BEKKŌ NI · Serves 4

Athough "tortoiseshell" (*bekkō* in Japanese) may sound like a strange name for a hearty pork and radish stew, the Japanese associate this name not with turtle meat (that's called *suppon* in Japan), but with hexagonal configurations (the pattern on the tortoise's back is made up of six-sided shapes) and with the mottled reddish-brown color of soy-braised chunks of food (they resemble the variegated shades of a tortoise's shell).

As this savory meat and vegetable stew simmers in its soy-seasoned broth, it takes on a variety of warm earth tones, giving this dish its unusual name. The pieces of meat are succulent, though firm, and the radish and onions are left with a bit of crunch to them. *Bekkō Ni* is a cold-weather favorite in many Japanese households.

> 1 pound pork shoulder, or loin
> ½ pound *daikon* (Japanese white radish)
> 1 large onion, about 7 ounces
> 1 tablespoon vegetable oil
> 1½ cups *dashi* (basic sea stock, p. 48)
> 1 tablespoon *saké* (Japanese rice wine)
> 2 tablespoons soy sauce
> 2 teaspoons sugar

Cut the pork into 1-inch cubes, trimming away excess fat. If you want to use the radish peel to make the sauté recipe on p. 253, wash the radish well and peel it in broad strips with a knife. Cut the radish into 1-inch cubes, too. Peel the onion and slice it in half through the middle. Place the cut surface on your cutting board and slice each half into four wedges, by making an X through it with your knife.

In a Dutch oven or other heavy-duty pot, heat the oil and brown the meat lightly. Add 1 cup of the stock and adjust the heat to maintain a steady simmer. Cook the meat, covered, for 10 minutes. Add the rice wine, soy sauce, and sugar and continue to cook, covered, for another 10 minutes. Remove the cover, add the radish pieces, and cook for 5 minutes. Add the remaining ½ cup of stock with the onions and cook for 5 more minutes, stirring to break up the onion wedges. There should be very little richly colored "gravy" left in the pot, but this should be served with the pork and radish.

Menu Suggestions: Serve this braised meat-and-vegetable main course with a warm loaf of crusty bread and a green salad, perhaps one with ginger vinaigrette (p. 261). Or be more traditional and serve *Bekkō Ni* with steaming rice (p. 218) and a colorful assortment of commercially prepared pickled vegetables, such as *takuan* (yellow pickled radish) and *shiba-zuké* (purple pickled eggplant), or homemade Lemon-Pickled Cabbage (p. 254).

Glazed Chicken Roll

TORI NO YAHATA MAKI · *Serves 4*

Wrapping and rolling one ingredient in another is a favorite technique in the Japanese kitchen. Unlike mixing or blending, encasing one food in another allows each ingredient to maintain its own characteristics while combining a variety of tastes, textures, and colors. Most often, the Japanese use only a few ounces of tissue-thin meat when wrapping another ingredient, but here's a hefty roll similiar to a French *galantine.*

2 whole chicken breasts, with rib meat, skin, and bones intact, about 1½ pounds in all

marinade: ⅓ cup *saké* (Japanese rice wine)
1–2 teaspoons freshly grated ginger

stock: bones from above chicken
2½ cups *dashi* (basic sea stock, p. 48)
2 tablespoons *mirin* (syrupy rice wine)
3 tablespoons *usukuchi shōyu* (light soy sauce)
3–4 ounces onion, peeled and cut in 1-inch wedges
1 small carrot
2 ounces fresh string beans
1½ tablespoons vegetable oil

glaze: 1 tablespoon soy sauce
1 tablespoon *mirin* (syrupy rice wine)
1 tablespoon cornstarch
1 tablespoon cold water

Bone the chicken breasts, being particularly careful not to cut or remove any skin. For each, slide a knife under the rib meat and cut away and out. Use fingers to separate the breast meat from both sides of the carcass; the fillets will cling to the breastbone. Pull breast meat down and off the bone. Trim off excess fat. With your fingers, sepa-

 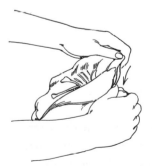

rate the fillets from the bone. Each strip of fillet meat will have a stringy tendon down the center; to remove it, pull it toward you as you hold the fillet with the tip of your knife. Save the bones for stock making.

Combine the marinade ingredients in a shallow pan large enough to hold the two full breasts in a single layer. Score the thick breast meat lightly and marinate the meat, skin side up, while making the stock (about 30 minutes).

Place the bones in a 3- or 4-quart pot and add the sea stock, syrupy rice wine, light soy sauce, and onion. Bring to a boil rapidly, then reduce the heat to maintain a steady simmer. Cook the stock for 20 minutes, then strain, discarding any solids.

Remove the chicken from the marinade and pat dry on paper towels. Lay each breast flat, skin side down. Take one strip of fillet meat and lay it down the center line of each breast, then another fillet strip across the top.

Peel and trim the carrot so that it's as long as the widest section of breast meat. Cut the carrot into four strips, lengthwise. Trim the string beans and divide them into two bundles. For each breast, lay two carrot strips and one bundle of string beans across the width. Roll the chicken snugly over the vegetables, tucking in the rib meat on both sides. Tie the chicken so it will hold together well in cooking.

Heat the oil in a Dutch oven that's large enough to accommodate both rolls. Sear the rolls, turning them to brown evenly. Pour off any excess fat. Add the strained stock, lower the heat, and simmer the rolls, uncovered, for 15–20 minutes. Turn the chicken several times to ensure even cooking. Test for doneness by inserting a sharp skewer into the chicken and through the vegetables. If the skewer is easily removed and the juices are clear, the roll is cooked. If you meet with much resistance or the juices are tinged with pink, cook for an additional 4–5 minutes.

Remove the rolls from the Dutch oven and cut away the trussing strings. Season the stock with the soy sauce and syrupy rice wine, and keep simmering. Mix the cornstarch with the cold water to make a smooth paste. Add this to the stock and bring to a boil, stirring to thicken. Replace the chicken rolls and shake the pot to glaze the meat. Remove the rolls; slice each into four to six circles. Serve two or three slices per person with the cut edge up. Spoon extra sauce over the slices, or serve it on the side if you wish.

Menu Suggestions: Plain steamed rice (p. 211) makes the perfect backdrop for this hearty and succulent chicken dish. The Japanese would serve the rice separately, perhaps with some pickled vegetables on the side, but most Americans will prefer to present the chicken over a bed of rice to soak up all the lovely sauce. Pleasantly tart, crunchy Orchard and Field Salad (p. 251) would make a nice contrast of tastes and textures to the tender, savory meat. Radish and *Shiso* Salad (p. 258) or Lemon-Pickled Cabbage (p. 254) would also be a good choice.

Bubbling Beef-in-a-Pot

SHABU SHABU · Serves 6

The Japanese language is filled with words that sound like their meanings. *Shabu Shabu* mimics the sound of meat being swished through bubbling liquid and thus becomes the name for this enticing meal-in-a-pot. In Japan this is considered an extravagant dish, to be either enjoyed in restaurants devoted to beef dishes, or made at home for some special occasion. Thankfully, in the United States the price of top-quality beef isn't as prohibitive as it is in Japan. You'll need tissue-thin slices of lightly marbled sirloin that will cook instantaneously but not toughen. Either you or your butcher will have to partially freeze the meat to facilitate slicing.

	1½	pounds very thinly sliced sirloin beef
	¾	pound *hakusai* (Chinese cabbage)
	4–6	ounces *shungiku* (edible chrysanthemum leaves) OR fresh spinach
	6–7	scallions (white and green parts)
	8–10	ounces fresh mushrooms (button, dark *shii-také,* or slender white *enokidaké*)
	4	ounces *harusamé* ("spring rain" cellophane noodles)
	1	block *yaki-dōfu* (grilled bean curd)
bubbling broth:	20–25	square inches *kombu* (dried kelp for stock making)
	3	cups cold water
dipping sauce:	1½	tablespoons white sesame seeds
	3	tablespoons fresh lime juice
	⅓	cup soy sauce

Arrange the slices of beef attractively on a large platter. The slices should be laid domino style, one slice leaning slightly upon another, for greater ease later in cooking.

All the vegetable ingredients are probably best arranged on a separate platter. Rinse the cabbage under cold water to remove any residual gritty material. Drain and slice it into 2½-inch lengths. Mound these toward the back of your platter. Rinse the chrysanthemum leaves well under cold water and shake dry. Trim off any tough stems and discard any flowering buds. If using spinach, rinse well, shake dry, and trim away tough stems. Lay the green leaves to one side of the serving platter, leaning them against the pile of cabbage. Rinse and trim the scallions, cutting them into 2-inch lengths. Stack these near the cabbage. Trim the mushroom stems and discard any moldy tips. With a damp cloth, wipe the mushroom caps and slice them in half if small, or into quarters if large. If using *enokidaké* mushrooms, rinse the clump under cold water, shake dry, and remove the lower half of the stems. Mound the mushrooms against the green chrysanthemum or spinach leaves. Soak the *harusamé* noodles in warm water to cover for 10 minutes. Drain the softened noodles and place them near the mushrooms. Drain the grilled bean curd and slice it in half, lengthwise. Cut across five times to yield twelve small rectangular blocks. Stack these near the scallions.

Lay the kelp in your cooking vessel and pour in the cold water. Over medium heat, bring the water to a boil. Remove the kelp (and save for use in one of the recipes on p. 116, 200, 262 or discard, as you like) and keep the broth at a steady bubble.

In a clean dry skillet, roast the sesame seeds over medium-high heat for 30–40 seconds until they begin to color slightly or a few pop. Shake the pan to keep the seeds in motion. Empty them onto a clean, dry cutting board and mince the seeds to crack them. Place the cracked seeds in a shallow bowl and add the lime juice and soy sauce, stirring to mix.

Bring the bubbling pot to the table and keep the liquid cooking on a portable stove unit. Place the platters of meat and vegetables on the table. Each diner should have a small bowl with some of the dipping sauce in it.

The scallions, mushrooms, and bean curd require 3–4 minutes' cooking in the simmering pot, the cabbage and chrysanthemum or spinach leaves just 1 minute or so. The noodles are best added last, to soak up the complex flavors of the broth. The beef is merely swished in the broth and extracted immediately. The diners help themselves to what they want from the main pot, dip it into their bowls of sauce, and eat. (If froth accumulates around the edge of your pot as the meat and vegetables cook, skim it away.) The resulting broth is sometimes ladled into the remains of the dipping sauce and drunk as a soup at the conclusion of the meal.

Menu Suggestions: In Japan, a platter of *sashimi* (fresh fish) is usually brought to the table before the bubbling pot appears, and the diners help themselves while the cook finishes last-minute kitchen preparations. Sliced Fresh Tuna with Lime and Soy (p. 118) or Fresh Fluke in Smoky Vinaigrette (p. 120) would make a pleasant first course, even in America. Piping-hot steamed rice (p. 218) is the perfect backdrop to the meat and vegetables.

Rustic Japanese-Style Roast Chicken

TORI NO MARU MISO YAKI · Serves 6

*I*f you hear a Japanese say he has eaten meat at a meal, he's probably referring to a dish that contained no more than 2–3 ounces of poultry. Chicken is the most popular meat in Japan, and it's sold ground like hamburger meat (this is the cheapest and most common form), in parts (fillet strips are considered the greatest delicacy), and whole (for those who have home ovens in which to roast the bird). This recipe combines a cooking technique relatively new to the Japanese—oven roasting—with more traditional seasoning: the fermented bean paste called *miso*. It's a positively winning combination, particularly when served with plain rice, or crusty rolls to soak up the delicious gravy.

> 3½- pound roasting chicken
>
> 2 tablespoons chicken fat (rendered as described below)

1 cup julienned root vegetables (carrot, parsnip, and fresh burdock root {*gobō*} are recommended)

2 tablespoons *saké* (Japanese rice wine)

neri miso
(glossy bean-
paste sauce):

⅓ cup *aka miso* (dark fermented bean paste)

3 tablespoons sugar

3 tablespoons *saké* (Japanese rice wine)

Remove the lump of fat from the neck and breast of the chicken and place it in a heavy skillet over medium heat. Turn the lump of fat several times as it melts. Render 1 tablespoon of fat to use later (pour this off and set it aside), then render another tablespoon of fat in the skillet before discarding whatever remains of the original lump.

Sauté the vegetables in the skillet with the fat, stirring constantly, for 1 minute. Add 2 tablespoons of rice wine, lower the heat slightly, and continue to simmer for 2 minutes.

In a small saucepan, combine the ingredients for the *neri miso* sauce. Stir together well before placing the saucepan over medium heat and cooking for 1 minute or until bubbly, glossy, and smooth. Set the sauce aside.

Add 1 tablespoon of the *neri miso* sauce to the simmering vegetables and cook them for 1 more minute or until nearly all the liquid is absorbed. Set aside the vegetables with whatever sauce remains in the skillet and allow the vegetables to cool slightly.

Set the oven for 475 degrees. Rinse the chicken, inside and out, with fresh cold water and pat dry on paper towels. Blot up any liquid from the chicken's cavity before stuffing it with the vegetables. Either truss the bird's legs to keep the stuffing from falling out, or stitch the opening closed.

Lay the stuffed chicken on its side on a rack set in a roasting pan. Brush the top surfaces of the chicken with some of the reserved rendered chicken fat and roast for 20 minutes. Turn the chicken to expose its other side, brush it, and roast for another 20 minutes.

Reduce the oven temperature to 375 degrees, rearrange the chicken breast up, and brush all exposed surfaces with some of the *neri miso* sauce. Roast for 10 minutes. Brush all surfaces with more sauce or pan drippings, and continue to roast for a final 10 minutes. Remove the bird from the oven and allow it to rest for 10 minutes. Pour off the pan juices and remove the fat from them. (Quick chilling in the freezer followed by spooning off solidified fat is one method; there are newly designed cups with spouts to pour off sauce below liquid fat, too.) Mix whatever remains of the *neri miso* sauce into the de-fatted pan juices and stir ⅓ cup of water into this mixture to make a fairly thick gravy. Taste, and add a few more drops of water if the gravy seems too intense for you. Heat the gravy just before serving.

Remove the vegetables from the chicken before slicing the bird. Arrange all on a heated serving platter and serve with gravy on the side.

Menu Suggestions: I like to start my meal with gingery pumpkin and yam soup (A Bowl of Sunshine, p. 80) or zesty Tomato and *Shiso* Bisque (p. 78). The vegetable stuffing from the roasted chicken is usually sufficient to serve as a side dish, although a crisp green salad might be welcome, too, especially one dressed with ginger vinaigrette (p. 261).

Steak with Wasabi *Butter*

GYŪ HIRÉ NO WASABI BATĀ KAKÉ · Serves 4–6

*I*t's true! Kobé steers really do guzzle beer and have their bodies massaged daily. And Japanese beef is justly famous—exquisitely marbled, incredibly tender, richly flavorful, and astronomically priced! Here in America, fine fillet of beef is far less costly, affording the opportunity to experiment with new presentations. The following dish resulted from playing with various flavored butters one day, and I think you'll agree it's simple, but sumptuous.

> ½ stick (2 ounces) fresh sweet butter
> 2–3 teaspoons *wasabi* powder (fiery Japanese horseradish)

suet (ask your butcher for a 2–inch piece)

salt and pepper

4–6 filet mignon steaks, each about 6 ounces and 1 inch thick

2 tablespoons *saké* (Japanese rice wine)

2 tablespoons soy sauce

Bring the butter to room temperature, but don't let it melt. With a whisk or fork, beat the butter until it's fluffy. Gradually beat into the powdered horseradish. Fill a small dish with the butter mixture, smooth the surface with a knife or spatula, and chill until extremely firm. (The butter will keep well, covered, for weeks in the refrigerator.)

Melt the suet over medium heat in a heavy skillet (wrought iron is best). Sprinkle a pinch of salt and a shake of pepper over the steaks on both sides. Raise the heat to high and sear the meat for 1 minute. Flip the steaks and sear the other side for another minute. Reduce the heat to medium, cook for 1 more minute on each side, then add the rice wine and soy sauce and cover the skillet for 1 minute more. Flip the steaks and cook another 30 seconds for rare, or 1 minute for medium-rare, meat. Transfer the steaks to individual preheated plates.

With a decorative butter scraper or a melon baller, scrape or scoop the chilled *wasabi* butter and lay some on each steak. Serve immediately with the butter melting naturally on the hot meat to create an aromatic and slightly fiery sauce.

Menu Suggestions: This cross-cultural steak goes well with Tumble-About Potatoes (p. 239) or Autumn Rice with Wild Mushrooms (p. 224). Any green vegetables would be welcome on the menu—it could be chilled Cabbage and Spinach Rolls with Sesame Vinaigrette (p. 242) or warm Glazed Zucchini with Sesame (p. 247).

Grilled Veal Chops with Sanshō Butter

KO USHI NO SANSHŌ YAKI · Serves 4

The Japanese herb *sanshō* is wonderfully aromatic and quite lovely with grilled meats and fish. Here I've used it to flavor butter that melts into a rich sauce, highlighting the subtle flavor of grilled veal chops.

½ stick (2 ounces) fresh sweet butter
2 tablespoons chopped parsley
1 teaspoon grated lemon zest
2 teaspoons *sanshō* (fragrant Japanese pepper)
¼ teaspoon salt
2 teaspoons *saké* (Japanese rice wine)
4 small veal loin chops, each about 6 ounces
   and no more than 1¼ inches thick
1 teaspoon vegetable oil

Bring the butter to room temperature but don't let it melt. With a fork or small whisk, whip the butter until fluffy. Beat in the parsley, grated lemon zest, and Japanese pepper until thoroughly incorporated. Fill a small dish or bowl with the butter, smoothing the surface with a knife or spatula. Chill the butter until really firm. (The butter will keep well, covered, in the refrigerator for several weeks—beyond that time the delicate fragrance of the pepper fades.)

Preheat your broiler or outdoor grill. Rub the salt and rice wine into both sides of the meat and let it rest for 5 minutes. Brush the surfaces of the chops very lightly with the oil to keep them from sticking, and broil or grill them over intense heat for 2 minutes. Turn the chops and continue to cook over high heat for another 3–4 minutes. Either lower your broiler to medium heat or move your chops to a less hot area of the grill, and cook for 5–6 minutes more on each side for rosy veal (an internal temperature of about 160 degrees). Remove the chops to preheated individual plates and place a generous pat of herb butter on each. If you like, the butter can be decoratively scooped into a sphere with a melon baller, or scraped into curlicuelike shavings with a butter hook. Serve at once, allowing the butter to melt naturally, forming a sauce for the veal.

Menu Suggestions: The subtle, herbal nuance of this meat entrée is nicely complemented by soy-braised Tumble-About Potatoes (p. 239) and Glazed Zucchini with Sesame (p. 247). An entirely different approach might be to set off the delicate veal and its butter sauce by serving it with piquant side dishes: either Orchard and Field Salad (p. 251) or Flower Turnips (p. 265).

Lamb Chops with
Fresh Wild Japanese Mushrooms

RAMU NO KINOKO SOÉ · *Serves 4*

There's no tradition of eating lamb in Japan—there has never been pastureland to support grazing herds—but in recent years lamb from New Zealand has been sold in some supermarkets in large Japanese cities. Perhaps it's the slightly gamy aroma of roasted lamb that keeps most Japanese home cooks from trying it. Since imported meat is expensive in Japan, I'm sure a certain reluctance to experiment with costly ingredients has also contributed to the lack of popularity of lamb in Japanese home cooking today. But Japanese food professionals—chefs trained or experienced in cooking outside their homeland—have discovered the versatility and meaty pleasures of lamb. Lamb dishes appear on many menus in Japanese–French restaurants in America. I'm particularly fond of the following rendition, in which the garlic, *saké,* and soy marinade tenderizes and tames any inclination toward gaminess, while the fresh wild mushrooms add an elegant touch to the dish.

4 loin lamb chops, about 6 ounces each

marinade: 1 small clove garlic, finely minced
¼ cup *saké* (Japanese rice wine)
¼ cup soy sauce

6–8 ounces fresh *enokidaké* (slender creamy-white mushrooms) OR fresh *shiitaké* (dark oak mushrooms) OR combination of both

Trim as much fat as possible from the chops and render it in a heavy skillet (wrought iron is best) until it yields about 1½ tablespoons. Pour this off and set aside for later. Wipe out the skillet with a wad of paper towels.

Lay the lamb chops in a single layer in a glass or ceramic dish. Combine the marinade ingredients and pour them over the chops, allowing 20–30 minutes at room temperature, or up to 3 hours in the refrigerator, for full flavor to develop. Turn the chops once or twice if the marinade doesn't cover the meat.

If using *enokidaké* mushrooms, rinse gently under cold water, then shake dry. Trim and discard the bottom halves of the stalks. If using *shiitaké* mushrooms, remove the stems and save them for enriching stock (p. 50), if you wish, or discard. Rinse the caps under cold water to remove any dirt or sand, and gently press them between the palms of your hands to get rid of excess moisture. Slice the caps into ⅛-inch strips. Set aside.

Lift the chops from the marinade and pat dry on paper towels. Heat the rendered fat in the skillet and quickly sear the edges of the chops. Brown the sides of the chops, about 1 minute per side. Lower the heat, pour in the marinade, and partially cover the skillet. Cook the lamb chops for 1 more minute if less than 1 inch thick, 2–3 more minutes for chops 1¼–1½ inches thick, for rosy meat (to reach an internal temperature of about 150 degrees). Turn the chops during this final cooking.

Remove the chops from the skillet to warmed plates. Toss the prepared mushrooms into the skillet and stir them over high heat until just barely wilted. Divide the mushrooms among the four plates, draping them over the chops. Moisten the chops and mushrooms with any remaining pan juices.

Menu Suggestions: A clear clam broth such as the one on p. 66 might be a good way to start the meal, or, in a different mood, the creamy fresh pea soup on p. 76 would be a nice beginning. Warm Herbed Rice (p. 228), Homemade Cold Citron Noodles (p. 235), or Homemade Cold Herb Noodles (p. 236) would complement the entrée lamb chops.

Tosa-*Style Grilled Beef*

GYŪNIKU NO TOSA-ZUKURI · Serves 6–8

*H*ere's a simple yet succulent grilled beef dish that cleverly adapts a classic Japanese technique to an American meat-centered menu. The original dish is made with *katsuo* (bonito) in Japan. The waters of Tosa Bay off the Kōchi coast teem with bonito, which are harvested year-round to produce *katsuo bushi,* the dry-roasted fish flakes so important in traditional stock making. In the early summer months, though, fresh bonito is a delicacy. At that time, the fish are filleted, keeping the silvery skins intact. The fillets are then skewered and seared over intense heat to tenderize the skins yet keep the flesh rare and moist. A quick plunge in ice water stops the cooking process while forcing any oils or fats to solidify, facilitating their removal. The lean, rare fish fillets are patted dry and marinated in a heady combination of soy, ginger, garlic, and scallions, before being sliced and served chilled or at room temperature.

My Japanese sister-in-law, Yohko Yokoi, has lived in suburban New Jersey for many years and entertains her American neighbors frequently. Her summer barbecues attract a large and hungry crowd, particularly when she serves her beef version of the Tosa fish classic. For special occasions she prepares the dish using filet mignon, which is truly magnificent. In a more frugal mood, she makes use of London broil, which becomes tender and tasty when prepared in the Japanese way.

After sampling her beef grill several years ago, I knew this dish would win a wide American audience, and I began incorporating it into my summertime classes. This recipe is particularly popular with those who use outdoor barbecues often. After an informal cookout, the hot coals are just right for searing the beef. The marinade is quickly combined and the next day all you have to do is slice the meat.

1½ pounds beef, preferably filet mignon,
    though London broil is fine
2 cloves garlic, peeled and cut into slivers
1 tablespoon vegetable oil
¼ teaspoon salt
½ teaspoon freshly ground black pepper
   ice water

marinade: ½ cup soy sauce
2 tablespoons *saké* (Japanese rice wine)
2 tablespoons rice vinegar
1 tablespoon lemon juice
1 tablespoon ginger juice (extracted from
   freshly grated ginger)
½ cup honey
2 scallions, trimmed and finely minced (green
   and white parts), about ¼ cup

garnish: ¼ cup freshly snipped chives (optional)

dip: juice of 1 lemon
¼ cup soy sauce

Choose a slender filet mignon or a piece of London broil that's no thicker than 1¼ inches. Make several shallow slits in all the surfaces of the meat and insert slivers of garlic into them. Brush the meat with a thin layer of oil, then salt and pepper both sides.

Sear the meat over hot coals or in a very hot preheated broiler. Turn it once after 5 minutes, or when well browned. Sear the other side of the meat, too. (If using a rounded filet, you may have to turn the meat at quarter turns to brown evenly.) The meat should be quite rare, though not raw, inside. You can judge the degree of doneness by lightly squeezing the meat with blunt tongs at the thickest section; the firmer the feel, the better done the meat is. Ideally, you'll encounter a bit of resistance at the surface, but feel the core to be more flexible. The internal temperature will be about 140 degrees.

Remove the meat from the grill and plunge it into a bowl of ice water. Gently lift the meat out of the water, leaving any fat behind. Pat the meat dry on several layers of paper toweling.

In a glass or ceramic container large enough to allow the grilled steak to lie flat in a single piece, combine the marinade ingredients. Stir well to distribute. Let the meat sit in the marinade, covered, at room temperature for 3 hours, or in the refrigerator overnight. If the marinade doesn't completely cover the steak, turn the meat several times to ensure even flavoring.

Serve chilled, or at room temperature. Just before serving, remove the meat from the marinade. Slice the steak across the grain into ¼-inch slices. Arrange these slices, domino style, on a large platter. Cover the top with snipped chives if you wish. Combine the lemon juice and soy sauce to make a dipping mixture, which is served separately.

Menu Suggestions: I like to pair this beef dish with a platter of *sushi,* such as Miniature Hand Rolls with Three Fillings (p. 149) or circles of Rainbow Roll (p. 144) or Plump Rolls (p. 146). Dessert could be a refreshing fruit ice like Cantaloupe Sherbet (p. 281) or the richer Green Tea Ice Cream (p. 279).

Sweet and Spicy Grilled Leg of Lamb

RAMU NO SHŌGA YAKI · *Serves 8–10*

The Japanese rarely eat large quantities of meat, and most home kitchens don't have an oven large enough to accommodate a 5- or 6-pound roast. The roasted leg of lamb may seem terribly English at first, until you taste the rich ginger and soy glaze; it assures a happy cross-cultural culinary experience!

to 6-pound leg of lamb

2 large cloves garlic

　　　generous ½ teaspoon salt

2 large knobs fresh ginger, about 3 ounces in
　　all

¼ cup *saké* (Japanese rice wine)

½ cup soy sauce

3 tablespoons sugar

2 tablespoons *mirin* (syrupy rice wine)

1 teaspoon vegetable oil

　　　watercress, parsley, OR *tsumamina* (radish
　　　sprouts), optional

Trim away all excess fat from the leg of lamb. Peel the cloves of garlic and slice each, lengthwise, into five or six pieces. Make shallow slits at random in the meat and bury a piece of garlic in each. Rub the salt well over the meat.

Peel the ginger, saving the peels for later use. Grate the ginger and mix it with 1 tablespoon of the rice wine. Use this mixture to cover the meat entirely. Wrap the meat in clear plastic wrap and allow it to marinate for 2 hours at room temperature, or overnight in the refrigerator.

In a small saucepan combine the remaining rice wine, soy sauce, sugar, and syrupy rice wine and add the peels from the ginger. Bring the mixture to a boil, stirring, over medium heat. Reduce the heat to maintain a simmer and cook the sauce for 20 minutes, or until it thickens slightly. Strain the sauce. This glaze can be made several days ahead and stored, covered, in the refrigerator.

Preheat your oven to 425 degrees. Scrape off and discard the grated ginger coating on the lamb and rub the entire surface lightly with the vegetable oil. If the bone is exposed, cover it with foil. Place the meat, rounded side up, on a rack in a shallow roasting pan. Roast the meat, uncovered, for 30 minutes. Reduce the oven temperature to 350 degrees and brush the lamb with the gingery soy glaze. Cover and roast for 1½–2 more hours, or until a meat thermometer registers 150–160 degrees, for beautifully rosy meat. Brush the lamb with additional glaze every 20–30 minutes while roasting. Uncover the lamb for the final 20 minutes. If during that time the juices that have accumulated in the bottom of the roasting pan should appear to be in danger of scorching, add a few drops of cold water to the pan.

Allow the leg of lamb to sit for at least 15 minutes and up to ½ hour before carving. If you're concerned about serving your sliced meat hot, make a cover of foil to enclose the roasted leg while it rests and remove the lamb from the oven when the thermometer reads 150 degrees. To carve, lift the leg bone and cut down along it in thin slices. Arrange the slices slightly overlapped in domino fashion on a serving platter. Garnish the platter with watercress, parsley, or radish sprouts, if you wish. Serve the remaining gingery soy glazing sauce on the side.

Menu Suggestions: Any of the warm seasoned rice dishes on pp. 222–228 would be fine served with this rich lamb dish. Chilled Potato Salad with *Wasabi* Mayonnaise (p. 240) would be a different but delectable choice. Green Salad with Walnut and Bean Dressing (p. 260) or Asparagus Salad in Smoky Sauce (p. 248) would be good with the lamb, too. My favorite dessert with this is the rich Pear Ice Cream (p. 278) or vanilla ice cream with kumquat sauce (p. 280).

Side Dishes...

*R*ice and noodles, vegetables and salads, condiments and pickles—those small accompaniments that support the leading role, including an autumnal mélange of wild, woodsy mushrooms and rice, home-made citron noodles, Orchard and Field Salad, Tumble-About Potatoes, Glazed Zucchini with Sesame, Lemon-Pickled Cabbage, and a green salad with ginger vinaigrette

*T*raditionally the Japanese plan their daily meals around rice. In fact, the Japanese word for cooked rice, *gohan,* can also mean a meal. Noodles are eaten as a snack in Japan, where they're served chilled in the warm weather and steaming in bowls of broth in the winter. In Japan, potatoes are thought of as just another vegetable and often appear at the same meal with rice.

In contrast to this, American menus usually call for two vegetables to be served in conjunction with the main course: one that's starchy—most often potatoes, though occasionally noodles or rice—and another that's not. In the United States a recent emphasis on nutrition and health has led many people to include salads as part of their noon and evening meals as well.

This chapter begins with a basic recipe for unseasoned rice and proceeds with several flavored-rice preparations. In Japan these flavored-rice dishes are the central focus of the meal; in America they're more likely to be served as side dishes to the main-course recipes in this book. The noodle recipes that follow the rice ones are suitable for light lunches in any culture. They might also be served, like pasta in Italy, as a first course to a Continental meal.

A number of vegetable side dishes, such as Eggplant with Pungent Bean Sauce, Asparagus Salad in Smoky Sauce, or Glazed Zucchini with Sesame, will provide you with new ways of enjoying familiar vegetables. Other recipes, such as Kelp Squares with Fragrant Pepper, or Radish and *Shiso* Salad, will introduce you to some fabulous new vegetables (marine and terrestrial) and herbs. Although many of the vegetable tidbits in this chapter are eaten with plain rice in their native Japan, they're just as enticing when served as condiments with a Western-style entrée. You'll quickly discover how varied and versatile the recipes in this section are.

Basic Boiled Rice

GOHAN

The Japanese serve unseasoned, unadorned, cooked short-grained rice with nearly every meal. Its subtle flavor becomes the perfect foil for other, more complex dishes. The list that follows shows the amount of fresh cold water needed to cook various quantities of raw rice. The yield of cooked rice is about double the quantity of raw rice used. It's extremely difficult to cook less than 1 cup of raw rice, and I recommend making 1½ cups or more at a time. Leftover rice responds well to freezing and microwave reheating.

> For 1 cup raw rice, use 1 cup plus 2 tablespoons cold water
> For 1¼ cups raw rice, use a scant 1½ cups cold water
> For 1½ cups raw rice, use 1¾ cups cold water
> For 1¾ cups raw rice, use 2 cups plus 2 tablespoons cold water
> For 2 cups raw rice, use 2⅓ cups cold water

Place the rice in a bowl and cover with cold water. Stir the rice vigorously; it will become cloudy with starch from the rice grains. (Occasionally small pebbles or bits of straw are found mixed with the rice; discard these bits, which were used as abrasives to help separate the hull from the kernel after the rice was harvested.) Strain the rice, discarding the cloudy water, and repeat the washing procedure with fresh cold water. Continue to rinse, swish, and strain until the rinsing water runs clear. This will probably require three or four washings. Drain the washed rice well after the final rinse. You'll notice that the rice has become slightly more opaque; the kernels have begun to absorb moisture from the washing process and this will ensure tender cooked rice.

Place the rice in a sturdy, straight-sided pot. For a single cup of rice use a 2-quart pot; for 2 cups of raw rice a 3- to 3½-quart capacity is best. Measure in the indicated amount of fresh cold water. Ideally, the rice should sit in its measured water for 10 minutes before cooking, but if you're pressed for time, add a few drops more water and cook right away. Cover the pot with a tight-fitting lid.

Over high heat, bring the water in the pot to a rolling boil. It's best not to remove the lid to check on the rice's progress. Instead, rely on other clues; you can hear the bubbling noises and see the lid begin to dance. This should take 3–5 minutes. Reduce the heat and continue to cook until the water is absorbed. This will take about 5 minutes and you may hear a low hissing sound. If you must check, peek quickly, replacing the lid immediately. Increase the heat to high again for 30 seconds to dry off the rice. Remove the pot, still tightly covered, and let the rice stand for at least 10 minutes. Even if you wish to serve it piping hot, these final minutes of self-steaming are necessary to achieve the proper texture.

Special Note on Newly Harvested Rice:
The Japanese have always prized the freshly harvested rice crop that comes to market in the fall; most Japanese willingly pay a premium for *shin mai* ("new rice"). In recent years, California has begun to market its Japanese-style short-grained "new rice" here in America, and happily at the same price as the storage crop. During the months of October and November, ask the people at your nearest Japanese food store if they have *shin mai*. If they do, you're in for a treat. Washing procedures remain the same but *shin mai* requires less water for cooking. During October and November, equal quantities of rice and water should be just right. If you still have some *shin mai* left to cook in December, it's best to take a middle-of-the-road approach to measuring the cooking water; every cup of raw rice should be cooked with 1 cup plus 1 tablespoon of cold water. By the beginning of the new year, all the rice sold in the stores will be from the storage crop and should be cooked according to the basic list above.

Decorative Rice Bundles

MAKU NO UCHI BENTŌ · Makes 15

The Japanese take for granted the versatility of rice as a picnic food, since they enjoy eating rice at room temperature, molded into a number of attractive shapes. One of the most popular shapes is called *maku no uchi* or "between the curtains." The name refers to the boxed meal that, in the old days, was taken to the theater and eaten between acts. Using molds or *kata,* as they are called in Japanese, the rice is coaxed into five bite-sized cylinders, which are then decoratively garnished with strips of seaweed or a sprinkling of black sesame. In America, Decorative Rice Bundles are as perfect for a tailgate party (or any other outdoor meal) as for a buffet table.

1½ cups cooked rice, still warm (p. 218)
    scant ¼ teaspoon salt
1 teaspoon *kuro goma* (black sesame seeds) OR
  ½ sheet *yaki-zushi nori* (toasted paper-thin seaweed)

If you'll be packing the rice for a picnic, it's particularly important to salt it right after it has been cooked, as this acts as a preservative. Sprinkle the salt over the rice and toss lightly to mix well.

Separate a *maku no uchi kata,* or mold, into its three component parts: a rectangular frame and two strips, each with five curved and hollowed "valleys" and six pointed "mountains."

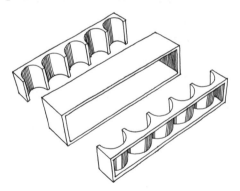

Dip the rectangular frame in cold water and lay it upon your work board. Dip one of the strips in cold water and fit it into the frame so that the pointed "mountains" face up. With hands dipped in cold water, scoop up one third of the warm salted rice and fill the mold evenly with it. Take the remaining strip of the mold and dampen it in cold water. Insert it, "mountains" pointing down, into the frame. Press down firmly but evenly on the top strip, while gently lifting the frame up, over, and off the molded rice. Peel off the top strip, invert the rice,

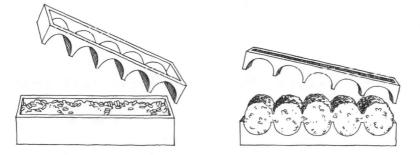

then peel off the remaining strip of mold. With fingers dampened in cold water, separate the five bundles of rice. Repeat the molding procedure to make fifteen bundles in all.

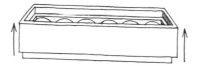

In a clean, dry skillet, toast the black sesame seeds over high heat for about 30 seconds. Shake the pan to keep the seeds in motion. Garnish the rice bundles with a few black sesame seeds in the center of each cylinder. Or, with scissors, cut the seaweed into fifteen strips, and use one of these to encircle each bundle of rice.

Arrange the bundles in rows, or stack them in pyramidlike hills. Cover with clear plastic wrap to prevent the edges from drying if you wish to make the rice bundles more than 30 minutes in advance of serving. The salted, molded rice will keep well at room temperature for 5–6 hours. The Japanese figure five or more cylinders per person, but most Americans will want only two or three.

Note:

Maku no uchi molds usually make five cylinders of rice at a time, but occasionally you'll find a mold that creates seven smaller bundles at once. There are plastic, metal, and wooden molds in a variety of other shapes and sizes for sale in many Oriental groceries. All molds should be dipped in cold water just before using, to keep the rice from sticking to them. Most molds aren't meant to be washed in a dishwasher; soak them in warm sudsy water when you're finished, then rinse and let dry.

Steamed Clams and Rice

ASARI GOHAN · Serves 4

There are many kinds of saltwater and freshwater clams in Japan, and they're enjoyed in a variety of dishes. Here, soft-shell clams are steamed and their broth is used to cook rice. The clam meats are then tossed into the rice and the dish is garnished with parsley and sea herb flakes. In its native Japan, this pilaflike dish might be served with just a *miso*-thickened soup and pickled vegetables for a light meal. In America it could provide the perfect backdrop to almost any meat, fish, or vegetable entrée.

> 2 **dozen steamer clams OR other soft-shell variety**
>
> 10–12 **square inches *kombu* (dried kelp for stock making)**
>
> 3 **tablespoons *saké* (Japanese rice wine)**
>
> 3 **tablespoons water**
>
> 1 **teaspoon *usukuchi shōyu* (light soy sauce)**
>
> 1½ **cups raw rice, preferably short-grained Japanese style**
>
> ½ **teaspoon parsley flakes**
>
> ¼ **teaspoon *ao nori* (sea herb flakes)**

Make a salted water solution to cover the clams. (It should taste briny, like the ocean.) Soak the clams in it for 1–2 hours. Stir up the water, scrubbing the clam shells with a brush to remove gritty material. Rinse the clams under fresh cold water, then drain.

Place the kelp in the bottom of a sturdy pot large enough to hold all the clams in a single layer. Add 3 tablespoons each of rice wine and water, then put the scrubbed and drained clams into the pot and cover it.

Over high heat, bring the liquid in the pot to a rolling boil. Soon thereafter, you'll hear the sound of the clam shells popping open. Lower the heat slightly and continue to cook, covered, for 2–2½ minutes after the shells have opened. Remove the pot from the heat and pour the broth through a cloth- or paper-lined strainer or colander into a measuring cup. Set the clams and kelp aside; you'll need them later in this recipe. Season the broth with the light soy sauce, then add enough water to make 1¾ cups. Set this liquid aside to use in cooking the rice.

Wash the rice with cold water, rinsing until the water runs clear. Drain the rice before placing it in a sturdy, straight-sided 4-quart pot. Rinse the kelp that was set aside after steaming the clams, and lay it over the rice.

Pour in the seasoned clam broth and cover the pot securely. Over high heat, bring the liquid to a rolling boil. This will take about 5 minutes and you'll hear the liquid bubbling and may see the lid dance a bit, too. Reduce the heat to maintain a steady simmer and continue to cook the rice, tightly lidded, until all the liquid has been absorbed. This will take about 5 minutes and you'll be able to hear a dry, hissing sound from the pot. Take a quick look inside to check the rice's progress if you must, but replace the lid immediately. Remove the pot from the heat and let the cooked rice sit for 10–15 minutes, lidded and undisturbed.

Remove the clam meats from their shells. Rinse the meats quickly if necessary to rid them of any sandy material. Remove and discard any membrane coverings on the "feet" of the clam meats (the part that extends from the shell). Pat the clams dry and mince coarsely. Toss these pieces into the cooked rice after discarding the kelp from the rice pot.

In a small bowl, combine the parsley flakes with the sea herb flakes. Crush the mixture with your fingertips, then sprinkle over the hot rice. This will add a delightfully fresh and briny aroma to the rice dish. Serve immediately, or allow the rice to cool to room temperature if you prefer.

Menu Suggestions: I like to serve Steamed Clams and Rice in lieu of bread stuffing with roasted poultry. It also makes a marvelous backdrop for Soy-Braised Duck Salad (p. 169) or Sweet and Spicy Grilled Leg of Lamb (p. 211).

Autumn Rice with Wild Mushrooms

AKI NO SANSAKU · *Serves 6*

I love the fall, when the leaves change color and fresh wild mushrooms are in abundance. The glory of this particular dish lies in the extravagant enjoyment of fresh wild mushrooms, and the pleasure of seeing nature being echoed on your plate with garnishes of "maple leaf" carrots and "pine needle" green beans. I like to serve this rice dish outdoors in its natural environment, with a picnic assortment of savory tidbits such as Seashore Chicken Swirls (p. 104), Japanese-Style Breaded Fried Oysters (p. 98), Chicken Dumplings (p. 87), Flower Turnips (p. 265), or Spicy Sautéed Radish Peels (p. 253). If I serve this dish indoors, I prefer to pair it with Sweet and Spicy Grilled Leg of Lamb (p. 211), Steak with *Wasabi* Butter (p. 204), Soy-Braised Duck Salad (p. 169), or Glaze-Grilled Salmon Steaks (p. 179).

8	ounces fresh wild mushrooms (see Note below)
2	cups *dashi* (basic sea stock, p. 48)
3	tablespoons *saké* (Japanese rice wine)
3	tablespoons *mirin* (syrupy rice wine)
2	tablespoons *usukuchi shōyu* (light soy sauce)
2	cups raw rice, preferably short-grained Japanese style
1	teaspoon *shichimi tōgarashi* (blend of 7 spices)

garnish:		
	4–5	ounces fresh, young, slender green beans
	½	sheet *Asakusa nori* OR *yaki-zushi nori* (paper-thin seaweed, plain or toasted)
	8	large carrot rounds, each ⅛ inch thick

With a damp cloth or mushroom brush, dust fresh mushrooms such as *matsutaké, shiitaké,* or chanterelles to remove residual dirt. Trim the stems to remove any moldy tips and with your fingers pull the mushrooms apart, lengthwise, into strips. With a knife cut these into ½-inch lengths. With your hands, tear any large caps into 1-inch pieces.

If you're using *enokidaké,* remove them from their plastic bag, rinse the heads under cold running water, and shake dry. Remove and discard the bottom halves, cutting the remaining stems into ½-inch lengths.

If you're using the pearly-gray *shimejitaké,* they need to be rinsed under cold water and gently squeezed dry. Trim away the moldy parts of the stems and, with your hands, separate each mushroom from the larger mass. If the caps of the mushrooms are more than ½ inch across, cut these in half lengthwise before slicing into ½-inch lengths.

Season the stock with the rice wines and light soy sauce. Bring this mixture to a boil over medium heat. Add the mushrooms, reducing the heat if necessary to maintain a steady simmer. Cook the mushrooms for 2–2½ minutes, then strain them, pressing gently to extract all cooking liquid. Reserve both the mushrooms and the liquid separately. Add water, if necessary, to the seasoned mushroom liquid to measure 2⅓ cups in all.

Wash the rice thoroughly and let it drain completely. Place the drained rice and the mushroom liquid in a 3- to 3½-quart pot, one that has straight sides and a tight-fitting lid. Cook over high heat for 5 minutes or until the liquid is bubbling. Lower the heat and continue to cook for another 5 minutes or until all the liquid has been absorbed. You can usually hear the changes in the cooking stages, but if you must peek inside to check the rice's progress, do so quickly, immediately replacing the lid.

Remove the pot from the stove and let the rice self-steam for at least 10 minutes (this ensures tender grains of cooked rice) but no more than 20, since it's best to season this dish while still warm. Toss in the reserved mushrooms and gently fold them into the rice. Season with the seven-spice blend and toss again for even distribution. Mound the mushroom-and-rice pilaf on a large platter, or pack it into a plastic container for picnicking.

Trim both ends of the green beans and cut them in half if longer than 2½ inches. Bring a large pot of salted water to a rolling boil and blanch the beans for 1 minute. Drain the beans immediately and, while still hot, slit each lengthwise leaving ¼ inch intact at one end. Open the slit beans just enough to let them straddle the side of a bowl and let them cool to room temperature in that position.

With scissors, cut narrow strips of seaweed, approximately ⅛ inch wide and 1–1½ inches long. Each green bean will use one of these strips. Wind a strip of seaweed around the intact end of each bean,

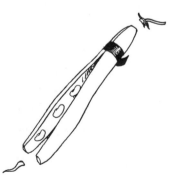

sealing it with a drop of water if necessary. Trim off whatever uncut tip remains so that the band of seaweed is flush with the top.

If you have a maple leaf cutter, use it to cut out shapes from the carrot rounds. If not, cut the carrots in half to make half-moons. Blanch the cut carrots for 1–1½ minutes in boiling salted water, then drain.

(You might want to make the green-bean and carrot garnishes ahead of time, which is fine as long as you keep the precut "autumn foliage" at room temperature while you prepare the mushrooms and rice.)

Scatter the "maple leaf" or half-moon carrots and the "pine needle" green beans across the rice, to give the illusion that the leaves and pine needles have fallen on the forest floor. The Japanese name for this dish translates as "Autumn Stroll."

Serve the rice warm, or let it cool to room temperature and cover with a damp cloth and clear plastic wrap if you wish to keep it for several hours before eating. No refrigeration is necessary for up to 5 hours; in fact if you do refrigerate the rice, you'll need to "freshen" it in a microwave (15 seconds on "boil") or a double boiler (10 minutes over low heat) before serving. Garnish only after reheating.

Note:
In Japan, October and November are the months to splurge on *matsutaké*—those wildly priced (ten dollars and up for a single one), incredibly aromatic (you can smell the pine trees near which they grow) mushrooms. A pale-colored relative to the Japanese dark *matsutaké*

grows in symbiotic bliss with the indigenous pine trees of the American Northwest. There's a ferry that shuttles between Seattle and Bremerton, Washington, and every fall it's crowded with amateur and professional mycologists who are out to forage for the fabulous fungi.

This boat has been nicknamed the *Tokyo Express* because of the large numbers of Japanese and Americans of Japanese extraction who travel on it. Everyone jealously guards a secret territory and many make a handsome profit on sales to gourmet and specialty shops.

If you live in the Northwest, by all means make the special effort to locate a store selling fresh *matsutaké* (pine) mushrooms; failing that, substitute your abundant and meaty fresh chanterelles. Dark Japanese *shiitaké* (oak) mushrooms have begun to be cultivated in Virginia, and slender, creamy-colored *enokidaké* are being successfully farmed in California. In addition, fresh pearly-gray *shimejitaké* mushrooms occasionally appear in oriental groceries in the larger metropolitan areas.

Herbed Rice

SHISO GOHAN · Serves 4

Broad, green, flat-leafed *shiso* is one of the most alluring of Japanese herbs. Vaguely reminiscent of both basil and mint, yet clearly unique in its aromatic appeal, *shiso* combines well with almost any food. Here its gentle, herbaceous flavor enhances white rice that could accompany fish, seafood, poultry, or meat.

4 cups freshly cooked white rice, still warm
(p. 218)

½ teaspoon salt

10–12 leaves fresh *shiso* (flat-leafed Japanese herb)

Toss the rice in a large bowl to break up any lumps. Sprinkle the salt over the rice and gently toss to incorporate well.

Rinse the herb leaves under cold water and shake dry. Trim away the stem, then slice the leaves in half, lengthwise. Stack the half leaves then cut across them to make fine shreds. Toss and fold these into the rice, distributing well. Serve immediately.

Buckwheat Noodles with Fresh Tomato Sauce

SOBA-GETTI · *Serves 4*

The inspiration for this bicultural pasta came from Cafe Seiyoken, a chic New York establishment that prides itself on making waves on the culinary shores of the American east coast.

1 pound plum tomatoes (fresh ones are best,
but use drained, canned plum tomatoes if
fresh are unavailable)

1 tablespoon olive oil

1 small clove garlic, peeled and minced

½ small yellow onion, peeled and diced

¼ teaspoon salt

1 teaspoon *mirin* (syrupy rice wine)

10–12 ounces dried *soba* (Japanese buckwheat
noodles) OR 1 pound fresh whole-wheat
noodles

4–5 leaves fresh *shiso* (flat-leafed Japanese herb)
OR 10–12 leaves fresh mint

¼ teaspoon freshly ground black pepper (optional)

Bring a pot of water to a boil and, one at a time, blanch the tomatoes for 4–5 seconds. Transfer the tomatoes to a bowl of cold water. Slice them in half and peel off the skins. Coarsely chop the tomatoes and set aside.

Heat the olive oil in a heavy-duty skillet, then sauté the garlic and onion over medium heat until the vegetables are fragrant and translucent. Add the chopped tomatoes and season the mixture with the salt and syrupy rice wine. Reduce the heat to low and simmer the tomato sauce, stirring occasionally, for 5–6 minutes or until the tomatoes are tender and the sauce slightly thickened. If the mixture should look in danger of scorching, add a few drops of cold water to the skillet.

In a large pot, bring at least 3 quarts of water to a rolling boil. If you're using dried noodles, scatter them across the boiling water and stir when they become pliable. As soon as the water returns to a boil, add 1 cup of cold water. Start timing the noodles after the water returns to a second boil. Cook for 3–4 minutes. Test a strand; it should be firm but tender. If you're cooking fresh noodles, cook them for 2–3 minutes after the water returns to its first boil. Drain the cooked noodles and rinse lightly under warm water to remove excess starch. Drain thoroughly.

Toss the cooked and drained noodles into the tomato sauce and cook for 1 minute, or until warmed through.

Rinse the *shiso* or mint leaves under cold water and trim away their stems. With your fingers, tear the leaves into small pieces and use these to garnish the noodles with tomato sauce. Serve immediately with freshly ground black pepper, if you wish.

Menu Suggestions: This dish makes a light but satisfying lunch when served with a green salad and some fresh fruit. Or serve smaller portions as a first course to a meat entrée such as Steak with *Wasabi* Butter (p. 204) or Lamb Chops with Fresh Wild Japanese Mushrooms (p. 207).

Udon *Noodles with Clam Sauce*

UDON-GETTI · *Serves 4*

This recipe combines Japanese *udon* noodles with an Italian clam sauce. I first ate *Udon-getti* at a small, "punky" pasta parlor called Kabé no Ana ("A Hole in the Wall") in the Shibuya district of Tokyo about seven years ago. At that time, I thought it was a delicious comment on culinary migration: Noodles thought to have originated in China, brought to Italy for European refinement, were being returned to the Far East for Japanese enjoyment. I complete the worldly travelogue by bringing this cross-cultural wonder to the United States.

2 dozen cherrystone OR other hard-shell clams

2 tablespoons *saké* (Japanese rice wine)

2 tablespoons cold water

2 teaspoons soy sauce

1 teaspoon *mirin* (syrupy rice wine)

1 pound fresh *udon* (thick white noodles) OR ½ pound *hoshi udon* (dried thick white noodles)

2 teaspoons olive oil

1 small clove garlic, peeled and minced

pinch salt

½ sheet *yaki-zushi nori* (toasted paper-thin seaweed), cut into very thin 1-inch strips

Scrub the clam shells to remove surface dirt. Soak the clams undisturbed in salted water (it should taste briny like the ocean) for 1–2 hours, then stir up the water and discard. Place the cleaned clams in a sturdy pot large enough to hold them comfortably. Add the rice wine and 2 tablespoons of cold water, and cover the pot. Over high heat, steam the clams just until they open. Pour the broth through a cloth- or paper-lined strainer or colander, then season it with the soy sauce and syrupy rice wine. Remove the clam meats and discard their shells and any unopened clams. Cut each of the clam meats in half, or into quarters if really large.

Bring a large pot of water to a rolling boil and cook the fresh noodles for 4–5 minutes; they should be firm but tender. If using dried noodles, toss them into deep, vigorously boiling water and stir. When the water returns to a boil, add 1 cup of cold water. Continue to cook over high heat for 5–6 minutes after the water returns to a second boil. Test a strand; it should be translucent with no opaque core. Drain the noodles immediately after cooking. Rinse the noodles under running warm water for a few seconds to remove excess surface starch, then toss them with 1 teaspoon of olive oil and set aside.

Heat the remaining 1 teaspoon of olive oil in a large, heavy-duty skillet. Sauté the garlic in it for 2 minutes over low heat. Add the clam meats and raise the heat to high as you toss them about in the garlic and oil. Season with a pinch of salt. add the cooked noodles to the skillet and toss to incorporate. Add the reserved and seasoned clam broth and continue to sauté, stirring for 1 more minute, or until there's barely any liquid left to the sauce.

Divide the noodles and clam sauce into four portions and garnish the top of each with one quarter of the seaweed strips. Serve immediately.

Menu Suggestions: Like the preceding recipe, this noodle dish could either be featured on a lunchtime menu or begin an evening meal of roasted meat or poultry. In either case a crisp green salad with Ginger Vinaigrette (p. 261) is a nice addition. Green Tea Ice Cream (p. 279) would make a delicious conclusion.

Cold Noodle Salad with Smoky Sesame-Citron Sauce

HIYASHI UDON · Serves 4

This is a popular snack in Japan in the summer and I think that you, too, will appreciate its refreshing qualities on a warm day. Make the sauce in the cool of the previous evening if you like; it will keep well in the refrigerator for at least a week. The noodles, may be cooked and refrigerated, and the vegetables prepared hours ahead of meal-time, too.

dipping sauce:	
1½	cups *dashi* (basic sea stock, p. 48)
3	tablespoons *usukuchi shōyu* (light soy sauce)
2	tablespoons *mirin* (syrupy rice wine)
1	package (5 grams) OR about ⅓ cup *katsuo bushi* (dried bonito flakes)
1	ounce dried *wakamé* (sweet sea tangle)
2	small unwaxed cucumbers, about 5 ounces in all
1½	pounds fresh *udon* (thick white noodles) OR 10–12 ounces *hoshi udon* (dried white noodles)
1½	tablespoons white sesame seeds
	zest of ¼ lemon, finely slivered

In a small saucepan, mix the stock, light soy sauce, and syrupy rice wine and heat through. Remove the pan from the heat and sprinkle the bonito flakes over the mixture. Allow them to steep for 3 minutes, then pour the broth through a cloth- or paper-lined strainer or colander. Chill the sauce in the refrigerator for at least 2 hours before serving.

Place the sea tangle in a bowl of warm water to cover for 15–20 minutes. Drain, then rinse the sea tangle thoroughly under fresh cold water. Pat the sea tangle dry on paper towels; then, with a knife, trim away any tough stems. Coarsely chop the sea tangle and set it aside.

Wash the cucumbers well and slice off a ½-inch piece from the stem (darker green) end of each. Using this stem piece, rub the cut surface with circular motions until a thick white foam appears; rinse it away.

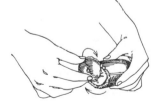

This is what the Japanese call *aku nuki* or "bitterness removal." Trim the opposite end of the cucumber, then cut it into thin slices slightly on the diagonal. Stack several of these slices at a time and cut them into narrow julienne strips. The strips will be tipped in dark green, while the centers will be pale. Set aside the cucumber strips, covered with clear wrap to keep them fresh.

In a large pot of boiling water, cook the noodles over high heat. If using fresh noodles, cook them for 7–8 minutes after the water has returned to the boil. Test a strand; it should be firm but tender, with no hard core. If using dried noodles, scatter them across vigorously boiling water. Add 1 cup of cold water as soon as the water returns to a boil. Cook the noodles for 10 minutes after the water returns to a second boil. Test a strand after about 8 minutes just to be sure. There's tremendous variation in cooking times depending upon brand choice. Drain the cooked noodles immediately, showering them with fresh cold water to remove surface starch and cool them. Drain again and chill until ready to serve. You may cook the noodles several hours in advance of mealtime.

In a clean, dry skillet, roast the sesame seeds over medium-high heat for 30–40 seconds or until they begin to color slightly or a few pop. Shake the pan to keep the seeds in motion. Set aside.

Assemble the noodle salad just before serving. Rinse the noodles under fresh cold water and drain them. The Japanese often serve cold noodles on either a slatted mat, to allow excess water to drain to the plate beneath, or submerged in ice water in a deep bowl. Choose the easiest method for yourself. Garnish individual or communal dishes or bowls with a mound of the chopped sea tangle and a pile of cucumber shreds. Serve the chilled sauce separately, adding the sesame seeds and the slivers of lemon zest to it at the last minute. Each person lifts noodles from the mat or bowl of ice water, dips them into the chilled sauce, and merrily slurps them down (in Japan, the more noise you make, the better!). The sea tangle and cucumbers are also dipped in the sauce and eaten. The sesame seeds and lemon zest cling to the noodles and vegetables as they're dipped in the smoky sauce.

Menu Suggestions: These chilled noodles make a nutritious meal in itself, although smaller portions might be served as a first course before a fish, seafood, or poultry entrée.

Homemade Cold Citron Noodles

YUZU KIRI SOBA · Serves 4

Here's a delightfully different kind of homemade pasta that I discovered at a neighborhood noodle shop when I lived in Ogikubo in Tokyo. The recent appearance of Japanese citron oil in most Oriental groceries has encouraged me to develop this recipe for fellow Americans. Although there's a subtle and wonderful difference between *yuzu* (Japanese citron) and the American lemon, the zest and juice of the latter makes a delicious seasoning for the noodle dough, too. The Japanese eat noodles such as these as a snack, though you may find them more useful as a refreshing starch accompaniment to a hot-weather meal.

> ⅓ cup whole-wheat flour
>
> ⅔ cup all-purpose flour
>
> 1 large egg
>
> 2 tablespoons *yuzu abura* (citron oil) OR 1 tablespoon vegetable oil, 1 teaspoon lemon juice, and 1 teaspoon grated lemon zest
>
> ¼ teaspoon salt
>
> ½ sheet *yaki-zushi nori* (toasted paper-thin seaweed), cut into very thin 1-inch strips
>
> 1¼ cups dipping sauce (p. 233), chilled

In a shallow bowl, mix the flours thoroughly, then form a mound from them. Make a well in the center of the mound and break the egg into it. Add the citron oil and salt over the egg, and with a fork (or chopsticks) gently scramble the egg. Continue the scrambling motions, incorporating a bit of flour from the sides of the well as you go. Gradually beat in the flour to make a dough. (If using the plain vegetable-oil-and-lemon combination, incorporate the oil first before adding the juice and zest.)

Turn the dough out on a lightly floured board and knead it with the palms of the hands for a few minutes, until smooth and somewhat elastic. The dough should be the consistency that the Japanese call *mimi tabu* or "earlobe." Gently pinch the dough, then the soft, thick pad of your earlobe; they should feel about the same. Using a manual pasta machine, roll the noodle dough out to a thickness of $^1/_{16}$ inch. (Begin with the widest setting on your machine and gradually work to the next-to-thinnest setting.) Allow the broad strip of dough to rest for 3 minutes and lightly dust it with flour before running it through a narrow spaghetti-cutting attachment. Allow the noodles to air dry on a rack for at least 20 minutes and up to 2 hours before cooking them.

Bring a large pot of lightly salted water to a rolling boil. Cook the noodles, stirring occasionally, for 2 minutes. Strain the noodles immediately and shower them with fresh cold water. Drain well. If you wish to make and cook the noodles in advance, you'll need to shower them quickly in cold water again just before serving. Drain immediately.

The Japanese usually serve these noodles on woven or slatted mats with plates beneath. Large glass salad bowls make an attractive alternative. Garnish the cold noodles with seaweed strips just before serving. Chilled dipping sauce is served separately on the side. Each person lifts noodles from the plate or bowl and dips them in the sauce. Slurping from the dip dish held directly beneath your chin is the easiest, most authentic, and most fun way to eat them.

Menu Suggestions: These citron noodles can be served alone, or in combination with Homemade Cold Herb Noodles (p. 236) and/or Cold Noodle Salad with Smoky Sesame-Citron Sauce (p. 232).

Homemade Cold Herb Noodles

SHISO IRI SŌMEN · *Serves 4*

This herbaceous pasta is a variation on Homemade Cold Citron Noodles and was inspired by the recent availability in the United States of *shiso abura,* an aromatic spice oil. There's no simple substitute should this product be unavailable, but fresh mint oil makes an interesting, though differently colored and textured, variation on the theme. Whether made with Japanese spice oil or homemade mint oil, the resulting noodles are delicious alone, or served in combination with the lemony noodles on p. 232. Chilled noodles such as these, served with dipping sauce, are a popular snack in Japan. They can also become a tantalizing first course to a larger non-Oriental meal.

> 1 cup all-purpose white flour
> 1 egg
> 2 tablespoons *shiso abura* (herb oil) OR 2 tablespoons specially made mint oil (see Note below)
> ¼ teaspoon salt
> 1¼ cups dipping sauce (p. 233), chilled

Mound the flour in a shallow bowl. Make a well in the center of the mound and break the egg into it. Add the herb or mint oil and salt over the egg, and with a fork (or chopsticks) gently scramble the egg. Continue the scrambling motions, incorporating a bit of flour from the sides of the well as you go. Gradually beat in the flour to make a soft but not sticky dough.

Turn the dough out on a lightly floured board and knead it with the palms of the hands for a few minutes, until smooth and somewhat elastic. The dough should be the consistency the Japanese call *mimi tabu* or "earlobe." Gently pinch the dough, then the soft, thick pad of your earlobe; they should feel about the same. Using a manual pasta machine, roll the noodle dough out to a thickness of ¹⁄₁₆ inch. (Begin with the widest setting on your machine and gradually work to the next-to-thinnest setting.) Allow the broad strip of dough to rest for 3 minutes before running it through a narrow spaghetti-cutting attachment. Allow the noodles to air dry on a rack for at least 20 minutes and up to 2 hours before cooking them.

Bring 3–4 quarts of lightly salted water to a rolling boil in a very large pot. As the noodles cook, the water will foam and you must plan ahead for the necessary headroom. Cook the noodles in the boiling water, stirring occasionally, for 2 minutes. Strain the noodles immediately and shower them with fresh cold water. If you wish to make and cook the noodles in advance, you'll need to shower them quickly in cold water again just before serving.

The Japanese usually serve these noodles on woven or slatted mats with plates beneath. Chilled dipping sauce is served separately on the side. Each person lifts noodles from the plate or bowl and dips them in the sauce. Slurping them from the dip dish, held directly beneath your chin, is the easiest and most authentic way to eat them. Large glass salad bowls, with the sauce poured on the noodles at the last moment, makes an attractive alternative presentation.

Note:

If you cannot find *shiso abura* and wish to make mint oil in its stead, you'll need to make a minimum of ¼ cup to engage the blades of a blender or food processor. You'll have to use only 2 tablespoons of the aromatic oil to make the noodle recipe above. The remaining oil can be stored for several weeks in the refrigerator (it may cloud a bit, but that's fine), or use it with a few drops of lemon juice to dress crisp lettuce.

> **1 cup loosely packed fresh mint leaves**
> **3–4 tablespoons vegetable oil**

Rinse the mint leaves and pat dry. Place the fresh leaves in the bowl of a food processor fitted with the metal blade. Pulse-process until the leaves are uniformly and finely chopped. You may have to stop and scrape down the sides several times to accomplish this.

With the motor going, dribble in 3 tablespoons of the oil. Stop and scrape down the sides as often as necessary to combine the chopped herb and oil well. Add more oil, dribbling it in, if the mixture seems dry.

Store the oil in a covered glass or ceramic container. The mint will settle to the bottom of the container after a few moments. When making the noodles, use the thick sediment from the bottom of your container. When using the oil for salad dressings, stir it up well before measuring.

Tumble-About Potatoes

JAGAIMO NO NIKKOROGASHI · *Serves 4*

The Japanese language is very onomatopoetic and the name of this dish, *nikkorogashi,* is taken from the sound of small whole potatoes being shaken about in a pan as they cook. These potatoes are delicious served hot or at room temperature.

> 1½ pounds small new potatoes
> 1½ cups *dashi* (basic sea stock, p. 48)
> 3 tablespoons *mirin* (syrupy rice wine)
> 3 tablespoons *usukuchi shōyu* (light soy sauce)

Take each potato and lightly score it around its middle. This will make peeling easier later on. Either steam the potatoes for 12–13 minutes, or bring a pot of water to a boil and parboil the potatoes for 7–8 minutes, then drain. In either case, a toothpick should pass easily through the potato at its thickest point. Using a towel to protect your hands from the heat, hold the potatoes, one at a time, so that the original scored mark isn't covered. Twist the skins off by moving one hand clockwise, the other counterclockwise. Discard the skins.

In a pan just large enough to accommodate the potatoes in a single layer, bring the stock, syrupy rice wine, and light soy sauce to a boil. Place the skinned potatoes in the bubbling liquid and cook over medium-high heat for 10 minutes. As the liquid reduces, shake the pan, "tumbling" the potatoes about. Continue to cook until nearly all the liquid has reduced and the potatoes are colored a rich reddish brown.

Menu Suggestions: In Japan, these potatoes are packed into many a lunch box for school, and you might find them a welcome change from potato salad for your picnic with cold cuts. Tumble-About Potatoes are good served hot or cold with roasted or grilled meat or fish, too.

Potato Salad with Wasabi Mayonnaise

JAGAIMO NO WASABI MAYO AÉ · Makes 2½–3 cups for 4–6 servings

The incendiary Japanese horseradish called *wasabi* is traditionally served as a condiment to fish, particularly in *sashimi* or *sushi* style. I've used it here to enliven a potato salad that would go well with any picnic or cold buffet. I've given the *wasabi* mayonnaise as a separate recipe, immediately following this one, since it has a personality all its own.

> 1¼ pounds red-skinned potatoes
> 1 tablespoon finely chopped scallion (green part only)
> 1 small carrot (about 3–4 ounces)
> ¼ teaspoon salt
> ½ cup *wasabi* mayonnaise (p. 241)

Place the potatoes, with their skins still on, in a large pot with cold water to cover. Over high heat bring the water to a boil and cook for 15 minutes. (A toothpick should easily go through each potato.) Drain the potatoes and let them cool enough to handle comfortably. Peel and slice them into 1-inch chunks. Allow the potatoes to cool thoroughly, uncovered.

Soak the scallion in ice water for 5 minutes, then drain and gently pat dry before setting aside.

Peel the carrot, and cut it into 1-inch lengths. Slice it very thin, then stack the slices and cut them into threadlike julienne shreds. Toss the carrot shreds with the salt, squeezing to wilt them. Rinse the carrot shreds under cold water and squeeze dry before setting aside.

In a bowl, mix the cooled potato chunks with the *wasabi* mayonnaise. Use gentle folding motions with a rubber spatula to keep from bruising the potatoes. Toss in the scallion, then the carrot, folding in each addition gently but thoroughly. Cover and chill the salad for 5 minutes, or serve at room temperature.

Note:

The oomph behind the *wasabi* fades with exposure to high heat and/or air. If you wish to make this salad well in advance of serving it, cover and chill the potatoes until ready to assemble. Prepare the scallion and carrot, too, covering and chilling these separately. If using mayonnaise prepared more than 3 hours before, you may wish to spark it up by whisking in an additional ¼ teaspoon of *wasabi* powder mixed with a drop of cold water. For best results, just before serving dress the potatoes with the mayonnaise and then toss in the scallion and carrot.

Wasabi *Mayonnaise*

WASABI MAYO · Makes ½–⅔ cup

*J*apanese horseradish is a small nubbly root with broad, ruffle-edged leaves that grows in marshy fields. The inland areas of the Izu Peninsula are known for their prized *wasabi* fields, which are irrigated by the cool mountain streams nearby. The sharp, clean zing of this fresh condiment has won many fans on both sides of the Pacific.

The fresh root is occasionally sold in the United States, but far more common is the dried and powdered form. Playing with the powder one day in my New York kitchen, I discovered it had the most amazing emulsifying properties when making mayonnaise. The resulting dressing had a delightful punch to it. I find *wasabi* mayonnaise to be incredibly versatile and use it to dress potatoes and other vegetables, seafood, poultry, beef, veal, and lamb.

> 1 yolk from extra-large egg, at room temperature
> ⅛ teaspoon salt
> 2 teaspoons rice vinegar
> 1 tablespoon *wasabi* powder (fiery Japanese horseradish)
> ½ cup vegetable oil
> 1 tablespoon lime juice

In a clean, dry bowl combine the egg yolk, salt, rice vinegar, and horseradish. Whisk them together until well combined. Add the oil, drop by drop, beating vigorously as you add it. Keep adding the oil until you get a thick dressing. Whisk in the lime juice to thin the dressing to a proper consistency. Cover the mayonnaise with clear plastic wrap and let it rest for 10 minutes before using. Store any leftovers in a tightly sealed jar in the refrigerator.

Note:
The mayonnaise is at its best from 10 minutes to 2 hours after making it; thereafter it tends to lose some of its power. Just before serving it can be revived. Mix an additional ¼ teaspoon of *wasabi* powder with a drop of cold water, then whisk this into the mayonnaise.

Cabbage and Spinach Rolls with Sesame Vinaigrette

OHITASHI · *Makes 16 pieces, 2 or 3 per serving*

The technique of rolling or enclosing one food in another is a favorite of the Japanese. Here Chinese cabbage and spinach are formed into a stunning two-toned pattern of concentric circles. Pieces sliced from the roll are later dressed with the sesame vinaigrette and garnished with whole seeds. Although this recipe requires advance preparation of both the vegetable roll and the dressing, it's neither difficult nor time consuming. The cabbage and spinach rolls can also be used, undressed, in casseroles or stews such as the seafood one on p. 175.

½ pound fresh spinach
6 leaves *hakusai* (Chinese cabbage)

sesame vinaigrette:
3 tablespoons soy sauce
3 tablespoons rice vinegar

2 tablespoons *mirin* (syrupy rice wine)

1½ teaspoons *goma abura* (aromatic sesame oil)

1½ teaspoons white sesame seeds

Wash the spinach in lots of cold water to remove all traces of dirt. Gather the stems together and tie the spinach into two bundles with kitchen twine. Bring a pot of lightly salted water to a rolling boil, then turn off the heat. Hold the spinach by the stems with either fingers or tongs and dip the bundles into the hot water until just barely wilted. Remove them immediately to a bowl of ice water to stop the cooking process. Remove the spinach from the cold water, squeeze out all liquid, and set aside on paper toweling.

Bring the pot of hot water back to a boil and quickly blanch the cabbage leaves until barely wilted. I put the leaves, one at a time, into the pot with long cooking chopsticks, hold them under the hot water for a count of 10, and fish them out right away. Plunge the wilted cabbage leaves in the bowl of cold water to cool them, then gently pat dry.

It's easiest to assemble the vegetable rolls on a slated bamboo mat called a *sudaré*, but you could manage with just a clean kitchen towel. Each roll will use three leaves of cabbage and one bundle of spinach. Lay the cabbage leaves across your mat or towel to create a rectangular area approximately 8 by 5 inches. The stem portions should point alternately right and left, and the leafy portions should be spread to cover the area.

Trim and discard the tied stems from the two spinach bundles, then divide each into two bunches. The spinach should be laid horizontally across the cabbage at the edge closest to you, with the stem ends of one bunch flush to the right, the other bunch flush to the left. Lift the cabbage with the help of the mat or cloth and flip it over the spinach. Continue to roll snugly until all the cabbage has encircled the spinach.

Repeat this procedure with the remaining three cabbage leaves and two bunches of spinach to make a second roll.

Using string or rubber bands to hold the cloth or *sudaré* mat in place, tie the ends of each roll and refrigerate for at least 1 hour or, covered, up to 1 day. Some liquid may drip from the tightly wound roll, so it's best to place it on paper toweling on a plate.

In a small bowl, mix the dressing ingredients. Chill the dressing, if you like. It can be stored in the refrigerator for several weeks.

In a clean, dry skillet, toast the sesame seeds over medium-high heat for 30–40 seconds until they begin to color slightly or a few pop. Shake the pan to keep the seeds in motion.

When ready to serve the salad, remove the rolls from their mats or cloths and, with a sharp knife, slice each into eight pieces. A single serving could be two or three pieces. Stand them on flanged plates or in shallow bowls so that the concentric pattern is clearly visible. Spoon some of the dressing over each piece and garnish with the whole toasted sesame seeds.

Menu Suggestions: These vegetable rolls are good with any meat or fish entrée, especially those that are fried (such as *Tatsuta* Deep-Fried Soft-Shell Crabs with Ginger on p. 177) or grilled (like Grilled Veal Chops with *Sanshō* Butter on p. 206, or Lamb Chops with Fresh Wild Japanese Mushrooms on p. 207). The sesame vinaigrette can be used to dress other vegetables and adds a spritely touch to sliced tomatoes and cucumbers.

Eggplant and Green Pepper Sauté

NASU TO PĪMAN NO MISO ITAMÉ · Serves 4

A Japanese friend living in New York, Kyoko Schwartzman, showed me how to make this wonderful ratatouillelike dish. It combines two of my favorite summer vegetables, bell peppers and eggplants, and flavors them with mellow bean paste and sesame seeds. This dish goes well with grilled fish, meat, or poultry. It also makes a marvelous filling for an omelet!

2 tablespoons white sesame seeds
2 tablespoons *shiro miso* (light fermented bean paste)
2 teaspoons *mirin* (syrupy rice wine)
1 medium-size eggplant, about ¾ pound
1 large sweet green pepper, about 4 ounces
2–3 tablespoons vegetable oil
⅓ cup *dashi* (basic sea stock, p. 48) OR water

In a clean, dry skillet, roast the sesame seeds over medium-high heat for 30–40 seconds until they color slightly or a few pop. Shake the pan to keep the seeds in motion. Transfer the seeds to a cutting board and mince them with a sharp knife, much as you would parsley. Set the seeds aside.

In a small bowl, combine the bean paste and syrupy rice wine, stirring to mix well. Set aside.

Peel the eggplant, then cut it lengthwise into ¼-inch-thick, 2-inch long julienne strips. Remove the seeds and white ribs from the green pepper and slice it lengthwise into ¼-inch julienne strips.

Heat 2 tablespoons of oil in a skillet and sauté the eggplant over medium-high heat for about 1 minute, stirring constantly to keep the eggplant from scorching. Add the cut peppers and continue to sauté, stirring, for 1 minute or until the peppers wilt ever so slightly. You may need to add another tablespoon of oil to the skillet as you sauté if the vegetables look in danger of scorching. Continue stirring the vegetables over direct heat for another minute until barely tender.

Add the stock or water, reducing the heat to low. Cover the skillet and let the vegetables simmer for 1 minute, undisturbed. Remove the cover, stir in the reserved bean-paste mixture, and simmer for yet 1 more minute. Sprinkle half the sesame seeds over the vegetable mixture and stir well to distribute. There should be a thick sauce enveloping the vegetables; if it appears thin and watery, raise the heat and reduce the liquid rapidly.

Serve hot, at room temperature, or even chilled. Garnish with the remaining sesame seeds just before serving.

Eggplant with Pungent Bean Sauce

NASU NO MISO AN KAKÉ · Serves 6

Although eggplants are available throughout the year in most parts of the United States, they're particularly good toward the end of the summer, when the hot sun seems to ripen them most gently. The pungent bean sauce in this recipe makes a nice contrast to the subtle sweetness of the flesh.

Versions of this classic dish appear on most Japanese restaurant menus in America, where they're often listed as *nasu no shigi yaki. Nasu* is eggplant, but *shigi* is the name of a long-beaked bird native to Japan. The elongated shape of Japanese eggplants reminds the Japanese of the bird. This name should only be used when slender eggplants are sliced in half, lengthwise. Here I make use of the bulbous American eggplant, cut into thick rounds.

> 6 **round unpeeled eggplant slices, about 3½ inches in diameter and 1 inch thick**
>
> **vegetable oil, for deep frying**
>
> 3 **tablespoons *aka miso* (dark fermented bean paste)**
>
> 1½ **tablespoons sugar**
>
> 2 **tablespoons *saké* (Japanese rice wine)**
>
> ½ **teaspoon freshly grated lemon rind, for garnish**

Shallowly score the flesh of the eggplant on both sides of each slice in a crosshatch pattern. This will help to cook the eggplant quickly and make eating it easier later.

Preheat the broiler at its highest setting.

You'll need oil at a depth of at least 1½ inches to fry the eggplant properly. Heat the oil to approximately 375 degrees (test with a sliver of skin or trimmed end piece; ideally the eggplant should drop ever so slightly below the surface of the oil and rise immediately to sizzle). Fry the slices in the oil, turning only once, until tender (about 2–2½ minutes in all). Don't crowd the pan. Remove the eggplant with a slotted spoon to paper toweling to drain.

In a 1-quart saucepan, stir together the bean paste, sugar, and rice wine. Over medium heat bring the mixture to a simmer, stirring constantly; it should be glossy, thick, and bubbling.

Spread a rounded tablespoon of the mixture over one side of each eggplant slice. Place the slices about 3–4 inches from the heat and broil until the sauce just begins to bubble, about 10–15 seconds. Garnish with the grated lemon peel and serve immediately.

Menu Suggestions: I like to serve this eggplant with subtly seasoned dishes like Snapper Steamed with Wild Mushrooms in Parchment (p. 181), or Bean Curd *Tempura* with Spicy Scallion Sauce (p. 183). Eggplant with Pungent Bean Sauce nicely complements fluffy scrambled eggs, too.

Glazed Zucchini with Sesame

ZUKKĪNI NO GOMA AÉ · *Serves 4–6*

In America, zucchini is incredibly abundant, as anyone with just a small vine in the backyard will attest. In Japan, though, it's a rare and imported delicacy. Since zucchini is such a versatile vegetable, blending well with all sorts of seasonings, it's no wonder that many Japanese living in America have been cooking with it. My favorite Japanese-style zucchini dish is this subtly nutty sesame sauté.

1 tablespoon white sesame seeds
3–4 slender zucchini squash, about 1¼ pounds in all
1–1½ tablespoons vegetable oil
1 tablespoon *saké* (Japanese rice wine)
1½ tablespoons soy sauce
½ teaspoon sugar

In a clean, dry skillet, roast the sesame seeds over medium-high heat for 30–40 seconds until they begin to color slightly or a few pop. Shake the pan to keep the seeds in motion. Set aside 1 teaspoon of whole seeds, but mince the rest with a knife on a dry board much as you would parsley.

Wash and pat dry the zucchini, then slice off about ½ inch from the stem end of each. Using this stem piece, rub the cut surface in circular motions until a thick white foam appears; rinse it away and pat the squash dry. This is what the Japanese call *aku nuki* or "bitterness removal." Trim the opposite end and cut each squash lengthwise into quarters. Cut these strips into 1½-inch lengths.

In a large skillet, heat the oil and sauté the zucchini over high heat for 1½–2 minutes. Keep the vegetable pieces moving constantly to keep them from browning and sticking. Add the rice wine, and continue to sauté for a few seconds before adding the soy sauce and sugar. Reduce the heat and cover the skillet, letting the zucchini simmer for 1 minute more. Remove the lid and you'll notice several tablespoons of liquid in the skillet. Sprinkle the minced sesame seeds over the zucchini, return the heat to high, and stir, cooking for another 10–15 seconds. The zucchini will take on a glazed appearance. Serve hot or at room temperature. Just before serving, garnish with the whole seeds that you set aside.

Menu Suggestions: This sautéed zucchini could be served as a vegetable accompaniment to any grilled or fried entrée. I particularly like to pair it with Steak with *Wasabi* Butter (p. 204).

Asparagus Salad in Smoky Sauce

ASUPARA NO OHITASHI · Serves 4

This dish is an adaptation of a Japanese classic that's typically made with spinach. Here the woodsy-sweet flavor of the asparagus is beautifully complemented by the bonito flakes that garnish the vegetable. Japanese asparagus is pencil thin and appears in the market from early spring through the rainy season in July. In America, the season for fresh asparagus is a bit longer, allowing us to enjoy this dish well through the summer and even into the fall.

tosa *sauce:*	1 cup *dashi* (basic sea stock, p. 48)
	1 tablespoon *mirin* (syrupy rice wine)
	1 tablespoon soy sauce, *usukuchi shōyu* (light soy sauce) preferred
	1 package (5 grams) OR about ⅓ cup *katsuo bushi* (dried bonito flakes)
	1 pound fresh green asparagus, slender stalks preferred

Season the basic sea stock with the syrupy rice wine and soy sauce, and bring to a boil over medium heat, stirring once or twice. Reserve 2 tablespoons of the bonito flakes for later and sprinkle the remainder of the package over the boiling seasoned stock. Remove the pot from the heat and let the stock steep for 3 minutes. Pour the liquid through a cloth- or paper-lined strainer or colander into a glass or ceramic dish (I find an 8½ by 4 by 2½–inch loaf pan the most convenient size and shape). Set aside.

Trim the asparagus discarding the woody bottoms, then cut what remains of the stalks in half. Bring a small pot of salted water to a rolling boil and add the lower, thicker halves of the stalks. Cook for 30 seconds or until the water returns to a boil, whichever is sooner. Add the tip pieces of the asparagus to the pot and cook for 1 minute or for 30 seconds after the water returns to a boil again, whichever is sooner. Drain the asparagus, both tips and stalks, promptly and place the pieces in the waiting *tosa* sauce.

Allow the sauced asparagus pieces to cool to room temperature before covering and chilling them in the refrigerator for a minimum of 30 minutes and up to 2 hours.

When you're ready to serve this dish, lift the lower halves of the asparagus out of the *tosa* sauce and divide them into four portions. The stalks should run parallel to each other and form a small bundle on each plate. (I'm particularly fond of serving this salad in shallow glass bowls.) Next, divide the tips of the asparagus into four portions and align these so that the tips all point in the same direction. Lay the tip pieces over the stalk pieces, forming each serving into a gentle mound. Sprinkle a half tablespoon of the reserved bonito flakes across the center of each serving of asparagus, just before bringing to the table.

Menu Suggestions: This asparagus dish makes an appealing vegetable accompaniment to Grilled Veal Chops with *Sanshō* Butter (p. 206), or *Miso*-Marinated Baked Chicken (p. 193). It's versatile enough though to go with almost any meat, fish, or poultry entrée.

Steamed Radish with Pungent Bean Sauce

FUROFUKI DAIKON · Serves 4

This dish is a cold-weather classic in its native land and I think you'll find it just as comforting and tasty here in the United States. The clouds of fragrant steam that billow forth from this dish remind the Japanese of their deep hot tubs (*ofuro*). They must blow (*fuku*) away the steam in order to eat the deliciously sauced radish, hence the name *furofuki*, or "steam bath blowing," radish.

4 large, 1½-inch-thick rounds *daikon* (Japanese white radish) OR rutabaga, about 8–10 ounces in all

neri miso (glossy bean-paste sauce):

¼ cup *aka miso* (dark fermented bean paste)

2 tablespoons *saké* (Japanese rice wine)

2 tablespoons sugar

2 tablespoons *dashi* (basic sea stock, p. 48) OR water

Peel the radish and save these peels for making the sauté on p. 253, if you wish, or discard. (If you choose rutabaga, since most peels are waxed you'll have to discard them.) Bevel the edges of the radish or rutabaga slightly. Place the rounds in a steamer and, over high heat, steam for 7–8 minutes. Test the vegetables with a wooden toothpick; there should be no resistance through the center (the hole you make in poking will be covered with sauce later). If you have to, steam the rounds for an additional 2–3 minutes until tender.

While the radish is steaming, make the sauce. Combine the remaining ingredients in a small saucepan and stir until you've made a smooth paste. Over low heat, cook the sauce, stirring constantly, until glossy and bubbly.

With a spatula, carefully transfer the steaming vegetable rounds to individual shallow bowls or flanged dishes. Spoon the bubbly hot bean sauce over the radish or rutabaga and serve at once. This dish is best eaten with a spoon.

Menu Suggestions: This dish goes particularly well with grilled fish and meat; Glaze-Grilled Salmon Steaks (p. 179) and Sweet and Spicy Grilled Leg of Lamb (p. 211) are my favorite choices.

Orchard and Field Salad

NI SHOKU NAMASU · *Serves 4*

*H*ere's an unusual fruit-and-vegetable mélange that nicely complements grilled or fried fish and poultry.

⅓ cup rice vinegar

2 tablespoons sugar

8–10 ounces *daikon* (Japanese white radish)

1 teaspoon salt

1 large Golden Delicious apple, about 7 ounces

3 ounces seedless green grapes

4 sprigs fresh mint, for garnish (optional)

Combine the rice vinegar and sugar in a small glass or ceramic saucepan, and heat the mixture slowly, stirring to dissolve the sugar. Pour it into a heat-proof pint-size glass or ceramic container and set aside to cool to room temperature.

Peel the radish and save the peels for making the sauté on p. 253, if you wish, or discard. Cut the radish into ¼-inch cubes and toss them with the salt, then let them rest for 10 minutes. Place the radish cubes in a strainer and shower them with fresh cold water to remove excess brine. Blot up the surface moisture with paper towels, then transfer the radish pieces to the vinegar and sugar mixture. Cover the container and allow the radish to marinate at room temperature for at least 30 minutes and up to 2 hours. Or refrigerate the radish for 4–24 hours.

Pour the radish and sauce into a large glass bowl. Peel and seed the apple, then cut it into ¼-inch cubed pieces and toss these well with the radish and sauce.

Pick all the grapes from their branches and discard any bruised fruit. Trim off the slightly discolored end that was attached to the branch and cut each grape in half, lengthwise. Toss these into the bowl and mix well. Chill the fruit and vegetables for at least 10 minutes and up to 2 hours.

Drain the fruit and vegetables of excess liquid just before serving. Garnish with sprigs of fresh mint, if you like.

Spicy Sautéed Radish Peels

DAIKON NO KAWA NO KIMPIRA · Serves 3–4

If you've bought some fresh *daikon* radish to cook as a vegetable, grate as a condiment, shred in a salad, or pickle in brine, I hope you saved the peels so you can make this splendid little side dish. I learned how to make Spicy Sautéed Radish Peels from some frugal Japanese friends, and quite frankly I often buy the *daikon* now just to make this dish.

> 6–7 ounces *daikon* (Japanese white radish) peels
> 2 teaspoons vegetable oil
> ⅛ teaspoon salt
> 1 teaspoon *saké* (Japanese rice wine)
> ½ teaspoon sugar
> 1 tablespoon soy sauce
> scant ¼ teaspoon *shichimi tōgarashi* (blend of 7 spices)

Rinse the radish peels to be sure they're free of dirt or other gritty material. Slice them into narrow julienne strips, approximately 1½ inches long. You should have about 1½ cups of radish strips. Rinse again, drain, and spread them out on a towel to dry.

In a skillet, heat the oil over medium heat and sauté the strips of peel, stirring constantly. When they begin to turn slightly translucent (after about 1–1½ minutes), sprinkle with the salt, then add the rice wine to the skillet. Continue to sauté for another minute or so before adding the sugar and soy sauce. Stir and cook for a final minute or so until the sugar is melted and the radish peels are glazed. Sprinkle with the seven-spice blend and stir to distribute evenly. Serve the radish peels piping hot or allow them to cool to room temperature.

Menu Suggestions: This vegetable sauté is often packed on a Japanese picnic and you might want to add it to your next outing. It goes well with many foods, particularly barbecued or grilled meats.

Lemon-Pickled Cabbage

HAKUSAI NO SU-ZUKÉ · Serves 6–8

This is a delightfully crisp and fresh-scented pickle with just a hint of fire. It's best when made from slightly wilted cabbage past its prime salad-making days—the perfect way to finish off the "other half" of a large head of Chinese cabbage. This pickle is particularly well suited to serving with braised, simmered, or stewed foods. My sister-in-law, Yohko Yokoi, who first showed me how to make this pickle, serves it with barbecued meats.

> 1–1¼ pounds *hakusai* (Chinese cabbage)
> 1 tablespoon kosher OR sea salt
> zest from ½ lemon, shredded
> ¼ cup rice vinegar
> 1 tablespoon lemon juice
> 1 teaspoon *mirin* (syrupy rice wine)
> 1 teaspoon *usukuchi shōyu* (light soy sauce)
> 1 *tōgarashi* (red chili pepper)
> soy sauce (optional)

Cut the cabbage into four or five wedges through the core and spread them out on a tray on a sunny window ledge for 2–3 hours. Or put the cabbage wedges in a closed plastic bag and place in a microwave oven on "boil" for 1 minute.

Rub the salt all over the wedges and scatter the pieces of lemon zest among the leaves. The cabbage needs to be weighted down for several hours. Traditionally large flat stones were used; more recently the Japanese have developed a special pot with a screw-top device. Called *shokutaku tsukémono ki,* such pots are often for sale at Oriental grocer-

ies for about ten dollars and will simplify this and other similar pickling procedures tremendously. However you can create your own weights with books, bricks, or even potatoes. Choose weights that are slightly smaller than the diameter of your container. Whatever you choose to use will sink down below the level of brine and get wet, so they must be wrapped in plastic first. You'll need 15–20 pounds of pressure to make this salad.

If you're using the special jar, place the cabbage and brine in the bottom of it and screw the lid on as snugly as possible. Check after 15–20 minutes to see if the screw needs tightening. A total of 3 hours of pressure should be sufficient. If you're devising your own weights, place the cabbage and brine in a glass or ceramic container and lay a flat plate over all; the plate must be an inch or so less in diameter than the bowl. On top of this plate, place your weights wrapped in waterproof material. Allow these weights to sit at least 8 hours, preferably overnight.

Unscrew the jar's inner lid or remove your weights, pouring off and reserving any brine. Squeeze the cabbage well, saving any brine. Combine the reserved liquids with the rice vinegar and lemon juice, seasoning with the syrupy rice wine and light soy sauce. Break the pod of a red pepper into several pieces and discard the seeds (unless you like very spicy foods, in which case add the seeds to the brine, too). Add the pod pieces to the pickling liquid.

Fit the cabbage snugly into a glass jar and pour the seasoned brine over it. Cover and let the pickle mature at room temperature for at least 2 hours and up to 5. Refrigerate until ready to serve (up to 2 weeks).

Just before serving, remove the cabbage from its seasoned brine, squeeze away excess liquid, and chop coarsely. If you like, pour a drop or two of soy sauce over the pickle.

Pickled Cabbage Salad

KYABETSU NO SHIO-ZUKÉ · *Serves 4*

This is a popular Japanese salt-pickled vegetable dish that's often packed along on picnics or enjoyed at home with grilled or broiled fish and meat. I suggest you serve it in much the same way you would cole-slaw.

> ½ head green cabbage, about 1 pound
> 2½ teaspoons salt
> 1 small unwaxed cucumber, about 3 ounces
> 1 teaspoon soy sauce (optional)

Cut the cabbage into very fine shreds and place them in a glass bowl. Toss the cabbage shreds with 2 teaspoons of salt and let them sit for 5 minutes.

Wash the cucumber well and slice off about ½ inch from the stem (darker green) end. Using this stem piece, rub the cut surface in circular motions until a thick white foam appears; rinse it away and pat the cucumber dry. This is what the Japanese call *aku nuki* or "bitterness removal." Trim off the opposite (light-colored) end, then slice the

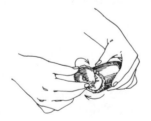

cucumber in half, lengthwise. Scoop out any seeds with a small spoon. Place the two cucumber halves on your cutting board, cut side down. Slice into very thin half-moons. Place these in a small glass bowl with the remaining ½ teaspoon of salt and toss to mix well.

Squeeze and toss the cabbage, keeping whatever liquid (brine) it exuded during the 5 minutes. When the cabbage is well wilted, combine it and its brine with the sliced and salted cucumbers. Continue to squeeze and toss the vegetables until limp and well mixed. Save all the briny vegetable liquid.

The vegetables need to be weighted down for several hours. Traditionally large flat stones were used; more recently the Japanese have developed a special pot with a screw-top device, called a *shokutaku tsukemono ki.* However you can create your own weighted jar with

books, bricks, or even potatoes. Choose weights that are slightly smaller than the diameter of your container. Whatever you choose to use will sink down below the level of brine and get wet, so they must be wrapped in plastic first. You'll need 5–8 pounds of pressure to make this salad.

If you're using the special jar, place the vegetables and brine in the bottom of it and screw the lid on as snugly as possible. Check after 15–20 minutes to see if the screw needs tightening. In all, you'll need to pressure your vegetables for only 45–60 minutes. If you're devising your own weights, place the vegetables and brine in a glass or ceramic container and lay a flat plate over all; the plate must be an inch or so less in diameter than the bowl. On top of this plate, place your weights wrapped in waterproof material. Allow these weights to sit for 2–3 hours, undisturbed.

If you plan on making this salad several days in advance, store the vegetables in their brine. Just before serving, or packing into your picnic basket, rinse the vegetables under cold water and drain. Squeeze to make sure no water remains. Toss the vegetables in a few drops of soy sauce for a more robust flavor, if you like.

Radish and Shiso Salad

DAIKON TO SHISO NO SHIO-ZUKÉ · Serves 4

The technique of salt-pickling vegetables is very old and this dish is a classic in its native land. The crunchy Japanese radish has a hint of fire that nicely complements the aromatic *shiso* leaf. A small mound of this salad is most refreshing with intensely flavored meats such as *Tosa*-Style Grilled Beef (p. 209), Sweet and Spicy Grilled Leg of Lamb (p. 211), or *Miso*-Marinated Baked Chicken (p. 193).

> ½ pound *daikon* (Japanese white radish)
> 1½ tablespoons salt
> 10 leaves *shiso* (flat-leafed Japanese herb)

Peel the radish and save the peels for making the sauté on p. 253, if you like, or discard. Slice the radish into very fine julienne strips. Place the radish shreds in a glass bowl and sprinkle the salt over them, tossing to distribute well. Set the radish aside to "sweat" for 5–10 minutes. Squeeze out all the liquid from the salted radish, reserving this brine for later use. Place the radish in a bowl and set it aside while you shred the herb leaves.

Rinse the *shiso* leaves and shake dry. Trim off the stems, then slice the leaves in half, lengthwise. Stack these and, cutting across the grain, slice the herb into very fine julienne shreds.

Mix the radish with the shredded *shiso*. The vegetables need to be weighted down for several hours. Traditionally large flat stones were used; more recently the Japanese have developed a special pot with a screw-top device, called a *shokutaku tsukémono ki.* However you can

create your own weighted jar with books, bricks, or even potatoes. Choose weights that are slightly smaller than the diameter of your container. Whatever you choose to use will sink down below the level of brine and get wet, so they must be wrapped in plastic first. You'll need at least 8 pounds of pressure to make this salad, and preferably 10–12.

If you're using the special jar, place the vegetables and brine in the bottom of it and screw the lid on as snugly as possible. Check after 15–20 minutes to see if the screw needs tightening. In all, you'll need to pressure your vegetables for only 45–60 minutes. If you're devising your own weights, place the vegetables and brine in a glass or ceramic container and lay a flat plate over all; the plate must be an inch or so less in diameter than the bowl. On top of this plate, place your weights wrapped in waterproof material. Allow these weights to sit for 3 hours, undisturbed.

If you wish to keep this salad for a day or two, refrigerate it, unpressured but in its brine, covered. Just before serving, drain off the brine. Quickly rinse the radish and *shiso* mixture under cold running water, drain, and squeeze dry immediately. Divide the mixture into four portions and gently coax each into a mountain shape.

Green Salad with
Walnut and Bean Dressing

KURUMI MISO AÉ · Serves 4

This salad is a delightful combination of crisp greens and crunchy nuts with an aromatic bean-paste dressing. Serve this with any meal—Oriental or Occidental.

salad dressing:

1 teaspoon *mirin* (syrupy rice wine)
¼ teaspoon superfine sugar
1½ tablespoons *aka miso* (dark fermented bean paste)
2 tablespoons rice vinegar
1 tablespoon cold water
2 tablespoons walnut oil
¼ cup coarsley chopped walnut meats

1 small head romaine lettuce, about ½ pound
3–4 tablespoons finely chopped scallion (green part only)

In the top of a double boiler, combine the syrupy rice wine, superfine sugar, and dark bean paste. Stir over medium heat until glossy and bubbly (about 2 minutes). Remove the pan from the heat and stir in the rice vinegar and water. Place the pan over a bowl of ice, or chill in the refrigerator until no longer warm. With a whisk, beat in the walnut oil.

In a clean, dry skillet, dry-roast the walnut meats for 20–30 seconds, or until the oil just comes to the surface, making the nuts appear a bit shiny. Stir the nuts into the salad dressing.

Wash the lettuce well, then spin or pat dry. Tear into bite-size pieces. Place the chopped scallion greens in a small bowl of cold water and let them sit for 2–3 minutes before draining. Pat the scallions dry. Toss the lettuce and scallions together, then mound them in a large bowl or on individual plates. Spoon some walnut and bean dressing over the lettuce and scallions and serve at once.

Note:
The walnut and bean dressing can be made ahead and refrigerated for up to 1 week.

Ginger Vinaigrette

SHŌGA SU AÉ · Makes about ⅔ cup

Here's a deliciously versatile dressing for salad greens, one that nicely complements any cross-cultural entrée and could be enjoyed at a purely Continental table, too. My source of inspiration was a classic Japanese sauce of rice vinegar, light bean paste, and ginger juice that's used to dress marine and terrestrial greens. On soft lettuces, such as Boston and red-tipped leaf, the spritely ginger vinaigrette is very appealing. You'll find this dressing perks up iceberg lettuce, or even sliced tomatoes and cucumbers, and makes these ordinary salad vegetables more tempting than you thought possible.

- 3 tablespoon rice vinegar
- ¼ teaspoon dry mustard
- 1 teaspoon ginger juice (extracted from freshly grated ginger)
- 1½ teaspoon *shiro miso* (light fermented bean paste)
- 1 teaspoon soy sauce
- ¼ teaspoon *mirin* (syrupy rice wine)
  pinch salt
- 3–4 tablespoons fruity olive oil
- 1 teaspoon *kuro goma* (black sesame seeds), optional
- ¼ teaspoon freshly ground black pepper, optional

In a small glass bowl mix the rice vinegar and mustard, then stir in the ginger juice. With a small whisk, incorporate the bean paste, then the soy sauce and syrupy rice wine. Whisk until smooth. Add a pinch of salt and start whisking in the olive oil. Taste the dressing after combining 3 tablespoons; if you feel the dressing is too tart, add a bit more oil, whisking it in.

I recommend washing and drying your greens and placing them in a large salad bowl where you can toss them easily. Start with just a bit of dressing and taste as you go along. I've found that 3 tablespoons of dressing is enough to toss into 8–10 ounces of greens. In the hot weather, I like to dress my greens, cover with clear plastic wrap, and chill for about 30–40 minutes before serving. Just before bringing the salad to the table, I season it with a mixture of black sesame and pepper. If you want to try it, too, dry-roast your black sesame seeds just before using. In a dry, clean skillet, roast the seeds over medium-high heat for about 30 seconds. Shake the pan to keep the seeds in motion. Empty them onto a dry cutting board and, with a sharp knife, mince the seeds as you would parsley. Their marvelous nutty aroma mixes well with the clean spiciness of freshly ground pepper. Make a mixture of the two and sprinkle it over your salad greens.

The ginger vinaigrette keeps well for several weeks in the refrigerator in a covered glass jar; after more than a month the fresh ginger sometimes develops a bitter aftertaste. For fullest flavor, stir or shake the dressing well before using.

Simmered Mushrooms and Kelp

SHIITAKÉ KOMBU · *Serves 4–6*

Here's a tasty way of using kelp left over from stock making. There's a hint of aniselike flavor to the dark, lustrous sea vegetable and the dried mushrooms add a lusty earthiness to the dish. Garnished with roasted sesame seeds, a small mound of these slivered vegetables makes a tasty and nutritious accompaniment to plain steamed rice.

about 100 square inches *kombu* (kelp), left over from making *dashi* (basic sea stock, p. 48)

1½–2 cups cold water

1 tablespoon rice vinegar

6–8 small dried *shiitaké* (dark Oriental mushrooms), about ½ ounce in all

⅔–¾ cup liquid from soaking mushrooms

1½–2 tablespoons *saké* (Japanese rice wine)

1½ tablespoons sugar

3 tablespoons soy sauce

1 tablespoon *mirin* (syrupy rice wine)

1 teaspoon white sesame seeds

Cut the kelp into strips about 2 inches long and ⅛ inch wide. Fill a small saucepan with 1½ cups of cold water and 1 tablespoon of rice vinegar, and bring to a boil. Add the strips of kelp, adjust the heat to maintain a simmer, and cook for 7–8 minutes. Remove a piece of the kelp and pinch it. If it gives easily, drain the kelp immediately. If it still feels resistant, add ½ cup more cold water and continue to simmer for 3–4 minutes after it returns to a boil. Drain the kelp and rinse under fresh cold water. Drain again and pat dry with paper towels.

Soak the dried mushrooms for at least 20 minutes in warm water to cover. Save this soaking liquid. Remove the stems and save them for enriching stock (p. 50), if you wish, or discard. Rinse the caps under cold water, being careful to remove any gritty material that might be clinging to the undersides. Slice the caps into ⅛-inch-thick slices and place these again in the original soaking liquid. Let the slices sit for at least 5 minutes. Squeeze the mushrooms, straining and reserving the liquid.

In a small saucepan, combine ⅔ cup of the strained mushroom liquid with the rice wine, and bring to a boil over high heat. Reduce the heat to maintain a simmer and add the strips of kelp and softened mushroom. Cook for 5 minutes, add the sugar, cook for another 5 minutes, then add the soy sauce, and cook for 7–8 minutes. Throughout the cooking, stir occasionally. If the vegetables look in danger of scorching, add a few more drops of mushroom liquid or water. Finally, add the syrupy rice wine and, shaking the pan, cook for 1½–2 minutes. The liquid will be very bubbly and the vegetables will be well glazed. Let the vegetables cool to room temperature in the pot.

In a small, dry skillet, roast the sesame seeds over medium-high heat for 30–40 seconds until they begin to color slightly or a few pop. Shake the pan to keep the seeds in motion. Toss half of the seeds into the mushroom and kelp mixture, reserving the remaining seeds for a last-minute garnish.

Note:
This dish will keep very well, covered and refrigerated, for 1 week to 10 days.

Kelp Squares with Fragrant Pepper

KOMBU NO SANSHŌ NI · Serves 10–12

If you make fresh *dashi* stock frequently, you'll find yourself with quite a bit of leftover kelp. Save the pieces in a plastic bag in the refrigerator for up to 10 days, and when you have about 48 square inches, make up a batch of these pleasantly spicy squares. Once prepared according to the recipe below, the kelp will keep, covered and refrigerated, for a month or more. A few squares will perk up a steaming bowl of plain white rice and add nutrition (particularly calcium) to your meal if you serve it as a condiment.

> about 48 square inches *kombu* (kelp), left over from making *dashi* (basic sea stock, p. 48)
>
> 6 tablespoons rice vinegar
>
> ¼ cup soy sauce
>
> 3 tablespoons *mirin* (syrupy rice wine)
>
> generous ¼ teaspoon *sanshō* (fragrant Japanese pepper) powder OR 1 scant teaspoon salted *sanshō* berries (see Note below)

Slice the kelp into 1-inch squares.

In an enamel, glass, or stainless-steel pot, bring 2 cups of water to a rolling boil, then add 3 tablespoons of rice vinegar. Reduce the heat to maintain a steady though not vigorous boil, and cook the kelp squares for 7–8 minutes. Drain the kelp and repeat this cooking process for another 5 minutes using 2 cups of fresh water and 3 more tablespoons of rice vinegar. These acid baths help to make the kelp tender and porous, but don't really affect the final taste. If the surface of the kelp squares seems sticky, rinse under fresh cold water and pat dry on paper towels.

Rinse your saucepan and fill it with the soy sauce and syrupy rice wine. Over medium heat, bring this mixture to a simmer, then place the parboiled kelp squares in it. Cook over fairly low heat for 4–5 minutes, stirring frequently. The liquid will become very foamy as it reduces rapidly. Season the kelp with the fragrant pepper powder, stirring to ensure even distribution. Remove the pan from the heat and let the dark, lustrous kelp squares cool to room temperature before serving or storing for future use.

Note:
If you're able to find whole *sanshō* berries instead of the powdered *sanshō* pepper, you'll be in for a real treat! Rinse the berries under cold water and pat dry. Mince with a sharp knife just before adding them to the simmering soy and syrupy rice wine. Leave the berries in throughout the cooking and cooling, serving them with the kelp squares.

Flower Turnips

HANA KABU · Makes 6

Sculpted to resemble chrysanthemums, these pickled turnips are a prized garnish in the cold months in Japan. Although the stark white of the vegetable strikes a marvelous contrast against the darker grilled and soy-simmered dishes that are usually served with it, the Japanese occasionally dye the flowers fuchsia or gold with natural food colors. If you want to make a multicolored bouquet, refer to the note at the end of the recipe.

amazu (sweet and sour) sauce:
- ½ cup rice vinegar
- ¼ cup sugar
- ¼ teaspoon salt

- 6 small white turnips
- 2 teaspoons salt
- 1 *tōgarashi* (red chili pepper), optional
- 1 teaspoon *kuro goma* (black sesame seeds)
- 6 leaves *shiso* (flat-leafed Japanese herb), optional

In a small enamel-lined or other noncorrodible saucepan, combine the sweet-and-sour-sauce ingredients and heat them over a low flame, stirring, until the sugar and salt dissolve. Remove the pan from the heat and allow the sauce to cool to room temperature, uncovered.

Peel the turnips to create a six-sided figure. Lay disposable wooden chopsticks on both sides of the turnip to keep your knife from cutting

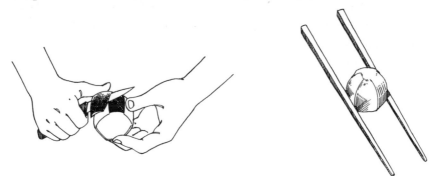

through to the board. Make many slices, then turn the turnip and repeat to make a crisscross pattern of slits. Repeat this procedure for the remaining turnips.

Salt the turnips and let them sit for 5 minutes. Gently squeeze to help wilt them. Once wilted, rinse the turnips under cold water and squeeze dry.

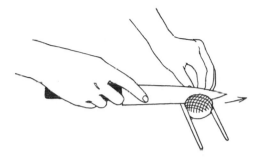

Place the turnips snugly in a wide-mouthed glass jar and pour the cooled sweet-and-sour sauce over them. If you want to add a touch of fire to the turnips, break the chili pepper in half and add both pieces to the sauce (the more seeds you keep, the hotter the final product).

Cover the turnips and let stand at room temperature for at least 2 hours, or refrigerated for a minimum of 8 hours. The pickled turnip flowers can be kept refrigerated for up to 3 months. When you're ready to serve, remove the turnips and gently press out excess sauce. Place each turnip on the open palm of one hand, cut side up. With your other palm flat against the cut surface of the turnip, rotate your hands in opposite directions to twist the "petals" of each "flower" open. In a skillet over medium-high heat, toast the sesame seeds for about 30 seconds. Shake the pan to keep the seeds in motion. Sprinkle the black sesame at the center of the petals to create the illusion of the pistils. If you like, place a *shiso* leaf beneath each flower to aid in the floral fantasy. The leaves should be briefly rinsed under cold water just before serving. Shake off excess moisture.

Note:
If you're able to purchase *aka-jiso* (a purple-leafed herb) pickled in brine, you can make charming pinky-purple flowers with an unusual aromatic nuance. Double the sweet-and-sour-sauce recipe, using half for untinted turnips and half for the dyed ones. Don't add chili peppers to the *aka-jiso* batch. Empty the contents of one package (ten *aka-jiso* leaves) into the sauce. It will take 3–4 days for the full color and aroma to mature.

The Japanese used to use dried gardenia pods (*kuchi nashi no mi*) to dye foods a golden yellow. Nowadays, these are extremely difficult to come by, even in Japan. I've substituted saffron threads on several occasions with interesting results. If you wish to make a tricolor arrangement, use one third of the doubled recipe for each color.

Menu Suggestions: I'm particularly fond of garnishing Glaze-Grilled Salmon Steaks (p. 197) and Sweet and Spicy Grilled Leg of Lamb (p. 211) with white pickled turnips; any color turnip is lovely with the Glazed Chicken Roll (p. 196).

Sweet and Sour Turnip Strips

SENGIRI-ZUKÉ · *Makes 1 cup*

This is a variation on the flower-shaped turnips in the previous recipe; here the vegetable is cut into thin strips. The delightfully piquant, crispy pickle that results is one of the five garnishes in Five-Colored *Sushi* (p. 156). Sweet and Sour Turnip Strips are equally suited to serving as a condiment with roasted or braised entrées such as *Miso*-Marinated Baked Chicken (p. 193).

amazu *(sweet and sour) sauce:*	½ cup rice vinegar
	¼ cup sugar
	¼ teaspoon salt
	2 white turnips, about ½ pound in all
	2 teaspoons salt

In a small glass or enamel-lined saucepan, combine the sweet-and-sour-sauce ingredients and heat them over a low flame, stirring, until the sugar and salt dissolve. Remove from the heat and allow the sauce to cool to room temperature, uncovered.

Peel the turnips and slice them into thin rounds. Stack a few of these at a time and cut them into narrow strips. In a bowl, toss these strips with the salt and let them sit for 5 minutes. With your hands, squeeze the turnip strips, trying to exude as much liquid as possible. The turnip strips should be pliable and limp. Rinse under cold water, then drain well. Fill a glass jar with the turnip strips, then pour the sweet and sour sauce over them.

Allow the turnip strips to marinate for at least 2 hours at room temperature, and up to 2 weeks in the refrigerator. Drain just before serving.

Desserts...

Varied sweets inspired by the traditions of Japan and flavored to suit the American palate, including Moss Pebbles (dark chocolate truffles lightly dusted with sweet green tea), Golden Purses (fabulous dessert crepes filled with almond-scented cream), fruity ices, and crisp gingery cookies

Although in Japan a meal traditionally concludes with the savory taste of pickled vegetables served with rice, the Japanese adore sweets, especially chocolate and elaborately decorated cakes. *Oyatsu*—an unofficial but staunchly observed "snack time" that roughly corresponds to three o'clock in the afternoon—is the occasion for indulging a sweet tooth in Japan. The ancient, but still practiced, tea ceremony provides another opportunity since the ritual includes partaking of exquisite candies and rice-flour and bean-jam pastries.

I've borrowed freely from both traditional and modern Japanese confections to create desserts for the American table. In some I've kept the look of traditional Japanese sweets while tampering with their taste to make them more compatible with American palates. In others I've done just the opposite; taken appealing Japanese flavorings such as *matcha,* the ceremonial green tea, and fresh (not powdered) ginger, and used them to flavor typical American cookies, ice cream, and candies. I've also combined East with West in a variety of fruit-flavored ices, sauces, and gelatin desserts. I've even included a fabulous honey sponge cake that was first introduced to Japan by the Portuguese hundreds of years ago. The varied cross-cultural desserts in this chapter will put a perfect finishing touch on any international meal.

Golden Purses

CHAKIN KURĪMU · Serves 6

This incredible dessert combines the best of both worlds: the graceful beauty of Japanese traditional form and the satisfying richness of Western confections. These elegantly tied, cream-filled pouches could be served at the conclusion of any meal, or as part of a midafternoon tea.

The Japanese technique for flipping thin sheets of omelet is illustrated and described in detail in the *sushi* chapter (pp. 133–134) and the same technique is useful here for making the crepes.

batter:
- ¼ cup all-purpose flour
- 2 tablespoons cornstarch
- ½ teaspoon sugar
- pinch salt
- ⅔ cup whole milk
- 2 large eggs
- 2 yolks from large eggs
- ½ teaspoon almond extract

- 1–2 tablespoons vegetable oil, for preparing pan (almond oil preferred)

filling:
- ½ cup heavy cream
- 1½ tablespoons powdered sugar
- ½ teaspoon almond extract

- 6 black licorice strings, each 18 inches long, for ties
- 2–3 ounces fresh berries, in season, for garnish (optional)

Mix the flour, cornstarch, sugar, and salt in a small bowl. Make a well in the center of this dry mixture and dribble the milk into it. With a fork or chopsticks, whisk in the milk, incorporating a bit of the dry mixture as you go until you have a smooth paste.

Break the eggs in a separate bowl, preferably one that has a spout to make pouring easier later on, and add the two yolks. Remove any opaque squiggles of albumen (these cause unpleasant streaks later), then mix the eggs thoroughly. Let any foam settle before you finish making the batter.

Pour the flour and milk mixture into the eggs in a thin, steady stream, stirring as you go. Add the almond extract and stir to incorporate.

Lightly oil a 6- or 7-inch skillet, or use a pan with a nonstick surface, and heat it over a low flame. Pour in about 3 tablespoons of the batter, tilting and swirling the pan to ensure an even coating. Cook over low heat until the edges begin to dry. Flip the crepe and cook for 5–10 seconds on the other side. Remove the finished crepe to a plate and repeat to make five more, stacking them as you go, shiny side up. Let the crepes cool to room temperature while you prepare the filling.

Whip the cream over ice until soft peaks form. Sprinkle in the powdered sugar and continue to beat until the cream stiffens. Add the almond extract and beat to distribute well.

Assembling the Golden Purses: Take a crepe, shiny side up, and fold it in half, then again into quarters. With a knife or kitchen shears, trim the rounded edge to remove any dry, crusty rim. Open the crepe and place one sixth of the flavored cream in the center. Bring the sides of the crepe up, pleating and gathering until you're able to totally enclose the cream. Take a length of licorice and tie the package with a bow. It's simplest to have a friend in the kitchen assisting in the tying, but if it must be a solo performance, loop the licorice over your pinky on the hand holding the gathers of crepe. Repeat to make five more cream-filled Golden Purses. Add a few fresh berries to the side, if you wish.

Note:
The recipe makes enough batter for one or two spare crepes. It's nice to have an extra just in case one of the others tears or rips. The crepes can be made hours ahead and refrigerated or frozen for up to 1 month. Make sure the crepes return to room temperature and blot off any moisture before using.

Pine Needle Candies

MATSUBA WAGASHI · *Makes about 50*

The Japanese often take culinary inspiration from nature, and pine needles are a popular motif in the fall and winter months. Perhaps you've already made green beans resemble pine needles and scattered them across the savory mushroom and rice dish on p. 224. Here's your chance to follow the theme through to dessert.

These "pine needles" are made from confectioners' sugar and egg white, in much the same way as royal icing. The slight bitterness of the *matcha,* which is the green coloring and flavoring agent, is beautifully balanced by the sugar. The dark tips of the sugar candies are colored and flavored with cocoa.

> 1 **cup confectioners' sugar**
> 1 **white from large egg, at room temperature**
> ⅛ **teaspoon cream of tartar**
> 1 **teaspoon cocoa powder**
> 2 **teaspoons *matcha* (powdered ceremonial green tea)**

Place the sugar, egg white, and cream of tartar in a deep bowl and beat the mixture with a hand-held mixer on low speed until smooth. Raise the speed to high and continue to beat for 3–4 minutes until the mixture becomes thick and very white and holds fairly stiff peaks.

With a rubber spatula, scrape up one quarter of the mixture and transfer it to another, smaller bowl. Sprinkle the cocoa powder over this frosting and stir it in until combined.

Sprinkle the powdered tea over the larger bowl of frosting and beat it in, on low speed, until completely combined.

Cover two cookie sheets with clear plastic wrap. Make two paper cones from cooking parchment; fill one with the green tea mixture and the other with the cocoa mixture. Snip the pointed end from the green tea cones so that the icing pipes out in ⅛-inch strings. Snip the pointed end from the cocoa cone so that the mixture pipes out in $1/16$-inch strings.

With the green tea mixture, pipe out long, narrow V shapes on the clear plastic surface. Pipe out an occasional 4 shape with the crossline extended. Don't crowd the candies. There will be enough icing to pipe out sixty or seventy pieces. The candies become quite brittle when they dry, and breakage occurs; even so, you'll end up with fifty or more delicate and lovely pine-needle sweets.

With the cocoa icing, pipe a few strokes across the spot where the sides of the V merge. This will aid the illusion of pine needle pairs.

Let the candies dry at room temperature for 3 hours or more. They should be stiff when you remove them from the plastic wrap. Gently peel back the wrap and lay the candies on a wire rack for a final hour of drying.

Store the candies on a loosely covered plate at room temperature for up to 24 hours. For longer storage, line a lidded plastic or metal container with paper towels to help prevent breakage and chipping, and carefully place the Pine Needle Candies on the soft lining. The candies will stay fresh for several weeks at room temperature and may be frozen for a month or more. When defrosting the candies, place them uncovered on a rack so that air circulates around all surfaces.

Menu Suggestions: I like to place two or three of the candies at a jaunty angle on a scoop of vanilla ice cream or use them to decorate a frosted cake. Pine Needle Candies make a lovely after-dinner sweet served alone or with Moss Pebbles (p. 293) or Felicity Swirls (p. 292). The sweets look particularly inviting when served on a two-toned folded-paper doily. For folding suggestions, see p. 300.

Pear Ice Cream

YONASHI NO KURĪMU · *Makes about 1½ pints*

Here's a gorgeous, velvety ice cream that captures the rich sweetness of sun-dried fruit. I began my experiments on this dish remembering the intense, luscious flavor of Japanese dried persimmons, which aren't readily available in the United States. Since California dried pears seemed to have a similar richness, particularly when simmered in plum wine, I decided to make use of them. I think this Pear Ice Cream stands well on its own or as an ending to any meal.

10–12 **ounces dried pears (choose soft, chewy ones and trim away any tough fibers or seeds)**
4 **cups water**
3 **tablespoons** *umé shu* **(Japanese plum wine)**
1 **teaspoon lemon juice**
2 **cups light cream**

In a noncorrodible saucepan combine the dried pears, water, and plum wine. Over medium heat, bring the mixture to a boil, then adjust to maintain a steady simmer.

Add the lemon juice and continue to cook for 10 minutes; the fruit will plump but pale considerably around the edges.

Puree the mixture until completely smooth, in a food processor fitted with the steel blade. Pour the pureed pear mixture into two metal ice-cube trays (with the dividers removed) and cover the surface with clear plastic wrap. Freeze until quite firm. Empty the pear slush into your food processor with the cream and pulse-process until thick and smooth. Return the mixture to the metal trays, cover again with clear plastic wrap, and freeze until solid. If you have an ice-cream maker, add the cream to the pureed pear mixture from the start and blend thoroughly. Place the pear and cream mixture in your machine and freeze according to the manufacturer's instructions for any fruit puree.

To serve, scoop out the ice cream into chilled glass or ceramic bowls. If the ice cream seems too stiff to scoop easily, let it rest in the refrigerator for 10–15 minutes first.

Green Tea Ice Cream

MATCHA KURĪMU · Makes 1 pint

This dessert appears on nearly every Japanese restaurant menu in the United States; it seems to be what most Americans have come to expect at the conclusion of their Japanese meal. Although I have many recipes in this book for East-West desserts that are far more unusual, I feel it's only proper to include my version of this newborn classic since it tastes so good and is so simple to make, especially if you have an electric ice-cream maker. I think it makes a wonderful end to just about any meal.

⅓ cup sugar
⅓ cup water
½ teaspoon *mirin* (syrupy rice wine)
2 teaspoons *matcha* (powdered ceremonial green tea)
½ cup whole milk
½ cup half-and-half

In a small saucepan, combine the sugar and the water and, over low heat, stirring, melt the sugar. Continue to simmer the syrup for 5 minutes. Stir in the syrupy rice wine and remove the saucepan from the heat. Take 1 tablespoon of this mixture to dissolve the powdered tea thoroughly, then return this concentrate to the saucepan and stir to mix evenly.

Stir in the milk and half-and-half. Pour this mixture into an electric ice-cream maker and allow it to chill and churn for 10 minutes. The final ice cream should be silky and smooth, not too hard.

If you're using freezer trays, fill them two-thirds full and freeze for 1–2 hours, or until nearly firm. Whip the mixture vigorously before refreezing firmly.

Kumquat Sauce

KINKAN NO KANRO SŌSU · Makes about 1 quart

Kumquats, stewed whole in heavy syrup after the pits have been painstakingly removed, are a traditional Japanese New Year's delicacy. The following recipe is an adaptation that I worked out after my daughter Rena, who was only three years old at the time, mangled most of the kumquats one day while "assisting" me in removing the pits. Wanting to salvage the bruised fruit (and her ego), I stirred some pectin in. The resulting sauce was heavenly, and every winter since, when the bright orange fruit has come to market, we've made a batch of kumquat sauce. I highly recommend it spooned lavishly over vanilla ice cream, or stirred into plain yogurt. It's also luscious when poured over custard pudding.

¾ pound fresh kumquats
2 cups water
1½ tablespoons *saké* (Japanese rice wine)
2 tablespoons lemon juice
1½ cups sugar
1 pouch liquid pectin

Wash the kumquats well, removing any leaves or stems in the process. Slice each kumquat in half and, with the aid of a toothpick, discard the seeds. Place the kumquats in a food processor fitted with the steel blade and pulse-process once or twice to chop the fruit coarsely.

Place the chopped kumquats in a deep, sturdy pot. Add the cold water and rice wine, and bring to a boil over high heat. Lower the heat to maintain a steady simmer, cooking the fruit for 2 minutes. Add the lemon juice and then half the sugar, stirring well to dissolve. Add the remaining sugar and continue to cook the mixture for 2 more minutes.

Bring the fruit mixture to a rolling boil and add the pectin. Stir well but maintain a hard boil. Cook, stirring occasionally, for 3 minutes. Remove the pot from the heat and, for long-term storage, ladle the sauce immediately into sterilized glass jars. Or, for more immediate use, pour the sauce into a heat-proof container and let it cool to room temperature before covering. Chill the sauce for at least 1 hour before serving with ice cream or yogurt.

Cantaloupe Sherbet

MERON MIZORÉ · Makes about 2 pints

This is a most refreshing, intensely fruity dessert that's light enough to serve at the end of even a heavy meal. In Japan, since melons of all kinds are very costly, this dish might be thought of as a bit extravagant. Here in the United States, where cantaloupes are available year-round at fairly reasonable prices, we can "indulge" ourselves regularly!

1 large, lushly ripe cantaloupe, about 20 ounces peeled and seeded
1½ tablespoons lemon juice
3 tablespoons *mirin* (syrupy rice wine)
3 tablespoons sugar syrup (see Note below)
2 tablespoons light cream (optional)

Cut the melon into 2-inch chunks and pulse-process in a food processor fitted with the steel blade until smooth. Add the lemon juice, syrupy rice wine, and sugar syrup and continue to process until the mixture is totally pureed and very smooth.

If you wish to make your ice a bit richer and silkier, include the optional light cream. Add it to the pureed mixture now if you'll be using an automatic ice-cream maker. If you'll be making the sherbet with a food processor only, wait.

Place the melon, or melon and cream mixture, in the bowl of an automatic ice-cream maker and proceed according to the manufacturer's instructions for any fruit puree. Or pour the fruit puree into two or three metal ice-cube trays (with the dividers removed), press clear plastic wrap across the surface, and freeze until nearly solid. Return the melon slush to the bowl of your food processor and pulse-process until smooth. Now is the appropriate time to add some cream, if you wish. Pulse-process to ensure thorough mixing. Refreeze the melon ice, covered with clear plastic wrap, for at least 2 hours, or until very firm.

If the sherbet seems too stiff to scoop easily, place it in the refrigerator for 10–15 minutes. At the same time, chill your serving bowls or goblets.

Note:
To make a sugar syrup, combine equal quantities of sugar and water in a small noncorrodible saucepan and cook, stirring, until the sugar melts. Continue to simmer the sugar for 5–8 minutes, or until slightly sticky. Allow the syrup to cool completely before using or storing away.

Since unused syrup will keep for months in a closed glass jar in the refrigerator, I suggest you make at least ½ cup of syrup with ½ cup each of sugar and water.

Honey Sponge Cake

KASUTERA · *Makes 18 pieces*

The Portuguese who lived in Nagasaki about 400 years ago made a honey cake very similar to this one. The Japanese were quite taken with it and developed their own version of the cake, without any butter. It has become a Japanese classic, taught in cooking classes devoted to traditional Japanese sweets, and is served with native green teas as well as with "foreign" black teas or coffee.

The generous amount of honey makes a moist cake with a rich, dark surface on both top and bottom, while the concentration of egg yolks makes the cake a deep yellow color.

I've included an optional fresh ginger icing for the cake, which I think transforms this classic into a tantalizing new dessert.

    4 large eggs, at room temperature
    3 yolks from large eggs, at room temperature
    ⅔ cup sugar
    ¼ cup honey
    1½ cups sifted self-rising cake flour
      vegetable oil and several tablespoons cake
      flour, for preparing baking pan (optional)

Preheat the oven to 400 degrees.

Beat the eggs and yolks with an electric mixer on medium speed until thick and creamy. Gradually add the sugar, beating all the while. Continue to beat at medium speed until the mixture is very thick, pale, and at least triple the volume of the original beaten eggs. Dribble the honey into the egg and sugar mixture, beating all the while.

Add the flour in two or three batches, folding to incorporate it into the batter.

Use a nonstick-surface 9-inch-square baking pan, or prepare your baking pan by greasing it lightly. Place a 9-inch-square piece of cooking parchment on the bottom of the pan and grease this as well. Lightly flour the lined pan.

Pour the batter into the prepared pan and gently tap on a flat surface to ensure removal of large air bubbles.

Bake the cake in the preheated oven for 25–30 minutes. The top surface will change to a rich burnished brown, and a skewer inserted into the middle will come out clean. (The cake looks best when smooth and flat on top. A fairly new product on the market, silver-colored asbestos quilted strips that encircle a baking pan, do a fine job of distributing heat and thus evening off any bumps or wrinkles on the surface. The reusable strips need to be dampened in cold water before being snugly fitted and pinned around the outside of the pan.)

Allow the cake to cool completely in the pan before removing it to a serving platter. Cut the cake into thirds, then across into 1½-inch pieces, for a total of eighteen. Peel off the bottom parchment as necessary. Serve one or two pieces per person.

OPTIONAL FRESH GINGER ICING:

¼ teaspoon cream of tartar

1 cup confectioner's sugar

1½ teaspoons ginger juice (extracted from
freshly grated ginger)

In a bowl combine the ingredients listed above and stir until completely smooth. Immediately pour the icing over the cake and let it air dry for 30 minutes or until the icing is no longer shiny. Cover the cake with plastic wrap if you're not going to serve it right away.

When I plan on icing my honey cake, I bake the cake in a nonstick 8-cup capacity *Bundt* tube pan. I place the baked and cooled cake on a rack over a plate and pour the icing over the entire top ridge. The icing forms a natural icicle pattern as it trickles down the sides, contrasting beautifully with the dark, smooth surface of the cake.

Fresh Ginger Cookies

SHŌGA NO KUKKĪ · *Makes 3 dozen*

This is a cookie that goes well with the melon sherbet and ice creams in this chapter, or for that matter with any frozen dessert. The assertive ginger flavor is typical of many Japanese dishes, though this cookie is also a little reminiscent of the Austrian *Linzer torte.*

½ cup unsalted butter, at room temperature

½ cup (about 4 ounces) packed brown sugar

½ cup (about 4 ounces) granulated white
sugar

1 cup ground almonds (can be prepared in a
food processor from about 8 ounces whole
or slivered nuts)

1 egg, lightly beaten

3 tablespoons ginger juice (extracted from
   freshly grated ginger)
1½ cups sifted all-purpose flour
1 teaspoon baking powder
½ teaspoon powdered cinnamon
1 teaspoon grated lemon rind

Preheat your oven to 375 degrees.

Cream the butter and sugars together until well combined and fluffy. (The Japanese traditional *suribachi* mortar happens to do a fabulous job of creaming untraditional materials such as butter and granulated sugar. Of course a blender, whisk, or even fork can perform the task simply enough.) Gradually beat in the ground nuts, then the egg and the ginger juice.

In a bowl, sift together the flour, baking powder, and cinnamon. Sprinkle this mixture over the butter and egg mixture, and beat to incorporate completely. Add the grated lemon rind and beat to combine.

Drop the cookie mixture by spoonfuls onto a parchment-lined cookie sheet. Bake the cookies for 10–12 minutes; they'll be nicely colored and still slightly soft to the touch. Let the cookies cool slightly before removing to a rack to complete the cooling. The cookies will stiffen considerably as they cool.

Store extra cookies in an airtight jar or tin for several weeks, or freeze for up to 1 month.

Green Tea Cookies

MATCHA NO KUKKI · *Makes about 30 cookies*

I've adapted a classic American refrigerator-type cookie to accommodate a traditional Japanese ingredient—powdered ceremonial tea. Instructions are given here for making elegant two-toned leaves and some swirls with the leftover dough. You might want to play around with the dough to make more distinctive or exotic designs of your own. No cookie, though, should be so large or so thick that it takes more than 15–20 minutes to bake in a preheated 300-degree oven, since the jade-colored tea powder becomes bitter and turns an unattractive olive shade when exposed to high heat, or even low heat, for an extended period of time.

> 1 stick sweet (unsalted) butter, at room temperature
> ⅓ cup sugar
> 1 large egg, beaten
> ½ teaspoon almond extract
> 1½ cups sifted all-purpose flour, plus 2–3 tablespoons for board
> 1½ teaspoons *matcha* (powdered ceremonial green tea)
> 1–1½ teaspoons cold water

Cream the butter in a bowl until light and fluffy. Gradually add the sugar and continue to cream the mixture for about 1 minute until all the sugar is completely incorporated. Reserve 1 tablespoon of beaten egg for later use and add the rest of the beaten egg to the creamed mixture. Add ½ teaspoon of almond extract, too. Beat in the egg and extract thoroughly.

Blend in the 1½ cups of flour, ¼ cup at a time, mixing well after each addition. The dough might be a bit crumbly, but when you exert gentle pressure on it, it will easily form a ball. Divide the mass into two equal balls.

In a small dish, mix the powdered tea with the cold water, a few drops at a time. Stir to make a thick, dark paste. Add this paste to one of the two balls of dough and knead it in thoroughly. Shape the green dough into a ball again. On a lightly floured surface, use your hands to flatten and pat the dough, coaxing it into a small rectangle 3½ by 4½ inches, and about 1 inch thick. Lay this rectangle on a piece of clear plastic wrap. Shape the plain dough in the same manner into an identical size.

Brush the surface of the green dough with the reserved beaten egg.

Place the white dough on top and gently press the two together. Wrap the double dough in the clear plastic wrap and chill it for at least 1 hour. The dough may be frozen after sealing it (allow this dough to return to room temperature before cutting and baking), or sealed and refrigerated for up to 5 days.

Preheat your oven to 300 degrees. Unwrap the double dough and slice it into ¼-inch strips, crosswise. Each of these should be placed on its side so that both green and white dough is visible; one color to the right, the other to the left. With a lightly floured 3-inch banquette

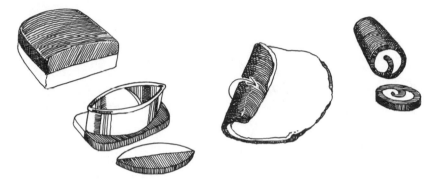

cutter, cut out "leaves" from each strip of two-toned dough. Gather up and set aside the surrounding dough, keeping separate piles for white and green; this excess dough will be reshaped. With a broad, lightly floured spatula, transfer the cut "leaves" to a foil-lined baking sheet.

Bake the leaves for 10–12 minutes, checking progress after 8 minutes. If the cookies seem to be browning, lower the heat in your oven. The cookies are done when they're firm, but uncolored. Remove the cookies to a wire rack and let them cool completely before serving.

While baking and cooling the leaf-shaped cookies, reshape the excess dough. On a lightly floured surface, roll out the white dough, then the green, keeping them the same size and no thicker than ¼ inch. Brush the surface of the green dough with some beaten egg, then lay the white dough on top. Roll them up snugly, jelly roll fashion. Wrap this roll in clear plastic wrap and chill it for at least 10 minutes. Unwrap the dough; cut the roll into about a dozen thin slices, each with a spiral design. Transfer these to a foil-lined baking sheet and bake at 300 degrees for 8–10 minutes. If the cookies seem to be coloring after 5 minutes, lower the oven temperature. Bake for a few more minutes, until the cookies are firm. Remove the cookies to a rack and let them cool before serving or storing them in a covered container. The cookies stay fresh for 2–3 days at room temperature; for longer storage, I recommend refrigeration.

Menu Suggestions: These East-West cookies are wonderful served with frozen desserts such as Cantaloupe Sherbet (p. 281) or Pear Ice Cream (p. 278). Green Tea Cookies are great with coffee, tea, or milk, too.

Jellied Orange Wedges

ORENJI KAN · Makes 24 wedges to serve 8–12

The Japanese have long known of the natural gelling properties of certain sea vegetables and have been making marvelous aspics and gelatins for centuries. Here a fruit that's relatively new to Japan, the navel orange, makes a lovely self-contained presentation. The final cut wedges of gelatin visually defy the laws of gravity!

> 2 sticks *kanten* (Japanese gelatin; agar)
> 6 large, thick-skinned, unblemished navel oranges
> 1–2 cups freshly squeezed OR pure pasteurized orange juice
> 3 tablespoons sugar

Tear the dry gelatin sticks into several pieces and soak in a bowl of cold water to cover for 15 minutes.

Meanwhile, cut the oranges in half through the stems. Carefully scoop out the insides. (You can start with a grapefruit knife or spoon, but the job is best done with fingers, peeling and tugging gently.) Do your scooping over a bowl to catch any juice. You should have completely smooth, white-lined cups of orange peel when you've finished.

Wrap the orange pulp in cheesecloth or muslin and squeeze to extract the juice. Add enough additional orange juice to make a total of 4 cups.

Squeeze the softened gelatin as you remove it from the water. The gelatin will now be very spongy and will shred easily. Shred the softened gelatin into an enamel-lined or glass saucepan with 2 cups of the orange juice. To save every bit of *kanten* gelatin, strain the soaking water through a fine-meshed sieve and add any salvaged bits to the saucepan. Add the sugar and cook the mixture for 5 minutes over low heat. Stir frequently until the gelatin melts. Simmer an additional 3–4 minutes before adding the remaining 2 cups of orange juice. Stir to mix evenly.

Arrange the orange shells on a large tray or fit them in a roasting pan so they don't rock back and forth. Fill the shells nearly to the top with the orange juice mixture. Lance any large bubbles with a toothpick; gently remove any foam from the surface with a bit of paper toweling. Let the gelatin cool at room temperature until it begins to set (about 30 minutes). Refrigerate, covered, for at least 2 hours and up to 24.

Before serving, cut each orange shell in half. Trim the shells so that the surface of the gelatin is flush with the edges of the orange skin. Serve two or three wedges per person. To eat, peel back the skin.

Honeydew Gelatin

MIDORI KAN · Makes 12 pieces to serve 4–6

This jellied fruit dish is served in small pieces as an extravagant palate cleanser in its native Japan, where melons are very costly. Here it might well be a light dessert to conclude any meal.

>   1 stick *kanten* (Japanese gelatin; agar)
>   1 exceedingly ripe honeydew melon, about
>   1½ pounds
>   ⅓ cup melon-flavored liqueur

Tear the dried gelatin stick into several pieces and soak in a bowl of cold water to cover for 15 minutes.

Meanwhile, peel and seed the melon, then cut into 2-inch chunks. Place these in a food processor fitted with the steel blade, and puree. Force the puree through a mesh strainer and measure the resulting liquid; there should be 1½ cups. Add water, if necessary, to make up the difference.

Squeeze the softened gelatin as you remove it from the water the gelatin will now be very spongy and will shred easily. Shred the softened gelatin into a glass or enamel-lined saucepan. To save every bit of *kanten* gelatin, strain the soaking water through a fine-meshed sieve and add any salvaged bits to the saucepan. Add the melon liquid and the liqueur, then cook the mixture for 5 minutes over low heat. Stir frequently until the gelatin melts.

Pour the liquid fruit gelatin into a smooth-sided glass or metal mold. Lance any larger bubbles with a toothpick and gently blot away foam from the surface with a strip of paper toweling. Let the gelatin cool to room temperature (and begin to solidify) before covering with clear plastic wrap. Chill for at least 2 hours and up to 24 in the refrigerator.

When ready to unmold, press gently on the surface of the gelatin near the rim to help release the edges. Place a plate, or cutting board, over the mold and invert. Cut the gelatin into twelve pieces.

Note:
The liquid gelatin can be poured into a small pan to a depth of ½ inch, unmolded as a sheet, and then cut into decorative shapes with cookie cutters. The final shapes can be carefully transferred to the serving platter with a broad spatula. Or the sheet can be cut into diamond shapes and transferred in the same manner.

Hawaiian Gelatin

HAWAI KAN · *Makes 6 servings*

*H*ere's another recipe that calls for *kanten,* a gelatin extracted from sea vegetation. I knew from previous kitchen experience with *kanten* that the chemistry of this substance was very different from that of ordinary gelatin, and when I was in Hawaii I decided to try it with fresh pineapple. It gelled! Another advantage of *kanten* over Western gelling powders is its ability to gel at room temperature. Although most fruit-flavored gelatins taste best when chilled, *kanten* doesn't have to be refrigerated to get it to gel. This means that dishes made with it won't "weep" when removed from the refrigerator, either. *Kanten* unmolds easily from any smooth-sided container, but here I've made use of crinkly foil muffin liners to add an interesting textural effect.

> 1 stick *kanten* (Japanese gelatin; agar)
> 1 cup cold water
> ¼ cup sugar
> 1½–1¾ cups pureed fresh pineapple (about ½ pineapple, peeled and trimmed)

Tear the dried gelatin stick into several pieces and soak in a bowl of water to cover for 15 minutes.

In a small saucepan, combine the cup of cold water with the sugar. Stirring, heat the mixture until the sugar melts completely.

Squeeze the softened gelatin as you remove it from the water. The gelatin will now be very spongy and will shred easily. Add the shreds to the sugar syrup. To save every bit of *kanten* gelatin, strain the soaking water through a fine-meshed sieve and add any salvaged bits to the sugar syrup. Cook the gelatin mixture for 5 minutes over low heat, stirring, to melt the gelatin thoroughly.

Remove from the heat and stir in the pureed pineapple. Line six muffin tins with foil liners and pour the pineapple mixture into the foil cups. Lance any large bubbles that appear on the surface. Allow the gelatin to stand at room temperature until cool and solidified (about ½ hour).

Chill the gelatin for at least 2 hours and up to 2 days. When ready to serve, remove the foil liners from the cups and invert each on a serving plate. Peel the foil away.

Felicity Swirls

KŌHAKU UZUMAKI · *Makes 18 pieces*

*H*ere's a marzipan and candied-ginger sweet that borrows its shape from a typical Japanese yam-paste-and-rice-flour pastry. The pink-and-white color scheme indicates felicity in Japan and confections of this sort would be served in conjunction with some celebration. I suggest you enjoy them at the conclusion of any festive meal. They look particularly pretty when paired with Moss Pebble truffles (p. 293) or Pine Needle Candies (p. 276).

> 7 ounces marzipan OR almond paste
> 3–4 tablespoons confectioners' sugar
> 2–3 drops red food coloring
> ½ tablespoon light corn syrup
> 1 ounce candied ginger, cut in long slivers

Divide the marzipan and work each half with 1 tablespoon of confectioners' sugar. The marzipan should be flexible but not sticky. Set one half aside and color the other with a few drops of red food coloring. Carefully knead this half into a smooth, rosy mass. If necessary, use a bit more confectioners' sugar to keep the marzipan from sticking to your hands, board, or bowl.

Lightly dust your board and pin with confectioners' sugar and roll out the uncolored marzipan in a rectangular shape approximately 3½ by 15 inches. Ideally the marzipan will be no thicker than ⅛ inch. Cut this piece into three strips, each about 5 inches long.

Now roll out the pink marzipan in the same manner.

Take one strip of pink and brush the top surface lightly with corn syrup. Lay an uncolored strip over it, matching up length and width so the edges are flush. With your brush dipped in corn syrup, lightly dab the top surface of the uncolored marzipan. Take about one third of the candied ginger slivers and lay them, right to left, across the width of the uncolored marzipan in a single layer. Starting with the edge closest to yourself, snugly roll the layers enclosing the ginger. Gently press the sides of the roll as you go to make these flush. Lay the roll seam side down, and repeat with the remaining materials to make two more rolls. If you're serving these sweets alone, make one of the three rolls with the colors reversed, to add more visual excitement. If you plan to serve these with Moss Pebble truffles or Pine Needle Candies, it's best to make them all as described above. Cover the rolls with plastic wrap and chill for at least 30 minutes and up to 2 days in the refrigerator.

Just before serving, slice each roll into six pieces. Stack them with the swirl pattern facing up, or arrange them standing (seam down) in diagonal rows.

Moss Pebbles

KOISHI MODOKI · Makes 30

In this recipe I've taken the shape of a popular Japanese sugar-coated bean confection and made it over in chocolate to appeal more to American tastes. This East-West sweet is best served with coffee or tea after a simple dessert of fresh fruit. Serve these cross-cultural chocolate truffles alone or paired with either Felicity Swirls (p. 292) or Pine Needle Candies (p. 276).

I'm indebted to my chocolate-adoring colleague Lori Longbotham for the glorious truffle-mixture recipe.

truffle mixture:	¼ pound bittersweet chocolate
	1 tablespoon sugar
	¼ cup heavy cream
	1 tablespoon sweet butter, at room temperature
dusting mixture:	3 tablespoons powdered sugar
	1 tablespoon *matcha* (powdered ceremonial green tea)

Break the chocolate into pieces, then chop it fine using the steel blade of your food processor. Transfer the chocolate to the top of a double boiler and melt it over simmering water. Stir gently.

In a small saucepan, mix the sugar and cream together. Scald this mixture.

Stir the scalded cream and softened butter into the melted chocolate. Stir to combine well, then allow the mixture to cool to room temperature. With an electric mixer, beat the mixture until it resembles buttercream. Cover and chill thoroughly. (You can even freeze it if you like.)

With a small spoon (or a large melon baller), scoop out thirty portions of the truffle mixture. Roll these in 1 tablespoon of powdered sugar and chill until ready to serve.

Combine 2 tablespoons of powdered sugar with the powdered green tea. Using half of this mixture, roll the truffles again. Place them on a tray and sift the remaining tea-and-sugar mixture over them. Ideally the shapes should be slightly rough, like pebbles, with a dusting of "moss."

Setting the Cross-Cultural Table...

*I*deas on how to set your table, including a discussion of thematic motifs from nature, suggestions on choosing plates and bowls, diagrams for making intriguing napkin folds and decorative ribbon ties

In Japan you might begin a meal with luminous slices of tuna served on a gently sloped mound of shaved ice, then be offered a landscaped arrangement of carved vegetables taking its cue from the season and served on a smooth but patterned porcelain dish. At the same meal, glaze-grilled salmon might be brought to you on a roughhewn slab of reddish-brown clay, while ornate but edible tidbits float in a delicate broth served in an elegant lacquer bowl, the pattern of which is discernible through the clear soup. Japanese tabletop artistry depends upon the interplay of shape, color, and texture of food and plate. Typically, each food is presented on a different surface, one that suits the particular food being served at that time and on that occasion. Traditionally there are no cloths, placemats, or napkins on the table in Japan, and utensils are limited to chopsticks only.

In contrast to this, Americans love to set their tables with starched linen and lace cloths, uniformly designed china and crystal, and at least three pieces of gleaming flatware: knife, fork, and spoon. For grand occasions, American tables are further adorned with festive flowers and perhaps candles.

Comparing the table presentations of the two cultures, I've often noted a curious culinary paradox: Although we tend to think of the Japanese as copiers and conformists rather than innovators and individualists, the tremendous diversity evident in Japanese food preparation and presentation belies that stereotype. It's the Western host or hostess, wanting to set an impressive table, who tends to rely upon constancy of pattern, color, and shape throughout the meal. In Japan, the plentiful number of courses, each garnished and served in accordance with its own theme, is one indication of the care given to the orchestration of the meal. Gastronomic harmony in Japan is achieved through a medley of tastes and visual effects, syncopating the tempo of food with plate. The American table is set like a metronome, in rhythmic unison, with each course from soup to dessert a mellow refrain.

Since outwardly, at least, the Japanese and American tables appear to be different, I've pondered the problems of setting an appropriate scene for cross-cultural fare. Although the table should hint of the Oriental overtones of the food to come, certain American tabletop conventions seemed important to retain—napkins for one, and the option of flatware for another. I feel that a single, large arrangement of flowers in the center of the table inhibits conversation and, since many floral motifs are used in garnishing the food itself, a central bouquet would be redundant. The Japanese shun flowers and plants on the table because of competing scents; the aroma of the food should be paramount while eating. An arrangement of branches or buds elsewhere in your home would be welcome, though, and you might wish to carry through whatever floral theme or color scheme you began at your table.

I looked to other Japanese arts and crafts to supply appropriate objects and themes to decorate the cross-cultural table. I found *origami,* the art of folding paper, applicable to cloth napkins, too. Japanese folded papers can also become trays, plates, or doilies on which to serve food. I've borrowed and adapted a few tying techniques from the Japanese art of *kumi himo* to create simple but unusual ribbon napkin rings.

Antique Japanese pottery and lacquerware, although exquisite, is too inaccessible and not necessarily appropriate for most modern American homes. Contemporary American craftspeople—potters, glassblowers, woodworkers, lacquerers, and textile designers—are creating stunning containers and surfaces for the serving of food. Although many of the craftspeople working in the United States today have been captivated and motivated by Japanese prototypes—the motifs, techniques, and technologies of classical Japan—their work remains American. For the photographs in this book, I chose to use baskets, plates, bowls, boxes, and dishes made by such contemporary artists living in America.

Look through your own collection of dishes and bowls; if you have solid-colored, unpatterned dinner plates, they'll be wonderful for serving elaborately garnished food or arranging several kinds of ornate fingerfoods together. Dark colors, even black, add a sense of drama to the presentation of many recipes, particularly if the food is yellow or green, though white, red, or brown looks sophisticated on a black background, too. Try juxtaposing textures as the Japanese do; serve sleek foods, like glazed steaks or roasts, on rustic pottery surfaces, while presenting ruffly, leafy lettuce or shredded vegetables on glassy-smooth plates. Experiment with mixing patterns and colors in your tableware, too. Try using a bright, solid-colored plate for a first course of geometrically arranged appetizers, followed by a gold-rimmed dinner plate with a meat or poultry entrée, and a few vegetable side dishes. You might finish with pastel porcelain cups and saucers for serving coffee, with dessert placed on dramatically folded papers. The cross-cultural cuisine in this cookbook is varied and ideally your table setting should reflect and enhance this diversity.

Just as Americans share specific associations with certain color schemes and motifs—orange pumpkins and black cats signify Halloween, while red hearts mean Valentine's Day—so the Japanese, too, have ornamental elements and colors that convey certain moods and seasons to them. Most Japanese culinary motifs derive from natural sources and are meant to enhance your meal by echoing the world of nature beyond your plate: Pink and white cherry blossoms mean spring; red maple leaves mean fall. There are also motifs and color schemes that convey felicitous feelings in Japan—the opened fan shape is one; the crane and tortoise are others. Often the complex shape of the original object is greatly streamlined and stylized, the tortoise becoming a hexagonal form (taken from the pattern of the shell) and the crane a series of isosceles triangles (evocative of the angle of neck and wing). Tied knots are auspicious in business and society in general, since they symbolize a relationship or commitment binding two parties. Red and white are the colors of felicity and festivity in Japan. Black, far from being funereal, is the color of formality, particularly when accented by gold and silver or red.

In the hope of inspiring you to include some Japanese themes at your table, I've included sketches of some of the more basic and recurring Japanese culinary motifs from nature.

The cherry blossom is the national symbol of Japan; the emphemeral flower symbolizes the fleeting quality of life. The pale-pink and

white petals are tossed everywhere by spring breezes early in April. The Japanese take flower viewing very seriously, and bring box lunches to eat while sitting beneath the blooming trees. The slightly indented, dimpled petal looks a bit like a heart shape to most Westerners; to the Japanese it's unmistakably a sign of spring.

Later, in the early summer, pale-lavender wisteria blossoms drooping from their trellised vines evoke a romantic mood.

The summer months in Japan get very warm and water, with its cooling properties, becomes a major culinary theme. Cold noodles are served on ice in bowls, or swirled on flat plates to resemble rivers and streams. Other malleable foods are coaxed into wave shapes, too.

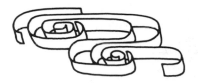

The autumn has many culinary motifs from nature associated with it, but the most frequently encountered are carrots cut to resemble maple leaves, and various vegetables and sweets shaped to look like pine needles or chrysanthemums. Since a stylized version of the flower

with sixteen petals is the emblem of the imperial family, it's reserved for official use only. Chrysanthemum motifs for culinary purposes must have fewer, or more, petals.

Two flowers blooming in the winter months that the Japanese are particularly fond of are the camellia and the plum blossom. Both red and white blossoms are common to both flowers and, since these col-

ors are considered auspicious ones in Japan, the camellia and plum blossom inspire *sushi* chefs and confectioners alike to make all sorts of tasty, festive foods. Carrots and *daikon* radishes typically get carved into plum blossoms from New Year's through March.

I've included some diagrams to help you fold paper and cloth, and tie ribbons to decorate your cross-cultural table.

The simplest of all is a "double mountain" effected from a single square sheet of paper folded slightly on the diagonal. An interesting

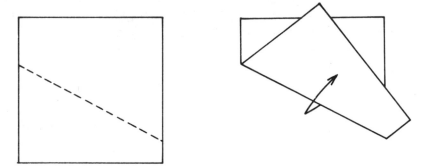

Fold once to form a double mountain; place the longest edge parallel to the table edge and closest to the diner.

variation is made possible by using two sheets of paper in contrasting colors. A small, 3- or 4-inch square makes a fine doily for a few cookies (such as those on pp. 284 or 285) or sweets (pp. 276, 292, or 293); a larger, 7- or 8-inch square makes a handsome liner for a dinner plate on which fried foods are to be placed. Gingery crabs (p. 177), fried oysters (p. 98), or noodle-coated shrimp (p. 93) look particularly lovely set against double-mountain papers. Fried foods should be well drained of excess oil before being transferred to the folded sheets. Specially coated paper is sold at many Oriental groceries (ask for *shiki shi*), though ordinary construction or writing paper is fine. If you plan to serve fried foods very hot, or sticky sweets, it's probably best to keep a plain white surface on top.

Still another variation on the double-mountain theme is possible by making an additional fold that creates a sheath to hold a small fork,

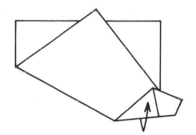

Fold the right-hand corner once to form a sheath.

spoon, or decorative pick (the Japanese use flat but pointed bamboo spears to eat some of their more traditional sweets). The sponge cake on p. 282 could be served on a folded paper such as this, with a dessert fork in the sheath. Using two sheets of different colors make these sheath-and-doily sheets look even more spectacular.

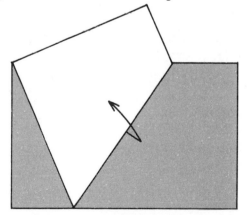

Fold the rectangle once to form a pentagon; place the longest edge parallel to the table edge and closest to the diner.

This next fold lends an interesting effect to ordinary rectangular cloth placemats, particularly those that are reversible and can create a two-toned appearance. This pentagon shape can also be made from two sheets of paper—perhaps one solid-color and one patterned sheet—folded together. The sweets shown on the third page of the color insert rest against red and white paper folded like this.

The next two sheaths can hold either chopsticks or flatware and can be fashioned from either paper or cloth. The simplest is the diagonal fold sheath; a slightly more complicated version is the pleated sheath.

DIAGONAL FOLD SHEATH

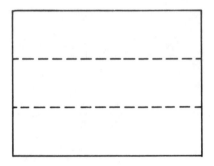

For a diagonal fold sheath, fold the rectangle lengthwise in thirds. Open up to display the creases.

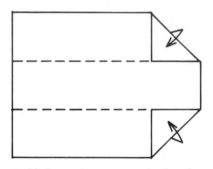

Fold down the upper right-hand corner; fold up the lower right-hand corner.

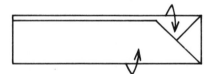

Fold again in thirds.

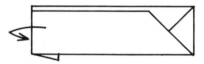

Flip the left-hand end under and fold. Tie with a decorative knot (optional).

THE PLEATED SHEATH

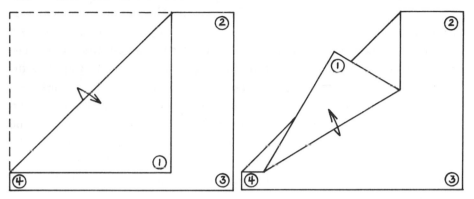

For a pleated sheath, begin with a rectangle. Fold down corner 1. Fold corner 1 back on itself.

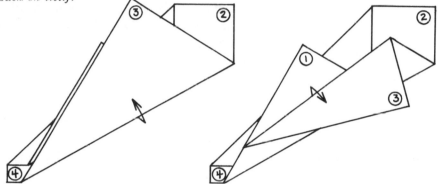

Bring corner 3 up and crease. Fold corner 3 back on itself.

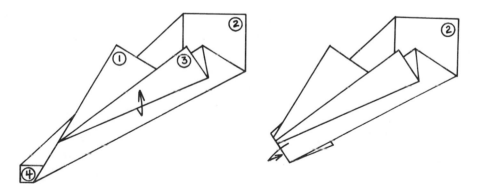

Bring corner 3 up again to pleat. Flip corner 4 under and fold. Tie with a decorative knot (optional).

These sheaths make neat, attractive packages at a buffet table, eliminating the juggling of many utensils at once. The sheaths also make an elegant, decorative contribution to a formal sit-down meal. A sheath made of paper can double as a placecard with your guest's name written on it (a simply folded napkin could rest beneath the paper sheath). In Japan, the eating ends of the chopsticks always point to the left, are aligned in parallel, and are placed down front from your plate or tray. For flatware, I think it might be best to have the eating end (i.e., the tines of the fork, the bowl of the spoon, and the blade of the knife) sticking out of your sheaths and pointing away from the diner. Your sheaths can be folded to lie flat, or tied with any of the beguiling ties below:

The two-toned loop shown here is a popular tie and fairly simple to execute. The Japanese always weave the ribbons so that the dark color is on the right side of the final presentation. There are two ways of completing this tie: one with "ears" that point up, called a flared loop; and one without "ears," a flat loop with the ribbons pulled to the back and knotted out of view. It's simplest to use thick, metallic twine or velvet rope; the textured surface keeps the finished knots from slipping out. Once you're used to the basic weaving technique, try four or five thinner strands taken together at one time. The traditional material used in Japan to make this and other ties is called *mizu hiki*, a covered cotton twine with amazing flexibility and strength. *Mizu hiki* is neither available here nor is it necessary. Go to a well-stocked notions store and see what ribbons, ropes, and other ties they have; experiment with a variety of materials.

FLARED LOOP TIE WITH EARS

For a flared loop, a single strand of light ribbon on the right is linked to a single strand of dark ribbon on the left. Both light and dark ribbons become double strands.

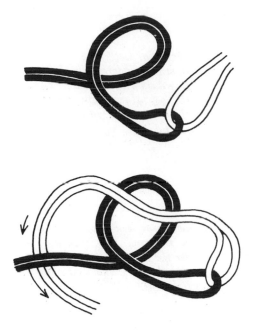

Make a loop with the dark-colored double strands and lay it flat on your working surface.

Lay the double strands of light ribbon over the dark loop, then weave them under the dark strands on the left.

Continue to weave with the double light strands: over, then under the dark ribbons, and then over the light and under the dark ones.

The completed knot, viewed from the rear.

FLAT LOOP TIE

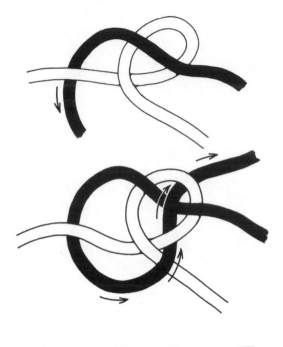

For a flat loop, make a loop from light-colored ribbon. Lay dark ribbon on top of the loop, then weave it under the left-hand light-colored strand.

Continue to weave with this dark strand: over, then under the light ribbons, then over the dark and under the light one.

Pull the knot snug; tie the light and dark strands together behind your napkin or sheath.

The wisteria cluster knot is similar to our square knot. It looks most like its namesake when made from two tones of mauve, though it's attractive in contrasting colors of a bolder nature, too. This knot is often used to tie the top strings of an *obi,* particularly on a young lady dressed for some special affair. Then, as at most other times, the trailing ends from both sides of the knot are discretely bound together out of sight. Here, I've suggested a variation on that theme, bringing the ends of the ribbon together around a folded napkin and knotting them to suggest clusters of dripping, dropping wisteria blossoms. Even though the smooth surface of satin or silk rope may prove a bit tricky at first, once you've mastered the technique of tying, I think the sheen from smooth surfaces adds a particularly graceful nuance to the final knot.

WISTERIA CLUSTER KNOT

For a wisteria cluster knot, holding a light-colored ribbon in your left hand and a dark-colored ribbon in your right hand, entwine them as shown. When finished, the upper right (light strand) and upper left (dark strand) point up.

Bring the dark strand across the top and under the light one.

Entwine as shown. Both light-colored strands end up on the left-hand side. Pull the knot snug; tie the loose ends together behind your napkin or sheath.

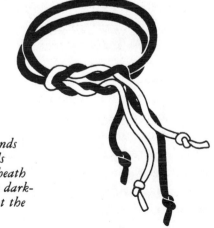

Turn the knot around so that the dark strands are on the left and the light strands are on the right. Bring both dark strands around to form a loop (your napkin or sheath goes through this space) and through the dark-colored loop behind the loose strands. Knot the ends of all four strands.

The three-looped knot is one of the most elegant ties. It's a bit more complicated than the others, though the principle of under-and-over weaving is the same. Practice with a single strand of textured rope, then try a variety of materials. Use several strands at once, alternating colors to create different effects.

THREE-LOOPED KNOT

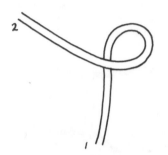

For a three-looped knot, make a single loop.

Bring end 2 back over the original loop to make a pretzellike shape.

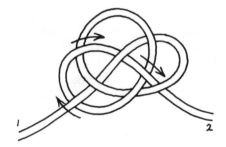

Take end 2 and weave it under end 1, then over, under and over, and finally under and out of the pretzel.

Pull the knot snug; tie ends 1 and 2 together in back.

For all of the ties, begin practice with 10–15 inches of twine, the longer lengths for thicker ropes. Once you've achieved the look you want, tie several, and trim them if necessary. Untie and measure to establish more accurate lengths for your final efforts.

Although the ties and knots described above, when used in lieu of napkin rings, will add a very special decorative element to the most mundane cloth napkins, folded cloths can make a spectacular impression, too. I've included detailed instructions for folding a flapped basket and a crane. Try the folding techniques first on 6-inch-square paper, then try a 10-inch square of synthetic cloth. I recommend using spray-starch while ironing the folds, to keep the final napkins crisp and neat looking. After a bit of practice you can graduate to linen of almost any size.

The flapped basket is particularly well suited to napkins that are decorated or monogrammed in just one corner. The final basket could hold individual name cards, flowers, or even a piece of fruit. Bread or rolls and/or individual butter pots look inviting nestled in a cloth basket, too. Croissants or other buttery rolls are not a good choice, though, since they often stain the napkin meant for a guest's lap.

FLAPPED BASKET

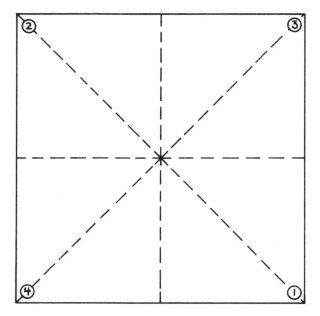

For a flapped basket, fold and press to crease where the dotted lines are. Open up.

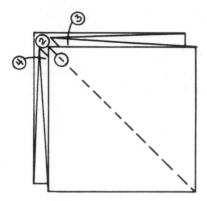

Bring points 1 and 2 together.
Fold in points 3 and 4. Press to
crease.

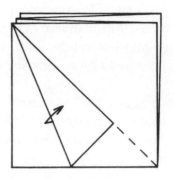

Fold the left-hand flap to the center line. Press to crease. Repeat
with the right-hand flap. Flip the
napkin over and repeat these folds
on the left- and right-hand flaps.

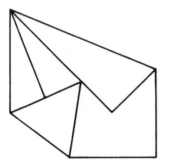

Fold back the left-hand flap; open
it and press. Repeat on the right-
hand side. Flip the napkin over
and repeat the open-and-press motions on both left- and right-hand
sides.

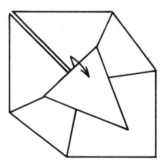

Bend the top point down. Flip the
napkin over and repeat.

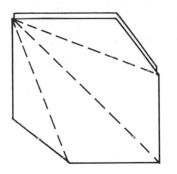

Lift the left-hand side up and fold over to cover the right. Flip the napkin over and repeat. (The dotted lines represent previous folds.)

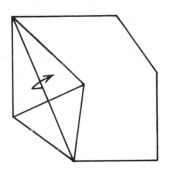

Fold back the left-hand corner to the center line. Repeat on the right.

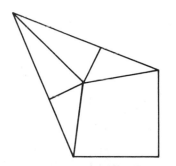

Flip the napkin over and repeat on the left- and right-hand sides.

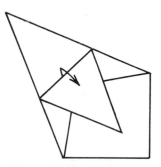

Fold the top flap down. Flip and repeat.

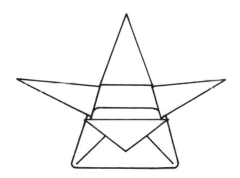

Open up.

The crane fold looks best, I think, when made from starched white linen and laid upon a large, patterned dinner plate. The final figure appears simple and elegant. No one will dispute the elegance, but it will take several concentrated practice sessions before the folding becomes simple. Once you've mastered the techniques, though, it will take only a few minutes to iron each.

THE CRANE

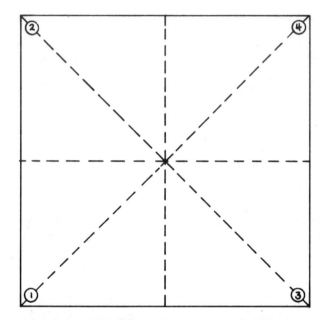

For a crane fold, fold and crease where the dotted lines are. Open up.

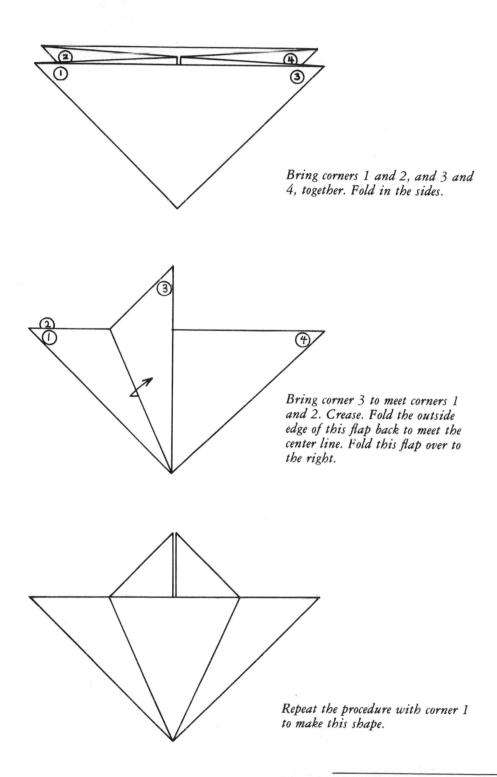

Bring corners 1 and 2, and 3 and 4, together. Fold in the sides.

Bring corner 3 to meet corners 1 and 2. Crease. Fold the outside edge of this flap back to meet the center line. Fold this flap over to the right.

Repeat the procedure with corner 1 to make this shape.

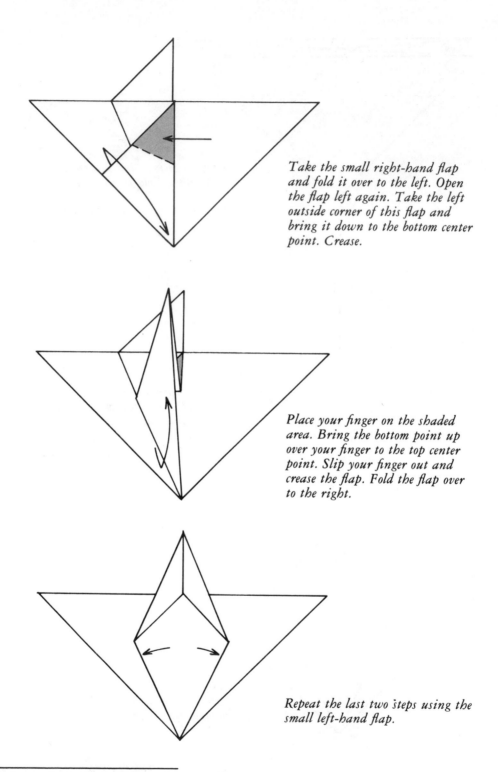

Take the small right-hand flap
and fold it over to the left. Open
the flap left again. Take the left
outside corner of this flap and
bring it down to the bottom center
point. Crease.

Place your finger on the shaded
area. Bring the bottom point up
over your finger to the top center
point. Slip your finger out and
crease the flap. Fold the flap over
to the right.

Repeat the last two steps using the
small left-hand flap.

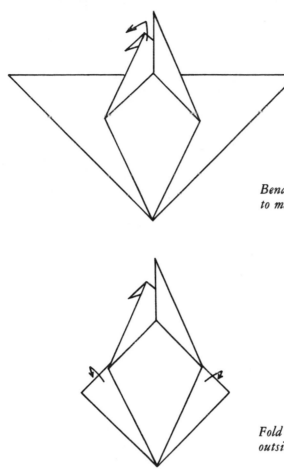

Bend back the left-hand center tip
to make a beak.

Fold back the left- and right-hand
outside flaps.

Photography Credits

Color photographs between pages 128 and 129 are by Aaron Rezny. The items displayed in the photographs were made by artisans and craftspeople in America.

Picnic basket with handle (jacket). *Lillian Crowe,* a member of the Eastern Band of Cherokee Indians, begins her weaving projects by gathering and preparing the natural materials necessary for her craft. Her work was lent courtesy of the Qualla Arts and Crafts Mutual, Inc., of Cherokee, North Carolina, an artisans' cooperative devoted to fostering Native American crafts and encouraging the artists to adapt their traditional skills to meet the needs of modern society.

Hand-stitched cloth (jacket). *Roxana Stamper,* a member of the Eastern Band of Cherokee Indians, created this design called "Road to Soco," which represents the winding trails and peaks of Soco Mountain. Her cloth was lent courtesy of the Qualla Arts and Crafts Mutual, Inc.

Wooden lunch boxes (jacket). The construction of these boxes is unique to the *Shaker community;* the joints or "fingers" ensure strength and durability. The simplicity of the boxes is in keeping with the Shakers' spare sense of design. These boxes were made by Connecticut Yankee, on Bainbridge Island, Washington.

Glass sushi plate (with tuna *sashimi*). *James Harmon,* a member of The New York Experimental Glass Workshop, Inc., creates glass objects of simple functionality. In designing this plate he was inspired by the geometric beauty of *sushi* and *sashimi.*

Silver chopsticks (with tuna *sashimi*). *Tchin,* an accomplished jeweler and sculptor of Blackfoot/Narraganset Indian and Chinese heritage, works in both gold and silver. These chopsticks, which he created to reflect his own unique background, were lent courtesy of Creative Resources, Inc., New York City.

Red teapot and cup (with sweets). *Sandra Wyner,* born in South Africa, has been living and working in Vermont for the last 10 years.

Shape and color are her primary concerns, as this delightfully angular, bright ceramic cup, saucer, and pot attest. Lent courtesy of Creative Resources, Inc.

Pottery dishes and bowls (with salmon dinner). *Romig Streeter,* a ceramic artist whose studio is in Millbrook, New York, crafted all the pieces shown here. Working in delicate porcelain, rugged stoneware, and unglazed wood-fired pottery, she creates a variety of effects. Having lived in Japan, she has been influenced by the idea of food and plate working together to create a specific design concept.

Black ceramic plate (with Clam *Sushi*) by *Romig Streeter*

Hand-printed paper (with Clam *Sushi*) by *Rena Andoh,* the author's daughter

Lacquer tray (with appetizers). *Patti King,* a furniture maker and lacquer worker residing in New York City, was inspired by elements of traditional Japanese design to create this very modern American lacquer tray.

Square white plates (with duck salad) by *Romig Streeter*

Ceramic soup bowl (with duck salad). *Ikuko Morino,* a friend of the author and formerly a member of The Potters' Guild in Ann Arbor, Michigan, made this traditional teabowl. Here it's used to serve a fresh pea soup.

Woven basket (with oranges). *Eva Wolfe,* a member of the Eastern Band of Cherokee Indians, wove this basket from river cane that she gathered and dyed herself. Mrs. Wolfe is recognized as one of the most skillful weavers among the Cherokee and has been awarded a grant from the National Endowment for the Arts that enables her to continue practicing her craft. Lent courtesy of the Qualla Arts and Crafts Mutual, Inc.

Mail-Order and Shopping Guide

Oriental ingredients have become increasingly popular and available throughout the United States. Should you have trouble, however, in obtaining certain items, write to the Japan Food Corporation. It is the major supplier of Oriental foodstuffs in the continental United States, and the people there will be glad to inform you of stores in your area that handle mail orders. The JFC has sales offices throughout the United States, but it's best to write to the head office for information.

> The Japan Food Corporation
> 445 Kauffman Court
> South San Francisco, CA   94080

Also:

- Find out what is available in your local supermarkets and greengrocers'.
- Consult the Yellow Pages of your telephone directory for Oriental markets, health-food markets, and gourmet cooking stores in your area.
- Contact your local newspaper's food department or local radio station's food-show host.
- Look in the hardware and gourmet cookware sections of your local department stores.
- Consult the catalogues of cookware specialty houses and mail-order outfits.
- Read through the advertisements in national food magazines, such as *Bon Appetit, Gourmet,* and *Food and Wine.*

You might also write to the following stores, services, and companies. They accept mail orders. Remember to ask whether they have minimum orders, if they require payment in advance or prefer COD, and whether they have printed catalogues and/or price lists.

CALIFORNIA

Anzen Hardware & Supply
220 E. 1st. Street
Los Angeles, CA   90012

Chico-San, Inc.
1144 W. 1st Street
Chico, CA   95926

The Chinese Grocer
209 Post Street at Grant
Ave.
San Francisco, CA   94108

Exotica Seed Company
1742 Laurel Canyon Boulevard
Hollywood, CA   90046

Kinoko Company
8139 Capwell Drive
Oakland, CA   94621

Kitazawa Seed Company
356 West Taylor Street
San Jose, CA   95110

Kongo Company
319 E. 1st Street
Los Angeles, CA   90012

K. Sakai Company
1656 Post Street
San Francisco, CA   94115

Nozawa Trading
870 S. Western Ave.
Los Angeles, CA   90005

Rafu Bussan, Inc.
326 E. 2nd Street
Los Angeles, CA   90012

Shing Chong & Co.
800 Grant Ave.
San Francisco, CA   94108

The Soyfoods Center
PO Box 234
Lafayette, CA   94549

DISTRICT OF COLUMBIA

Mikado
4709 Wisconsin Ave. NW
Washington. DC   20016

GEORGIA

Asian Trading Company
2581 Piedmont NE
Atlanta, GA   30324

ILLINOIS

Conte de Savoia
555 W. Roosevelt Road
Chicago, IL   60607

Oriental   Foods   and
Handcrafts
3708 N. Broadway
Chicago, IL   60613

Star Market
3349 N. Clark Street
Chicago, IL   60657

MASSACHUSETTS

Soyfoods, Inc.
Sunrise Farm
100 Heath Road
Colrain, MA   01340

Yoshinoya
36 Prospect Street
Cambridge, MA   02139

MICHIGAN

Kim's Korner
19517 West 7 Mile Road
Detroit, MI   48219

The Orient
PO Box 24
Portage, MI   49081

MISSOURI

Maruyama, Inc.
100 N. 18th Street
St. Louis, MO   63103

NEW YORK

Aphrodisia Products, Inc.
28 Carmine Street
New York, NY   10024

Flavors of Asia
Asianattic, Inc.
8 Briarwood Terrace
Albany, NY   12203

Kam Kuo Food Corp.
7–9 Mott Street
New York, NY   10013

Katagiri Company
224 E. 59th Street
New York, NY   10022

Tanaka and Company
326 Amsterdam Ave.
New York, NY   10023

OREGON

Anzen Japanese Foods and
Imports
736 N.E. Union Ave.
Portland, OR   97232

Nichols Garden Nursery
1190 N. Pacific Highway
Albany, OR   97321

PENNSYLVANIA

Bando Trading Company
2126 Murray Ave.
Pittsburgh, PA   15217

Mrs. De Wildt
RD 3
Bangor, PA   18013

International Supermarket
117 N. 10th Street
Philadelphia, PA   19107

UTAH

Le Jardin du Gourmet
West Danville, UT
05873

WASHINGTON

Specialty Spice Shop
2757 152nd Ave. NE
Redmond, WA   98052

WISCONSIN

Northwestern   Coffee
  Mills
217 N. Broadway
Milwaukee, WI   53202

AUSTRALIA

Buderim Ginger Growers'
  Co-Op Association
Box 114
Buderim
Queensland 4556
Australia

Index

Page numbers in **boldface** refer to illustrations.